John E. Pepper, Jr.
Former Chairman and CEO Procter & Gamble (1963 – 2003)
Recently retired Chairman of the Walt Disney Company

This is a unique story filled with deep and caring insight about the Russian people and their culture. It brings to life how a band of brave and committed peoples in both countries, have been anxious to learn from one another—and how they have helped bridge gaps in understanding between these two countries through the relationships they developed.

This is a deeply informed book and one that in my opinion is utterly objective in its appraisal of history and its view on the potential future of the two nations. Anyone who is interested in the enormous changes in Russia over the past two decades, and the difference ordinary people have made during one of the greatest societal transitions on our planet, will be informed and uplifted by this book.

Vladimir Pozner
Russian/American/French journalist & writer
"Pozner & Donahue" show (CNBC 1991-1996)
Host/Author "POZNER" - Channel One in Russia

This is a very special book. It tells a story that is one of both fortitude and faith. It tells the story of one woman's unwavering determination to fight and overcome the Cold War mythology that has formed the concepts that Russians and Americans have of each other.

Sharon Tennison is a lady who does not take "no" for an answer, who steadfastly pursues her goal, and, as is so movingly and powerfully demonstrated in these pages, achieves it.

William S. White
President of the Charles Stewart Mott Foundation

In the midst of the Cold War, Sharon Tennison dared to dream what "citizen diplomacy"— people-to-people exchanges—could do to dispel stereotypes and improve U.S./Soviet relations."

This nurse from San Francisco piqued my interest with her stories of roaming around the then-Soviet Union trying to find ways for Americans and Russians to exchange experiences and knowledge. Consequently, the Mott Foundation supported the Center for Citizen Initiatives and Sharon Tennison's unwavering commitment to help build a Russian civil society while dispelling stereotypes and enriching lives for literally tens of thousands of people in both post-Cold War countries. The C. S. Mott Foundation continues to support organizations working to build and strengthen the nonprofit sector in the Western Former Soviet Union, fondly remembering that it was Sharon who first introduced us to the region in 1989.

William B. Taylor, Jr.
U.S. Ambassador to Ukraine (2006-2009)
U.S. Coordinator of Assistance to Afghanistan (2003-2006)
U.S. State Department Coordinator of Assistance to Eastern Europe (1992-2002)

I want to add my support for CCI's heroic efforts in Russia—for encouraging mutual understanding, for educating both Americans and Russians about each other, and for sowing the seeds of both democracy and a market economy throughout Russia's eleven time zones.

Steve Wozniak
Co-Founder of Apple Computer, Inc.

I have supported CCI's far-reaching inspirational dreams and projects because they make sense. Cooperation rather than confrontation is the only way that will work when dealing with each other or with other nations.

Politicians should apply the same principles in dealing with other countries that we urge our children to use on their playgrounds: accept others' differences, recognize different points of view, be patient with each other, share with each other, help one another, settle differences by talking and mediation, and don't strike out at each other.

Suzanne Massie
Russia specialist
Author Land of the Firebird and Pavlovsk

Sharon Tennison is a remarkable woman who confronted the impossible and succeeded brilliantly in proving to us all how much a single dedicated individual can achieve and change, even in the international realm.

George Ingram
Former Deputy Assistant Administration of USAID
Responsible for the former Soviet Union

This is a story about the best of America—about how a few individuals helped change the world. CCI was a truly unique and effective endeavor in citizen diplomacy that helped facilitate the dual transitions of easing the hostile Cold War nature of U.S./Russian relations—and then helped Russian entrepreneurs navigate the path to market economics.

Arlie Schardt
CCI Board Chair for 20 years
Environmental Media Services, Founder/President
Former American Council on Foundations, VP
Former Environmental Defense Fund, CEO

To me, Tennison personifies "When the people lead, the leaders will follow." She is living proof of the power that one person can generate with a great idea, unswerving determination, and boundless energy.

CCI's greatest accomplishment has been to bring about a deeper understanding between untold thousands of American and Russian citizens. This is an immeasurable service to our world in which too many people choose to live with outdated stereotypes rather than recognize the natural alliance and forces for good that exist between Americans and Russians.

Enjoy, marvel, learn, and be inspired by this amazing story.

Thomas R. Pickering
Designated Career Ambassador
Ambassador to Russia 1993-1996
Ambassador to United Nations and six other nations

Sharon Tennison arguably met and talked with more Russians than any contemporary anywhere. She left her mark, and that of her organization, while repairing and rebuilding our relationship with that great country of Russia and its people. Breathtaking in its scope and focus, the book is a very good read about truly human ideas and episodes.

Paula Garb, PhD
Co-Director of University of California at Irvine
Center for Citizen Peacebuilding

I was living in Moscow with my two sons when Sharon and her colleagues first came there in 1983. No one could do better than she, in telling the stories of the extraordinary people in the United States, the Soviet Union, and post-Soviet Russia who have been brave enough to build bridges across the treacherous East-West divide in order to get to know the 'enemy' peoples.

Tennison documents how she and thousands of American and Soviet citizen diplomats broke through Cold War stereotypes of the 'other', one person at a time. These stories show how this movement grew to impact the new U.S./Russia policy in the 1990s.

Jack F. Matlock, Jr.
U.S. Ambassador to the USSR, 1987-91

Since 1983, CCI has organized and managed a series of remarkably successful efforts to bring Americans and Russians together to achieve a common goal. The group's efforts to replace misunderstanding on the personal level with habits of cooperation facilitated our official efforts, to bring the Cold War to an end and to cooperate with the Soviet Union's successor states.

This account of CCI and its various programs is an exciting and insightful read. It can also serve as a vade mecum, or resource book, for those interested in pursuing what has been aptly called "Track Two Diplomacy."

Dr. Vladimir Donskoy:
Professor of Business Ethics and Cross-Cultural Business Communication,
University of Irkutsk, Russia
District Governor 2004-2005, Rotary International, District 5010
Fulbright Scholar-in-Residence 1992-1993, California State University

To me, this book is a comprehensive chronicle of a dyed-in-the-wool American insider who has taken a 'seeing-is-believing' stance in describing the events during the tumultuous period of USA/Russia relationships at the turn of two centuries.

While reading the book, it was such a relief to see that the author does not spoon-feed the reader but encourages him or her to comprehend and internalize all of the complexities in the alternating rapprochement and alienation periods between our two great nations—also how we ordinary people can do extraordinary things toward creating and saving so fragile a peace. I am positive, she has accomplished a feat by making the reader feel that he or she has been a witness to a great turning point in history and proving, as the Russian proverb goes, that "even one person can be a warrior."

I strongly recommend this book to those who love Russia, to those who believe in Russia, in addition to those who trust Russia—but also to those who mistrust Russia, and even those are allergic to Russia . . . because even they may be appreciative of the efforts of the legions of proactive citizen diplomats who have worked in both countries to create better relations between the two former superpowers.

Patricia M. Cloherty
Chairman and CEO
Delta Private Equity Partners

It has often been said that " . . . it takes a village . . . ." For the U.S. and Russia to work cooperatively in this new era, it will indeed take all of us, as CCI recognized when it first commenced its bilateral training programs years ago.

I have had the great good fortune to have participated in many joint businesses between the two countries since 1994, and thus I have seen many positive steps taken to ensure that this forward progress continues. There is still work to be done, but the entrepreneurial spirit is alive and thriving in Russia.

Bernard Sucher
Entrepreneur
Former Chief of Merrill Lynch, Moscow
Former Manager of Alfa Bank Assets
Former Managing Director Troika Dialog

When Sting was singing, "I hope the Russians love their children too," Sharon Tennison, knew they did. Vision, courage and determination combined uniquely in this woman, who dared to tear at the Iron Curtain, and when it finally shredded, she patiently knitted together the lives of countless Americans and Russians. Sharon Tennison inspires across borders, and her story is a guide for anyone who has ever hoped to help heal our world.

Congressman Dennis J. Kucinich
10th Congressional District, Ohio

The Power of Impossible Ideas chronicles a journey of almost three decades taken together by American and Russian citizens who decided to make a difference between their two countries.

It is an inspiring history and it offers encouragement for others who want to reach across cultural divides to build trust and enable lasting cooperation.'

Yelena Khanga, TV journalist
Russia Today, English Speaking Channel
Channel 4, Princip Domino and Pro Eto

Congratulations on getting CCI's story into book form! I met Sharon on her first trip to the USSR. She came to our apartment to meet my mother, Lily Golden, and was shocked when the door was opened by an imposing, large black Soviet woman with a British accent! As a young journalist I wrote articles about CCI's work and watched as they created near-impossible programs to support us as we tried to break with our past and build a new and different kind of society.

Alexander (Sasha) Malashkin
CEO of Volma Corporation
Volgograd, Russia

My 1998 trip to North Carolina was a turning point in my business life. I understood that entrepreneurship gives unlimited opportunities to develop and improve. Shortly after that trip to U.S., I created three new businesses: a bowling alley for recreation, a trade centre, and a gypsum plant.

My second visit to the U.S. when we met Congress members and Secretary Powell is still unbelievable. I could not even imagine such organization of meetings—at such a high governmental level. This had a great influence on me. On coming home, I started to participate in social and entrepreneurial associations in my city to bring better politics to our region.

William T. Robinson, Attorney
International law, specializing in Russia
Corporate Governance, Rule of Law, Risk Management Practice
Rotary International US-Russia Inter-Country Committee

Having worked with Russia since the days of the Soviet Union, I have the greatest respect for CCI's tireless dedication and perseverance to develop a culture of ethical business conduct and community service across Russia. Sharon's strategy to go beyond Russia's two major cities, to provide business management training in Russia's regions was prescient; also CCI's involvement in developing Rotary clubs throughout Russia, and cultivating friendships and ties that are essential to building a civil society. The involvement beyond business, and time and work on the ground in the regions, has given CCI and me a shared perspective that is much more positive on Russia's transition than readers get from mainstream media or political commentary. I know of no other organization that has cast such a broad net to bring people together to build a strong foundation for the future of Russia.

Arthur Schultz
Certified Public Accountant
Philanthropist
Arthur B. Schultz Foundation

The Power of Impossible Ideas provides witness to those ideals that have forever driven visionaries and initiators. I am grateful to have worked along side CCI for over two decades to try to manifest what I believe is the highest form of responsible business. Together, I and CCI leaders tried to accomplish the following in Russia: 1) to harness and combine the energy of the free market place with social justice; 2) to blend capital with compassion; 3) to provide young Russian businessmen and women coming along in the entrepreneurial track with the means to absorb excellent business principles on which to develop their societies; and lastly, 4) to help Russia's young entrepreneurs to develop and apply philanthropic mentality and practices while running their businesses.

Vivian Castleberry
Castleberry Peace Institute, President
Peace Makers Inc., Founder
Former Women's Editor, Dallas Times Herald

Travel in this book with Sharon Tennison to the far away cities and towns of Russia to get glimpses into a fascinating world beyond western mainstream media headlines. Learn how you, too, can "step off of the end of earth on faith" and follow your own vision to inexplicable heights.

For those of us who have made trips with this "ordinary mother" over the past three decades, we have seen a prototype of what one person can do to make a difference in our world. Sharon is a consummate "citizen diplomat," gracious and humble, whether in the halls of Congress or in Russian villages. Her wealth of recorded material from years of traveling throughout Russia is now tightly condensed into this one volume. This chronicle allows the reader to follow the history, step by step, from the Cold War in 1983 to the present day. Enjoy and be challenged to look more deeply than headlines—and to step out on your own impossible ideas.

Jim Aneff
President, C-K Aneff Enterprises, Inc.
Past District Governor, Rotary International
CCI/National Field Coordinator for PEP
Abilene, Texas

CCI's PEP program opened the door for hundreds of Rotary, Kiwanis, Optimists and Lion's clubs across America, tens of thousands of civic club members and local citizens in over 500 American communities, as they connected with thousands of extraordinary dynamic

Russian business owners . . . in ways none of us could have ever imagined.

My years of working with PEP gave me a profound understanding of Russia. It changed my mentality and my life. I gained a deep appreciation for this vast and beautiful country. But most importantly, I now have good friends in every part of Russia. PEP was truly a grassroots, people-to-people program of the finest order. The positive results of PEP will be felt across Russia from one generation to another—and also remembered warmly in the minds and hearts of the many thousands of Americans who hosted these hopeful entrepreneurs in their businesses and homes.

Nancy Glaser, MBA Stanford
Current USAID Private Enterprise Officer, Afghanistan
Former Director of CCI's RISE Apparel Incubator
Formerly "Turn around specialist" for American businesses and non-profit organizations

Sharon has committed her last quarter of a century to improving relations between Russians and Americans like no other government action or program has achieved. This insightful book takes the reader through 30 years of Russia's recent history, as it was witnessed through the eyes of an everyday American citizen. The reader can't help but be impressed with the unexpected achievements recorded in Impossible Ideas, all of which occurred thanks to the dedicated efforts of many, many ordinary citizens, both Russian and American.

This book should be required reading for all government aid program officers and program implementers.

Craig Comstock
Formerly with the Ark Foundation
Currently writer for Huffington Post

The Ark Foundation gave Tennison the initial grant for "Soviets Meet Middle America" (SMMA) because she "thought big" and thus didn't say it was impossible to invite hundreds of Soviet citizens to visit this country, even though it had never been done before. With her colleagues, she had the tenacity and ingenuity to pioneer a game-changing exchange program between "enemies."

Impossible Ideas engagingly describes not only this early program, but also her organization's many other initiatives that practiced "citizen diplomacy," helped develop a civil society in the former USSR, while also correcting misguided views in the West.

Slava Stepashkin
PEP Facilitator and Interpreter
St.Petersburg, Russia and El Paso, Texas

My association with CCI gave me a unique opportunity to see hard-working grassroots America from within. We Russian interpreters who traveled with the delegations were the eyes, ears and voices for both Russian and American participants. We were also the cultural interpreters between the two peoples. It was an enormously important role in which to participate. I was able to see and understand business inside of American corporations, such as banking, hospitals, construction, retail, food services, architectural firms, and so on. It was the most exciting work I have ever done, knowing I was helping my fellow Russian compatriots, building bridges between the two countries, and being on a 45-degree learning curve myself. I observed lobbying of all sorts in a democratic society, even ethnic lobbying. Considering that America is a child of Europe, I have learned about the Armenian lobby, Israel lobby, Serbian lobby, and others in America.

I was greatly disappointed to learn that there is no Russian lobby in the United States. In this connection, I can truly claim that Sharon and CCI were effective instruments for educating and lobbying Russian people's needs in Congress and in American cities. They did this by bringing thousands of highly educated Russian entrepreneurs to the U.S. for training, which also gave opportunity for their opinions to be heard by Americans. I got to travel with three separate delegations of 100 Russians each that CCI brought to Congress members and foreign embassies in Washington, D.C. to discuss Russian-American relations and combating corruption. This was the pinnacle of my career!

The picture we got of America was very different from the Hollywood glitz and glamour, which most people around the world get to see about America on their television screens.

Don Chapman
Navy Captain, Retired
Delta Airlines, Captain, Retired

The Power of Impossible Ideas is a book that you will not be able to put down until you have finished the very last page. Every teenager in the U.S. should read this book so that they can understand what is possible if they follow their hearts and don't obsess about the salary or recognition. Sharon Tennison has given us a window into the art of making this planet a better place, and I salute her for her tireless efforts to bridge the huge gap that exists between Russia and the U.S.

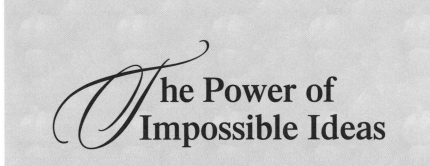

The Power of
Impossible Ideas

Ordinary Citizens'
Extraordinary Efforts
to Avert International Crisis

by Sharon Tennison

Odenwald Press

Published by Odenwald Press, Temple, Texas
Cover design by Mark Hendrick

Distributed by SMMA Distributors, 820 N. Delaware, Suite 405, San Mateo, CA 94401
(800-458-3387)

Library of Congress Cataloging-in-Publication Data

Tennison, Sharon.
  The power of impossible ideas : ordinary citizens' extraordinary efforts to
avert international crisis / Sharon Tennison.
      p. cm.
  Includes index.
  ISBN 978-1-884363-21-4 -- ISBN 1-884363-21-0
  1. United States--Relations--Soviet Union--Citizen participation. 2. Soviet
Union--Relations--United States--Citizen participation. 3. United
States--Relations--Russia (Federation)--Citizen participation. 4. Russia
(Federation)--Relations--United States--Citizen participation. 5. Center for
Citizen Initiatives (U.S.)--History. 6. Intercultural communication--Case
studies. 7. Exchange of persons programs, Soviet--United States. 8. Exchange
of persons programs, American--Soviet Union. 9. Antinuclear movement--United
States--History. 10. Antinuclear movement--Soviet Union--History. I. Title.
  E183.8.S65T43 2012
  327.73047--dc23
                                    2012013084

Printed in the United States of America

Dedication

To my adult children

Greg, Mike, Sherry, and Rob Ryan

who took the reins of their own lives

and completed growing themselves up

when I began trying to save the world from nuclear war.

Acknowledgments

It is impossible to acknowledge all of the extraordinary people who have been vitally important to the Center for Citizen Initiatives (CCI) over these past 30 years—it would take the remainder of the book to mention the names and the roles they have played. CCI is different from many institutional entities, in that tens of thousands of volunteers brought critical resources to us at specific times, then moved on, and others came in to add their unique contributions that kept up the momentum of our mission.

For fear of leaving out someone very important, it feels best to just say a grateful thanks to all of you who have given your talents and expertise so willingly at various junctures during CCI's history. Those of us who worked with you, Americans and Russians alike, remember your faces and your roles, the places where we intersected with you, and the gifts you brought to our common work.

Thank you! Thank you! Thank you!

As CCI's fundraiser, I want to extend gracious thanks to our major funders who made it possible for us all to succeed during these extraordinary years. Without their background support, the following history in these pages ahead could have never happened. Our deepest gratitude to:

> William S. White, President, and The Charles Stewart Mott Foundation
> Steve Wozniak, Apple Computer, Inc.
> Henry Dakin
> The Atlantic Philanthropic Trust (formerly the Anonymous Foundation)
> The Arthur B. Schultz Foundation
> Nika Pleshkova Thayer
> The United States Agency for International Development (USAID)
> The United States Information Agency (USIA)
> The United States Department of State

We are greatly indebted to CCI's Board of Directors who have been with us since 1990:

> Arlie Schardt, Chair of CCI Board
> Anthony Garrett
> Don Chapman
> Nancy Glaser
> Neil Young
> Pat Dowden
> Susanne Campbell

We are deeply grateful to the original pioneers of our work, whom you will meet later in the book. They took on the role of intermediaries between America and the "enemy." It is difficult to remember how dangerous those early years really were—when the whole world was divided into two camps, each armed with tens of thousands of nuclear weapons, many on launch pads ready to fire.

Bows to those of you who participated later in CCI's programs, who trained and home-hosted Russian entrepreneurs in your cities—you were the expertise and hearts of our programs—the conduits for transferring business information and personal goodwill between our two countries when political elites were caught up in zero-sum power politics.

Our extraordinary gratitude goes to hundreds of CCI staff members, both Americans and Russians, who brought their talents and knowledge to CCI over the past 27 years.

This book wouldn't be complete without honoring the Soviet people in the 1980s who risked careers and perhaps their lives, by taking us into their living rooms and hearts. They showed us the human side of their society and later helped us find ways to expand our common work. And to our Russian directors, facilitators, and thousands of Russian Fellows, colleagues and friends in the 1990s and 2000s, you served as Russian citizen diplomats and built tens of thousands of new bi-country relationships where none had existed before—we laud your work with us and treasure our memories of you.

Last, I want to acknowledge Vivian Castleberry, my role model, who has mentored me in the ways of activism and peacemaking since I was 22 years old. Of late, she was the taskmaster who relentlessly pressed me to write and complete this book. Until the final copy went to the publisher, she was still suggesting photos and tidbits for consideration. I wish all beginning writers could have such a muse on their shoulder. Kudos to Sylvia Odenwald at Odenwald Press for her patience as I obsessed over each line of the text. And to Boyd Brothers for their tolerance and support in getting the final production of the book completed.

Contents

PART III—2000-2010

REFLECTIONS OF THE 2000s

AT THE TURN OF RUSSIA'S 2000s

YEAR 2001

Glossary

Each organization has its own language—a lingo its members understand and use in communicating. We have tried to be clear about our terms, but the average reader could get lost in the language. The following is a list of terminology with the abbreviations used in this book.

AA	Alcoholics Anonymous
AI	Agriculture Initiative
CASW	Creating a Sober World
CCI	Center for Citizen Initiatives
CUUI	Center for U.S.-U.S.S.R. Initiatives
EDP	The Economic Development Program
EI	Environmental Initiative
EU	European Union
FARA	Foreign Agents Registration Act
FEMA	Federal Emergency Management Agency
FSB	Federal Security Service of Russia
GSOM	Graduate School of Management
IONS	Institute of Noetic Sciences
KGB	Committee for State Security
NATO	North Atlantic Treaty Organization
NGO	Non-Governmental Organization
OECD	Organization for Economic Cooperation and Development
OPORA	Organization to Protect Small and Mid-size Businesses
RISE	Russian Initiative for Self Employment
PEP	Productivity Enhancement Program
RAEF	Russian-American Enterprise Fund
SBDC	Small Business Development Center
SMMA	Soviets Meet Middle America!
USAID	United States Agency for International Development
USIA	United States Information Agency

From the Author

Dear Reader,

I find it necessary to provide disclaimers for this book. First, I am not a writer, have never taken a writing class, and find it rather ludicrous that I should try to write a book now at age 75. However, there is no one else to document this history; and if it doesn't get told, a small but truly extraordinary epoch of American history will be lost. I'm not willing to let this happen, since I believe there are important lessons within this period that must be preserved for future change makers. So I have been determined to find a way to get an account of this history in print—even if I have to write it myself. If only a few persons read this book and are inspired to act on their own ideas about how to make our world a better place for coming generations, my endless ruminating over the facts, dates and the real life vignettes recorded here, will have been worth it.

Second, I am not a Russian scholar or historian. Before traveling to the U.S.S.R. the first time, I decided to not burden my imaginations with history and entangling alliances. I wanted to have fresh eyes on contemporary Soviet life, unencumbered by others' opinions and prejudices. I wanted to know what did this enemy society look like, what kind of people lived in this closed off world, how did they think, and were they radically different from us in America.

At that time, I was only concerned with whether the world's next generation would survive—and if so, what it would take for both Americans and Soviets to get to some form of sane cooperation. Later I would begin pouring over the historical facts and diverse points of view regarding my own country and the U.S.S.R/Russia land mass. I hoped to understand what makes both populations 'tick'—thinking there might be a way to deal with the generations of fear and hostility that had developed over many decades.

This book has ended up being more of a collage and chronology of events, key players and programs—not a neatly flowing story line. So many diverse happenings occurred simultaneously throughout each year that there was no way to weave it all together in a normal book format. I checked with other authors; they agreed that this piece of history would need to be told in a different way. I trust you will be able to feel the essence of happenings that leave off in one place and pick up in another—and get a sense of the turbulent years during which these events were taking place.

The first draft of this book had to be cut in half. I painfully parted with pages and vignettes that revealed much more about the U.S.S.R. and Russia than the person or event being described. Wonderful material was truncated to the point where I feared the power of the book was getting lost. Still, I hope you can sense that this is a living "peoples' history," a history created and experienced by ordinary Americans and Russians who hoped against the odds that some larger meaning would come from meetings we had with each other—and as it turned out, unexplainable events began happening.

I have adhered strictly to my earlier writings for the text. However, memories are complex. Different eyes and minds see and store different aspects of happenings. If you were involved in events mentioned herein and recall aspects differently than recorded here, please forward me your perceptions so they can be added as addenda for researchers.

Last, I was obsessed by the idea to find a "win-win" relationship between the two superpowers. I don't pretend to understand this obsession … unless there is something to the notion of destiny. But I do know now, from my experience and the experiences of others, that when people are gripped with an impossible mission in their souls—and step out on faith … something in the "scheme of things" begins to acts like a giant magnet that draws in people, opportunities, and even funds to push the idea into reality, so …

Whatever you can do, or dream you can do, begin it. Boldness has genius, power, and magic in it."—Johann Wolfgang Goethe

May you be inspired to find your own power and magic,

Prologue

Events Prior to Travel to the U.S.S.R.

The Need to Document America's Early "Citizen Diplomats"

One piece of American history has yet to be recorded for posterity. The hoped-for détente of the '70s had come to a halt. Increasingly, enemy-making rhetoric erupted in both American and Soviet media. Tens of thousands of nuclear weapons held the entire world captive. International scientists predicted that if 10 percent of the weapons on launch pads were detonated, planet earth would be plunged into a "nuclear winter"—a dead cinder revolving in space.

Small groups of American citizen emissaries, independent of officials, began making a substantial, laser-like contribution to the reduction of tensions between the U.S. and the U.S.S.R. at a critical juncture in the 1980s. Reporting on this phenomenon, an American publication produced a cover story calling these groups of strange Americans, "Citizen Diplomats." This book documents part of that history.

The concept of groups of ordinary citizens-as-diplomats and their actions has not been recorded in history books, except for an instance between France and Germany during the late 1800s. It is reported that, to avert warring hostilities between their two nations, a small migration of French and German citizens crossed their borders without official permission to try to reduce tensions between their countries. Unfortunately, they were not successful.

A Shift in Thinking

In the early '80s, a quiet shift in mentality began happening across the U.S. Ordinary people in nameless nodes throughout America began asking themselves questions, "Why are we building all of these nuclear weapons—and will they protect us from nuclear war? What is fueling this enemy-ship between America and the U.S.S.R.? Might citizens stumble upon a non-political way to intervene in this catastrophe-waiting-to-happen?"

Unaware of each other's existences, these small groups began meeting in San Francisco, Seattle, Tucson, Palo Alto, Chicago, and upstate New York. They consisted of mainstream citizens—business owners, doctors, nurses, educators, lawyers, city planners, administrators, architects, ministers, and students—the backbone of local communities. "If national leaders can't find solutions, how can we?" they asked themselves. Yet they kept pondering because the specter of nuclear war was too horrendous to ignore.

A Powerful Idea Being Birthed

With no experience in organizing international efforts, no foreign language skills and no knowledge of the enemy's culture, we moved forward step-by-step to explore for ourselves if the Soviets were barbarian and out to destroy America. We figured out how to get to the U.S.S.R. and began crossing paths with others like ourselves on planes coming and going between the two countries. Most of us started with the idea of only one trip behind the Iron Curtain. Later we found ourselves scheduling second and third trips and taking friends and colleagues with us to meet with the "enemy" people.

Somewhere inside of us lurked a deep suspicion that there was more misunderstanding and fear between the countries and leaders, than diabolical intentions. It would remain to be seen whether or not this was true.

Why the Interest in Russia and How It Came About

Everyone asks how and why I, a non-academic, ordinary American woman, mother of four children have ended up working at the U.S.-Russia interface. It seems to others like an unimaginable career path. I agree. I had no previous interest in Russia and never could have guessed that I would spend a quarter of a century immersed in Russia's transition from communism to a market economy. The personal answer is rather straight forward. My four children were near leaving-the-nest in the late '70s—and the larger outside world, particularly the nuclear arms race, began impinging on my reality.

By autumn of 1979, the world felt full of forebodings. Information and talk about nuclear weapons and targets was omnipresent. Political campaigns were driven by the U.S.-U.S.S.R. relationship and the threat of nuclear war. Perhaps it had been so previously, but it had not registered with me until that time. All of a sudden it was in my face every time I switched on the TV or picked up a newspaper. I worried daily about my own children's futures. Would they get a chance to have families and careers of their own? If not, this wasn't acceptable to me. Something had to be done.

Looking for solutions, I became involved with astronaut Edgar Mitchell's Institute of Noetic Science (IONS), then directed by Dr. Willis Harmon, a "futurist" and professor at Stanford University. At IONS lectures, I met others like myself who were searching for answers. We formed a small group of professionals in Palo Alto, California. By 1981 we were increasingly perplexed and asking ourselves, "Has the world gone mad? Is anyone looking for alternative solutions to a nuclear war? Can ordinary citizens do anything to address this nightmare?" We felt that the 1980s would be a huge confluence of crashing ideologies and politics. Registering the same inner rumblings, our mentor, Willis Harmon, remarked in a lecture, "We may get through the 1980s unscathed, but if so, it will be one hell-of-a-wrenching." He encouraged us to get off our seats and on our feet. "Citizens," he said, "will have to become active in international relations to avert a future global catastrophe."

Lead-up Activities that Defined Our Work

A small number of us at IONS decided to create a first-ever conference to brainstorm the issues that we felt jeopardized our futures. Our personal address books helped identify big thinkers we had known from living in other states. We sent letters to the sharpest of these people asking them to join us for three days at the Asilomar Conference Center on the Pacific coast. Surprisingly, a flood of responses began coming in.

Throwing ourselves into this experimental conference, we designed an entirely new discussion format for the event. We would not listen to "talking heads" but instead would create an conference with no speakers. Small breakout groups would be organized to get hundreds of pressing ideas circulating. The outcome, of course, was totally unpredictable. By September of 1981 some 100 concerned Americans from across the country had confirmed attendance.

The conference day was soon upon us. With the sun setting on the Pacific, we opened the event with great apprehension. Willis was on hand to bolster our experiment. Soon one hundred conferees were taking turns telling why they had come across the country to an unknown event planned by strangers, and what their overriding concerns were for the future. Crosstalk wasn't permitted during the first long intense session. For three hours all ears were honed in on one voice after another. By the end of the long session, everyone in the room understood each other's concerns and knew with whom, and on what topics, they wanted to interact. We broke for individual conversations. The result was phenomenal. Participants immediately gravitated to various other conferees to explore ideas they had just heard voiced. After midnight, clumps of men and women were still in rapt discussions throughout the conference hall, out on the steps, and beyond on the grounds. What could have become a cacophonous 72-hour disaster became an orderly 24-hour-a-day brainstorm for three days. The discussion format worked. It included ground rules for listening and speaking during small breakout sessions. Then the main ideas were summarized for large group sessions. For the early 1980s, this was a novel way for a hundred people with no leader to voice their apprehensions and to come up with new ideas and directions.

The Asilomar conference was a turning point in our lives. A new national network was being born. We committed to go back to our cities and raise these international issues in every forum open to us—and to keep in touch with each other as we moved forward.

Quite a few, including me, felt drawn to the hottest of the issues … the U.S.-Soviet standoff and the nuclear arms race. Following the conference, ideas and possibilities began bubbling up.

Pursuing one idea after another, we found a logic of sorts emerging. We questioned our sanity, realizing how absurd it was to think that ordinary people might make a dent in international relations. But that didn't stop us. Two quotes became our mantras: Margaret Mead's, *"Never doubt that a small group of committed citizens can change the world; indeed, it is the only thing that ever has;"* and President Dwight Eisenhower's, *"When the people lead, the leaders will follow."* These bits of wisdom didn't change the impossibility of our task, but they kept us moving forward despite our trepidations.

Physicians for Social Responsibility—An Invitation to Act

The Alexian Brothers Hospital, where I worked in Intensive Care (ICU), received a request from the Federal Emergency Management Agency (FEMA), to set aside a certain number of beds in the event of a nuclear war. Several Alexian doctors had recently joined the newly forming Physicians for Social Responsibility (PSR) and were speaking out on the insanity of building more missiles. Over an unconscious patient, an epidemiologist asked me to join PSR and begin speaking with Bay Area audiences on the "Medical Consequences of Nuclear War." "But I'm not a doctor," I replied. He retorted, "You take care of burns, fractures, life and death, the same as we do. We need your help to take this issue to the public." Thus began an intensive effort on my part to learn how much firepower each superpower had, which American cities were targeted by Soviet missiles, the impacts of long and short range missiles, and how all of this would affect local populations if, or when, nuclear bombs were detonated.

More importantly, it was PSR's mission to show how ridiculous it was to even consider surviving a nuclear war. American hospitals could never handle a disaster of this magnitude regardless of how many beds were set aside. At the urging of PSR doctors, my hospital chose not to participate in the FEMA request.

Soon PSR was absorbing much of my spare time; nothing else seemed more important given the stark reality of nuclear conflagration. Audiences produced naysayers: "This woman is weakening our government's resolve to destroy Communism!" or "Would you like to live in the Soviet Union? Then listen to this lady!" Other comments revealed fear and paralysis. It was clear that some people had never entertained the hideous possibility of a nuclear war. Others spoke about going to bed at night fearing that nuclear weapons would destroy their families before dawn. Most were certain that the U.S.-USSR relationship would never change.

Writing to the President

President Reagan made a statement saying that 20,000,000 Americans dead in a nuclear war would be an acceptable number. One of his key officials floated the idea that Americans could survive a "nuclear exchange" by digging holes in the ground and placing doors over the tops. Today it's impossible to comprehend that such suggestions actually showed up in print media. I hastily wrote President Reagan a letter and told him not to consider me and my children part of his "20 million acceptable dead." In response, the White House sent a terse note saying that I had been "turned over to the U.S. State Department." I wondered if I had crossed an invisible line and whether there might be penalties in the future.

A Bolt-of-Lightning Idea

Walking through a friend's kitchen during a holiday party in San Jose, I was stopped short by a bizarre happening. Something inside my head communicated with arresting clarity, *"It's time to go see the enemy"* … then it was gone. In retrospect, it seemed more like a rapid ticker tape going off in the front of my cerebral cortex. It shook my insides. I am a practical woman. I don't hear voices; I don't see apparitions. Maybe it just popped up from my subconscious. I still don't understand this happening, but it was seminal to getting me to the Soviet Union for the first trip. When I awakened early the next morning, more ideas were coming. They were accompanied by a marked shunt of fresh energy—a restlessness to do something.

On January 1, 1983, our IONS group met in downtown San Francisco to celebrate the New Year. At one point I heard myself venturing to the group, "Maybe we should go see the enemy this year. Would anyone else like to go?" My friends' eyes resembled computers, quickly processing the idea. Some uttered a tentative "Yes," but it was clear that they were still weighing the pros and cons. We agreed it could not be an ordinary trip, but one in which we would be allowed to go to Soviet streets, meet real people and not be contained within foreigner hotels and official Intourist buses. Within weeks our group coalesced around this idea. The next step was to present this idea to the Soviet side; we doubted they would consider allowing what we hoped to do.

Meeting the Russian "Bear" at the Consulate in San Francisco—January 1983

The only Soviet Embassy or Consulate outside of Washington and New York is in San Francisco. A queasiness consumed me as I dialed their number. The following week, I drove up to the seven-story, brownish brick building and parked with apprehension. It was a typical sunny but chilly San Francisco day that was utterly silent. I stepped out of my Subaru onto Green Street. Not a car, not a human being, not even a cat could be seen or heard. It was surreal. A scary notion crossed my mind, "What if I should disappear behind the walls of this grim building?"

Ghosts of Stalin's purges, children dutifully informing on parents, and missile parades in Red Square leapt up in my mind. Fears of going into the lair of the enemy accompanied each step I took toward the spiked iron fence surrounding the building. Suddenly, as I neared the fence, a buzzer went off. The iron gate swung open. It revealed a walkway and several steps up to a door. As I approached the top, another buzzer released the official door for entry. Still I had not seen or heard a living soul.

Entering a drab brown paneled room, an ominous hammer and sickle was noted on the wall straight ahead. The place was stiff and cold. A stone-faced woman behind glass motioned me to take a seat. I did. Finally, a door opened. A voice said, "Ms. Tennison ... my name is Gennadi German; it's good to meet you, please come in." I was speechless. Before me stood a tall, handsome young man of perhaps 35 years. He was dressed in a gray tweed jacket with suede elbow patches. Before gaining composure, I heard myself saying, "You don't look like what I thought a Soviet would look like." He chuckled a bit and inquired what was I expecting.

Once behind the door in a smaller room, I quickly explained the reason for my visit. We wanted to know if it would be possible to go to the U.S.S.R., leave official hotels, and explore Soviet streets on our own, with the intention of meeting ordinary citizens. "Why?" he inquired. I replied, "We hope to learn more about your country's citizens and maybe even create a few informal strategies to diffuse fear and suspicion between the ordinary peoples of our nations." He agreed it was greatly needed and seemed to begin thinking how this prospect might be accomplished. He mentioned that the request was not routine and that he would need to seek permission from people higher than himself. It was unclear to me whether or not this was a ruse to pacify the American across the table. He proposed an appointment a week later for an answer. I walked out of the building in a less oppressive mood than when I entered.

A Chance Meeting at the Soviet Consulate

A week later I entered the Soviet Consulate to get their answer. The same buzzers went off, and I trudged up and into the same stark room. An aging woman sat nearby. After a few minutes she quietly inquired, "My dear, why are you here today?" Wondering if she was a plant, I replied truthfully that we had asked for rather unusual permissions to visit the U.S.S.R.—to get off the tourist buses and out of sanctioned hotels. She smiled kindly and said, "Then maybe you would like to meet my daughter who lives in Moscow?" Even more suspicious, nevertheless, my ears perked up. She introduced herself as Lillian Garb and said she was waiting to renew her visa. She ventured that her daughter, Paula Garb, was living in Russia raising her two Russian grandsons and that the three of them were expected in San Francisco in a couple of weeks. She asked if I would like to meet them. What an understatement. Lillian slipped me her telephone number. I was buttressed by this unexpected interaction when Gennadi appeared in the doorway. After pleasantries, he informed me that his Consulate superiors had agreed that more interface between our peoples was needed and offered the following: We would be assigned normal Intourist guides, but would have no problem going out on streets, getting off tour buses, and exploring the cities as we chose. He cautioned, however, that we were not to go outside the cities' limits. Was he telling the truth? The only way to know was to go and find out. The group was immediately informed that our trip was a "go."

Meeting Our Soon-to-be Unofficial Guide to the Soviet Union

One of our members chanced to meet Cynthia Lazaroff, a young American woman who studied Russian language in high school and university and then spent a year in Moscow. She agreed to travel with us as our unofficial interpreter and guide in the U.S.S.R. Cynthia informed us that Soviets are fond of lapel pins and suggested that we consider creating one to wear on Soviet streets, which we did. Next we began group language sessions. Some of us had far better language abilities than others. Sarah Seybold was rapidly absorbing Russian words and planning remarks for meetings in Moscow, and I was one of those for whom the Russian language sounded like grating noises from outer space.

My apartment became an office where we researched travel companies, took Russian lessons and prepared for the trip. News of this unusual undertaking traveled quickly. Others heard about our plans and requested to join us. The group grew rapidly to 20 persons—which we considered maximum.

Meeting the Garb/Danilenko Family

Two weeks after our initial encounter, I called Lillian Garb and got an invitation to meet her daughter and grandsons the day they arrived in San Francisco. After traveling from half a world away, they were exhausted but open to a short visit. Their story was intriguing. Lillian's husband was a child during the 1917 Bolshevik Revolution. He saw his parents killed by White Russians. Hence, he always believed in the Bolsheviks and communism. As an orphan, he was able to leave the U.S.S.R. and take a ship headed for the United States. He survived and eventually met and married Lillian. The two lived a simple life and raised two children, James and Paula.

Growing up, Paula was intent upon seeing her father's homeland. After graduating from high school, she got her first opportunity to visit the Soviet Union. Once there, she soon fell in love and eventually married a young man by the name of Danilenko. A year later she birthed their first son Andrei. Another son Gregory arrived five years later. The marriage became increasingly difficult, and Paula decided to move back to America with her boys. Once in California, she soon found that, without a degree, jobs were scarce.

Childcare was expensive; she was falling farther behind every month. Finally lacking alternatives, she decided to appeal to Soviet authorities to allow her to return to the U.S.S.R. based on the fact that her sons were Russian—they agreed.

In 1969 Paula left the Bay Area to raise her boys in Moscow where she hoped to get free education. Upon arrival in the U.S.S.R., she was given a small apartment, a job as a translator, and the right to apply for higher education. Free childcare was provided for her boys. Eventually Paula graduated from Moscow State University and later earned her Ph.D. at the Academy of Sciences Institute of Ethnology and Anthropology. Her sons grew up as Russian youth, and she became an anthropologist and author of two books: one on the Abkhaz population in Georgia, and the other about North Americans who immigrated to the U.S.S.R. starting in the 1920s.

The Garb/Danilenko family began playing an important role in our citizen diplomacy work and will reappear throughout the following pages.

Meeting My Two FBI Agents

In May of 1983 a call came from Seattle. "Sharon, Dannon Perry here. I hear you visited the Soviet Consulate?" "Yes, why?" "Chances are near 100 percent that your photo was taken from the building directly in front of the Consulate on Green Street. Your car license was photographed also. It's best that you go down to the FBI and check in." A gentle bear of a man, Dannon was a seasoned citizen diplomat and knew the ropes. I heeded his advice.

I found the Federal Bureau of Investigation listing in the phone book and made the call. On another spring day in early 1983, I entered the impressive granite FBI building in downtown San Francisco. It felt austere and unfriendly. Finally through a labyrinth of floors and halls, the appropriate corridor and room number appeared. Entering the room, I met not one, but two special agents, both women, already assigned to my case. The most active one was Gerry Tracy. Like good investigative journalists, both women knew the right questions to ask. Soon it was obvious that they knew more about me than most of my current friends. They asked about associations I had joined in past years and why I was involved with the Institute of Noetic Sciences, which I had not mentioned at that juncture. I could only surmise this show of information was to let me know how much they already had found out. With nothing to hide, my answers followed in a straightforward manner.

They warned that our group could only interfere with the serious intelligence work of the experts and that we should consider changing our direction. Their steely-eyed manner bothered me. Finally in parting I said, "Look, this is something that we must do. As organizer of this group, please know that I am an ordinary American mother of four children and am concerned about their futures. We will never do anything to compromise our country. You will be informed of our activities, but we will continue."

And so it was that the FBI began calling on us over the next several years. They kept in close touch during the planning of the first trip and told me when to meet them at the FBI building. I always complied. During those meetings, their chief interest was to warn us about what we would find in the Soviet Union. Only later did we learn that they had never touched ground in the U.S.S.R.; and not only that, but they would never in their lives be allowed to travel there. The last FBI meeting prior to travel brought grim warnings that we naive citizens might think that we could talk with ordinary Russian citizens, but, in truth, every person we would meet would be placed in our path and would be a KGB informer. We agreed that this might be so, but that we would have to discover it for ourselves. Prepared for the worst and expecting continuous encounters with KGB stooges, the group devised numerous ways to circumvent the best of Soviet schemes by the time we landed on ground in Moscow.

Meeting U.S. Government Officers Prior to Travel

We sent several letters to Washington, D.C. agencies: the United States Information Agency (USIA), the United States Agency for International Development (USAID), and the State Department telling them what we were planning. Soon an official letter arrived informing us that three officials from the USIA would travel to San Francisco and would like to meet with our group. Terrific! We assumed that they might want to work with us to offset tensions between the two countries.

Over 50 Bay Area members created a fabulous potluck dinner in Tiburon overlooking the Bay. We welcomed our guests and ushered them to the patio facing the water where tables were spread with delicacies. It was a magnificent San Francisco evening. The world seemed perfect. What could be better? A large U.S. government agency was interested in our grassroots approach to international relations!

Following dinner, we assembled inside for discussion. The newcomers explained who they were. One told about USIA programs and asked precisely what we were planning. We humbly told them everything about our coming trip, future intentions, and our belief that a different kind of diplomacy was needed for such grave times. They grew increasingly cynical. We answered questions only to receive more rebuffs for our naive ideas. "How many of you speak Russian?" we were asked. I rebutted, "Wait, the question should be, 'How many of us are studying the Russian language?' " Half of the hands in the room shot up. Interactions became more difficult. Finally we were told, "You need to cease your work. We are the real diplomats. You could be downright dangerous to the real diplomatic work being carried out with the U.S.S.R."

Clearly we had come to an impasse. I heard myself saying, "Thank you for your counsel. It seems we have come to the end of fruitful discussion. We leave you to do your work, as you deem necessary. And we assume that you, in good spirit, will leave us to do our work as we deem necessary." Within five minutes the three were out the door. We sat there speechless after they departed. How could we have been so naive? This encounter only made us more determined.

A Proposal from an Emmy Award-winning Documentarian

A flurry of wild activity was in motion as we scurried around to schedule our travel, stepped up Russian classes, interviewed trip applicants, and made sure that our normal responsibilities would be met in our absence from the U.S. In the middle of it all, an Emmy-Award documentarian telephoned, "We hear what you guys are up to … and if you can swing it, we would like to go along and document what happens." Fabulous idea we thought, but we couldn't imagine the Soviet Consulate granting permission for four additional members of a PBS film crew. Again I found myself sitting in front of Gennadi German at the Consulate. Listening patiently to our latest unorthodox request, he asked a number of questions and said he would check and let us know in a week.

The next week Gennadi had another green light for us, provided we accept that an officer from Gosteleradio (the U.S.S.R.'s huge central TV and radio complex) travel wherever the cameras went. It seemed reasonable. We informed the PBS-affiliated crew. For the first time, they admitted that they had no funds—and that we would need to raise money for their trips.

We had never raised money! Given the importance of a documentary on PBS, however, we decided to learn to become fundraisers. Bob Sayre, husband of traveler Lynda, contributed $5,000, and other friends from around America chipped in. Thanks to Bob, and to our surprise, we raised the rest of the $10,000.

An International Disaster—Korean Airliner 007 Shot Down by Soviets

Only days before our scheduled flight, an international catastrophe exploded in all media outlets. The Korean Airliner 007 was shot down by a Soviet aircraft killing all 269 passengers aboard. It was September 1, 1983. Our travel date was September 16. Worldwide condemnation of the Soviet Union was raging. International airlines began boycotting the U.S.S.R. Our flight tickets were cancelled. Believing it was more important than ever to make the trip, our group of 20 huddled and decided to try to get to Moscow by any means possible. On September 10, airline tickets were secured by routing through to Belgrade, Yugoslavia, a Soviet satellite country. From there we would take the Yugoslav JAT national airline into Moscow. With flight tickets resolved, I could finish up a couple of shifts at Alexian Brothers ICU before the travel date.

An Unexpected Meeting with the CIA

During this short interim, another surreal coincidence occurred on September 10. I rushed to the ICU for a 3:00 to 11:00 PM shift. Our departure date was still September 16, so there was time for me to take one more patient before leaving.

My assignment for the evening was given. It was a 50-year-old Korean man with a massive bleed in his head. His life hung by a thread. Upon entering the darkened room, familiar life-support sounds were heard—the whish of automated breaths to keep the body oxygenated, pumps keeping IVs regulated, and an occasional tinkle of an alert bell. The outgoing nurse gave her report. I checked equipment settings and vital signs. The patient's life was my responsibility for the next eight hours. In a corner of the dark room stood a silent family member who the day nurse had mentioned. My focus was solely on assessing the patient, the equipment, and making sure that everything possible was being done for his fragile condition.

He was an Asian man of short stature and thin build, who appeared much younger than his stated age. What could have produced a vascular accident in this body? Getting to a reasonable comfort level with the machinery and my patient, I was ready for more history.

Turning to the relative and allowing a little more light in the room, I was shocked. He was a fair-skinned, sandy-haired, tall, and a rather heavily built American. I quietly inquired, "What role do you play in the patient's life?" "The patient is part of my family," came a terse answer. "How long have you been family members?" "Decades now." "Has he had any health problems that would have indicated vascular disease?" "None." Puzzled, I went about routine documenting, changed an IV, and doing dressings checks. Meanwhile the family member stood by motionless and watching.

"Would you like to take a break and let another family member come in?" "No, I'm here to see that my relative is taken care of." At some point during the shift, it appeared that I was meeting the stranger's expectations. He started asking questions about equipment, chances for survival—those first inquiries that worried families make in life and death situations. After answering as best I could, he seemed satisfied. We finished out the evening shift with the patient's status unchanged.

On September 11, I had the same assignment. The big American was still in the darkened room. ICUs have a way of quickly breaking down barriers. With death pervading everything, even people who are not normally communicative have an instinctive need to reach out, particularly to nurses. Faced with grief and loss, life is seen for what it is—a delicate membrane between walking around and the unknown—perhaps nothing. A nurse's responsibility is to the patient, who may already be slipping beyond the membrane, and to be there for shocked and grieving family members.

The big man followed typical ICU family members' responses, being relieved to see that their loved one was well taken care of. Real communication between us began, I asked, "How did this man come into your family?" "He's my brother-in-law." Then the full story quietly poured out.

"I was a U2 pilot ... shot down over Korea and assumed dead by the U.S. This Korean family found me in the field. They hid me, and over the months they nursed me back to health. In gratitude, I vowed that if I ever got back to the '48' (states), I would bring as many of them as I could to America. They are all here now, and I am married to one of the daughters." This explained the mystery and also the hoard of little Asian people who were in and out of the hospital waiting area but never came in the ICU. This American, as it turned out, was the caretaker of them all.

The shift ended, and the following day's assignment was the same ... and again the protector of the patient was the same. During that shift, I could no longer hold back my big question. Warily I asked, "So, you were a U2 pilot ... what do you know about the shooting down of the 007 KAL Airliner over Sakhalin?" "Why do you ask?" "I am trying to get into the Soviet Union in a couple of days, and this information is of grave importance to me." A cautious pause occurred. Finally he replied, "Well, I can tell you this much. For years, each of those Korean passenger planes have been outfitted with a belly full of intelligence-gathering equipment the size of this room. It's been a calculated gamble that one of them would be taken down before now."

Shocked by his audacity, I began asking other questions such as how the commercial plane operated and whether the pilot knew what was going on in the belly of the plane. He said the pilot and person below had nothing to do with each other. One flies the plane, the other gathers intelligence. The answers came out so factually, so unemotionally, that I was stunned. "How can you be so sure, and, if you are sure, aren't you afraid to give out such information to an unknown person like me?" He reached in his pocket and pulled out a little red folder with his photo and identity as a CIA agent. Then said, "So many people know about this Korean Airliner situation; it will be in all the newspapers within a week. It can't be covered up. And, besides that, no one will touch me. I am part of a brotherhood of U2 pilots. We have pledged to each other that if any of us dies by other than natural causes, all the rest will tell everything we know—which the American public doesn't know. And we don't keep this a secret from our bosses."

I recalled seeing a short news blurb days before in the *San Francisco Chronicle*. It mentioned the outfitting of Korean planes with intelligence at Andrews Air Force base, but since no other news coverage had mentioned it, I considered there was nothing to it.

He changed the subject. "So you are going to the U.S.S.R.—what for?" I told him. His somber face slowly lightened up, "You will appreciate the Russian people—they have suffered a lot." Afterward, he spun story after story about Soviet people, their hard history, World War II, the devastation … making me wonder at first if he was a counter spy.

The next evening when I arrived at the hospital, he had brought old photos of himself with his Korean family, and a photo of himself as a young man with Gary Powers, (the famous American U2 pilot who was taken down over the U.S.S.R.). He mentioned that another plane he was piloting was shot down over Cuba, after which he was imprisoned with Fidel Castro in the mountains. Photos showed healing cigarette burns on their backs from jailers. He reminisced that President Kennedy sent him on a mission to deliver Castro the news that Kennedy couldn't support him as planned. The photos were real enough; the rest of the story I don't know about.

I would not return to the hospital before the trip to the U.S.S.R. He gave me his card and requested, "Get in touch with me upon your return; I want to know how you find the Soviet people."

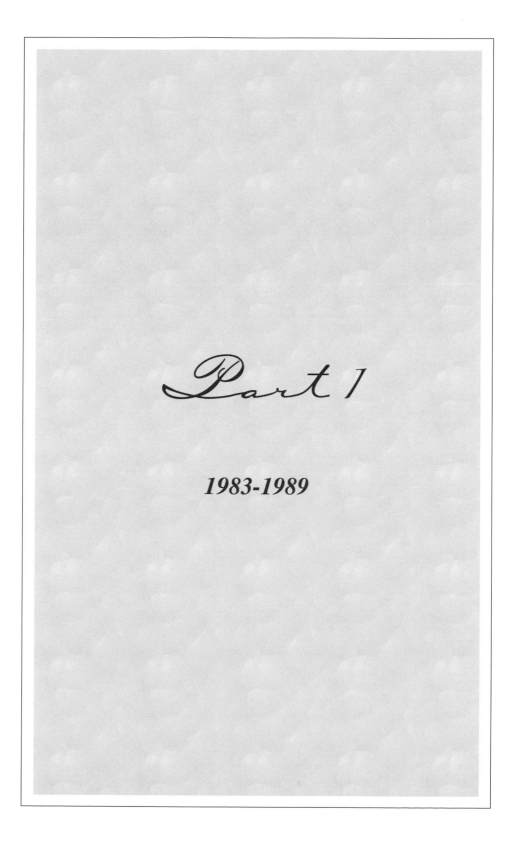

Part 1

1983-1989

The First Trip to the U.S.S.R.

Travel from the U.S. and Arriving in the "Land of the Enemy"

Twenty of us gathered at the San Francisco airport on September 16, 1983—but the normal excitement of group travel was missing. We seemed to sense the enormity of the situation upon which we were about to embark. Soon the camera crew showed up loaded down with gear: large shoulder cameras, boxes of film, lights, umbrellas for lighting, and boom boxes. British Airlines accepted it all as luggage.

It was particularly difficult to watch spouses and young children saying tearful goodbyes to travelers; if anything happened to them, the loss to their kin would be my fault, since I'd spun this whole venture into motion. An overwhelming uneasiness swept over us as we boarded the plane. It felt like entering another reality—a new place where the predictable past was of no help and new organs of perception had to somehow be quickly developed.

From New York to Frankfurt to Belgrade—the trip was uneventful but the foreboding didn't dissipate. Disembarking at the Belgrade airport, we knew for sure we were in a different world. Dingy kiosks dotted the sides of the waiting areas, lights were dim, and the place was gray except for a bit of color on a few cheap souvenirs. "Welcome to the Soviet Union," I thought.

We climbed up into a rickety-looking little JAT plane with perhaps 40 seats in it. By the time it was airborne, we found ourselves in the middle of a rapidly developing party. Fried chicken, boiled eggs, tomatoes, fresh greens, and bread were being passed among the passengers. We were kindly included. The local travelers were curious as to who we were and began struggling with their few words of English. I looked back and discovered that a member of our group, Barbara O'Reilly, had changed seats and was sitting in a nest of what looked like Russian airline pilots on their way back to Moscow. "Your name Varvara? Beautiful, beautiful name, yes, yes!" one delighted Russian fellow bellowed out with a big grin. The plane ride seemed to lighten up and so did our spirits. As we neared Moscow's lights in the distance, the entire planeload burst out singing *Moscow Nights* in harmony. Men, women, Americans, Russians, Yugoslavs—everyone was celebrating. We didn't know what, perhaps our meeting in the air, the sharing of food, learning new names, but most likely it was the relief that we'd met part of the enemy and they were just like us. Cynthia, our "informal" interpreter and guide, had been working overtime. We quickly learned how much one interpreter can handle when Russian speakers are 20 to one.

The tiny plane landed at Moscow's huge Sheremetyevo Airport at about 10:00 PM. To our amazement, the camera crew with equipment sailed right through Moscow Customs. For sure, someone had been apprised that we were arriving. The airport was dark and unfriendly. Two young Intourist guides, Masha and Vera, showed up to get us into our designated bus. By the time we made it to the hotel, we were dragging.

As we entered the Cosmos Hotel's lobby, flood lights became obvious. TV cameras were filming, and our new acquaintance, Paula Garb, unexpectedly appeared to greet us. How had she managed to arrange a welcome party in the center of the Cosmos lobby? Were we being used for propaganda purposes? My suspicious mind was ever at work. TV journalists asked questions about the KAL 007 crisis, and why we were coming to the U.S.S.R. when Americans here were leaving for the U.S.? We answered as best as we could, but must have been a disappointment to those hoping for tidbits of information to be used for propaganda purposes. Soon, we were off to our rooms to catch up on sleep.

New Experiences in a New Land

The following morning Masha and Vera inquired if we would like to meet Russians spontaneously on the streets or to take the regular city bus tour. Obviously they too had been prepped. We elected to see the top tourist sites first, which left plenty of time later for street encounters. Seeing the best during official excursions, made us wonder about other institutions not being shown to us. With "friendship" lapel pins in place, we began getting off the tour buses and finding metros to facilitate travel around the vastness of Moscow. We broke into small groups and started conversations with local youths in parks, young couples with prams, and grandmothers sitting on benches. Those we encountered were friendly once we introduced ourselves. Surprisingly local Russians smiled timidly and put on our pins without hesitation. Cynthia accompanied one group, then another. It was not uncommon to find Russians on the streets with some English capabilities. Several of our guys donned jogging togs and took to the sidewalks for morning runs— they must have looked aberrant to Muscovites on their way to work. It became obvious that no other joggers were on the streets. We disbanded in different directions. Through Cynthia we were able to get into a few Soviet apartments to visit with people she met during earlier stays in Moscow. Once behind locked doors, we were fascinated to hear a multiplicity of opinions on controversial issues among Soviet family members. On all Muscovites' minds were, "Why was the KAL airliner shot down—and will this event lead to war with America?"

Walking to the hotel one evening, Neil Forney was stopped by an aging woman on crutches with a leg missing. In broken English she asked if he was American. He replied that he was. She exploded, "Go home and tell your president, 'No War with America.' War took my leg. War hurts everyone. Tell him! 'No War!' " She hobbled off into the night.

Paula invited us to her apartment to discuss Soviet life. Sons, Andrei and Greg, ages 14 and 9, seemed delighted to talk about their lives in Moscow. Both were doing well in school and were eager to share their own ideas about being bi-cultural kids living in Russia. Life wasn't perfect, but for them it was good. As for the Cosmos lobby venue, Paula's work included arranging media events, so the welcome party wasn't difficult to accomplish.

At an official Soviet Peace Committee meeting, officials' propagandistic rhetoric and arrogant posturing about U.S. flaws infuriated us. Midway through the meeting, we began answering back and ended in a near shouting match. By the end, we agreed to disagree—with neither side feeling good about the fractious encounter.

Meeting Vladimir Pozner

Paula arranged a meeting with Vladimir Pozner, the Soviet Union's debonair TV personality. It was a shock to find him "so American." Pozner, it turned out, had been reared in New York up to age 16. His father, a Russian filmmaker rumored to be a spy during the McCarthy era, was forced to make a choice between the U.S. and the U.S.S.R. The elder Pozner took his family back to Moscow where teenage Vladimir had to adapt to Soviet life. He later explained, "For me coming here from America wasn't about democracy or communism—what I missed were hamburgers and Cokes!"

Our first meeting with Pozner was in a small conference room, which we assumed to be bugged. Even so, he was more forthcoming about the Soviet system than we expected. We heard none of the usual Peace Committee propaganda from him. However, he did believe that the KAL 007 airliner was on an intelligence-gathering mission. This meeting was the only one during the three-week trip when a Soviet official was straight with us. Pozner passed his telephone number as we departed. A long-lasting connection started that continues to the present.

Speaking from a Moscow Baptist Pulpit

We learned from another American that somewhere in Moscow there existed a working Baptist Church. Finally we obtained the location from a taxi driver. By the time we arrived, a mid-week service had already begun; familiar hymns were heard when we entered the doors.

The pre-revolutionary building appeared to have been a church from the beginning. The sanctuary was packed to capacity with folding chairs in all the aisles. Congregants were mostly babushkas in kerchiefs, some with their adult children and grandchildren. It looked to be a non-professional congregation. There was no room for us, but seats were cleared in the upper balcony to the left of the pulpit. Looking down on this sea of heads below, I wished my Baptist father could witness this worship service. This God-fearing, anti-communist American dad was seriously miffed that his daughter was traveling in the "land of the Godless enemy."

The minister came to the pulpit greeting the congregation in Christ's name and also greeted us, the unexpected visitors in the balcony. To our surprise, he asked if the leader of the group would come forward. We quickly decided that two of us would represent the group. Lynda Sayer and I weaved our way through the densely packed maze of congregants. We made unprepared remarks that we hoped made sense. Fortunately, photos taken from the balcony eventually provided evidence to my father that there were religious people in the Soviet Union.

Paula Garb with Russian sons, Andrei and Gregory Danilenko, in their small Moscow apartment in 1983. They soon became a favorite stop for American citizen diplomats arriving in Moscow.

Vladimir Pozner, Soviet TV anchor, with whom we discussed U.S.-U.S.S.R. issues in 1983. Pozner lived in New York until a teenager when his father was forced to move back to Russia as a result of McCarthy pressures. Once there Vladimir had to conform, learn to speak like a Russian and build his life in the Soviet Union.

We learned of a working Baptist Church in Moscow and took taxis to a service one evening. Showing up unannounced, we were seated in a packed congregation and ended up being invited to the pulpit to explain why we were there. Lynda Sayer and I tried to represent the remainder of the group as we looked over the congregation of mostly babushkas. This was September 20, 1983.

*3 x 5 gray cards were created to explain
our mission to Soviet citizens. They
were handed out on sidewalks, market
places, and metros for the next several
years. Soviets would put their telephone
numbers on the backs if they wanted to
continue discussions with us. Eventually
this was the way we built our Soviet
networks of citizens with whom we
interacted over the next few years.*

*We lost no time introducing our mission
to Soviet citizens, even on city metros.
To our surprise, this Soviet military
officer warmed up to our message.
September 1983.*

*Russian father putting a CUUI
friendship pin on his daughter. His
mother, out of camera range, was
cautioning him not to accept the
pin. September 1983.*

*Across the U.S.S.R., wedding parties
always went to the large memorials
around the cities which commemorated
the heroism of those who fought in World
War II. This is still tradition throughout
Russia, even now in year 2010.*

A Story Bigger than Life—Lily Golden

Another surprise—Paula inquired if I wanted to meet a close Soviet friend of hers. This was a coveted opportunity. We went to a suburban area where block houses were old and stairwells were in poor repair. Several flights up, Paula knocked at a door. It opened.

Before us, stood a large-framed, dignified-appearing black woman of about 45 years. In flawless British English, she welcomed us into her apartment. Standing beside her was a tiny, frail and aging white woman, whom she addressed as "Mama." The contrast was startling. Paula introduced me to Lily Golden, her mother, Bertha Bialek Golden, and Lily's 20-year-old daughter, Yelena Khanga. Thereupon I became privy to their larger-than-life story, which began in the early 1900s with Lily's black father, Oliver Golden.

Oliver grew up in Mississippi, where he gained experience in cotton growing. Brilliant and ambitious he enrolled in Tuskegee Institute and was a student of George Washington Carver. As a young man Oliver studied in the Soviet Union, during which he participated in agricultural projects. Back in the U.S. he recruited workers for Soviet contracts. In 1931, with the help of Dr. Carver, Oliver gathered a group of black specialists to go to Soviet Asia to help develop the Soviet cotton industry. His closest partner in this project was Bertha, who met him around 1927 in a New York jail after they both had been arrested for participating in an equal rights demonstration. This handsome black man and his tiny Jewish girlfriend eventually married. While living in New York, and before departing for the Soviet Union in 1931, Oliver was severely beaten for being with a white woman. His injuries would plague him long after his departure from New York. After several years working in Uzbekistan, he died of kidney injuries sustained from the mob beating. Bertha was left in the U.S.S.R. with their only child, Lily. She never went back to America.

When I met her, she seemed to be withering away ... except when I asked why she never returned to her homeland. Straightening up, she exploded with the vigor of a youth, saying that she adamantly believed in socialism and communism and had no interest in "going backward" or ever returning to the states where American relatives had disowned her. Bertha died a few years later. Lily will be revisited in following chapters.

Moscow Street Escapades

We were continually on the watch for the KGB, worried about 'bugs' in our hotel rooms and under dining tables. Traveler Bob Sturdivant was picked up by young KGB officers after photographing a skirmish in a park. The uniformed men wanted the film from Bob's camera. He refused. They took him to a nearby building for interrogation. Bob tried in broken language to explain that he was on a goodwill mission. He gave them the groups' lapel button showing two hands shaking. They were satisfied and quickly turned to the subject they really wanted to know about—the differences between American and Soviet football! Bob kept his film.

We spontaneously walked up to people on sidewalks, in market places, at civil wedding ceremonies, churches, and schools. Introducing ourselves, we shared our large lapel buttons and tried to get into personal conversations. Many of these encounters didn't amount to anything but superficial chat, but we hoped they left these Soviets with enjoyable encounters to think about the next time they read propaganda about America.

Prior to the trip, we were given contact information for Jewish "refusenik" families in the three cities to be visited. In Moscow we visited several tiny flats filled with Jews who were trying to leave the country—but were being kept captive by Soviet officials. We listened to their anger and accusations, and, of course, concurred with them that they and other Jews should be allowed to leave if they wished—which obviously they did. Among ourselves we brainstormed how we might be able to push the system for them.

So it went. We saw a mix of the best the Soviet Union had to offer through the official Intourist program. Admittedly, we were impressed with their early childhood care compared to the totally negative stereotypes we held prior to the trip. We experienced the worst sides of Soviet control through listening to the plight of the Jewish refusers and the ways in which their lives had been reduced to zero for bucking the system.

Trusting no one at our hotel, we spoke nothing of importance to each other while in our rooms. But we thought we had found a safe place to communicate. Each morning we met out of doors at the huge Cosmonaut statue across from the Cosmos Hotel. There we felt free to plot our day's strategy and share apartment stories with each other.

If the KGB had tried to arrange our experiences on the streets, it would have been impossible. We walked out of the hotel doors daily, went to the metros, and randomly split off in different directions. We didn't know where we were going, so how could the KGB have known where to be or who to set up? They could follow us, and appeared to do so on a few occasions. Our modus operandi was, "If you think you are being followed, stop at an ice cream vendor in the street and buy ice cream for yourself and for whoever you think is following you, and give it to them." The days were crammed full of adventures, and our minds were reeling with cognitive dissonance by the time we left Moscow.

Tbilisi, Georgia

Next we were off to the Soviet Republic of Georgia. It was a lovely, hilly, green place with fruit hanging on trees in mid-September. Compared to their light-haired Russian neighbors, Georgia's population had darker skin and hair. They displayed a sense of freedom and ease, waving off anything Soviet or Russian as beneath them. They claimed to be the masters of their own country. In Tbilisi, Cynthia introduced us to a group of Georgian psychotherapists and their mystic leader, Viktor. We were invited to their sacred spot up in the hills outside of Tbilisi. It sounded like such an adventure that we couldn't resist stretching the law requiring foreigners to remain in the cities.

We caught a rickety bus full of hefty Georgian women who were going home to their villages after a long day of selling produce at Thilisi's central farmers' market. Under their feet and on their laps they had produce, bread, and live chickens. Laughing and waving their arms wildly, they passed fruits, cilantro, and pig cracklings to us strangers. We were entranced by the spectacle of colors, smells and hilarity. The old bus finally made it up into the hills where the ladies deboarded at different small villages. Near the top, we debarked and came upon a friendly sheepherder and his clan of about thirty men, women, and children. With Cynthia's help, we caught the flavor of their poor but equally rich-appearing rural life before taking off on foot for even higher ground.

With the sky darkening, we trekked further up the incline. As the trail converged with another, we came upon the Georgian therapists, their leader and his wife, Larissa. Finally at the top of the hill, under a full moon, we laid down blankets, spread out food, and built a huge bonfire. Traveler Ray Gatchelon, captain of the Oakland Fire Department, had carried a peace torch halfway around the world to give to a Soviet of his choice. Up in the

Georgian children in Pioneer's uniforms, meeting Americans on Tbilisi streets. Sarah Seybold and Richard Bowen in back row.

Lily Golden, on the right, is an African/American/Soviet black woman we met in Moscow. Lily's father came to the U.S.S.R. in the early 1900s. The first meeting began a fascinating saga with Lily providing data and a personal story that deserves a film someday. Barbara Rinnan from Chicago and Tennison are on the left.

Our mountaintop experience with a Soviet mystic, Victor, and friends outside of Tbilisi. He is shown holding the bouquet of flowers. This event also started a long relationship for some members of the group with Victor and wife coming to the U.S. to visit later in the 1980s. September 1983.

Georgian hills that evening, Ray lit the torch and presented it to Viktor, who obviously was a man of great faith and peace. Here we were half a world away from our homes in America, working with our "enemies" to create a picnic. It made no sense at all. These were normal wonderful men and women just like ourselves.

Perhaps it was jet lag or culture disorientation, but on the mountaintop that evening, it seemed that there were no problems in the world that couldn't be resolved with sufficient exposure between opposing groups. Late that night, we had to find our way back to town through thickets and cow paths without the advantage of a flashlight. As Tbilisi's city lights became visible in the distance, we moved in a single line toward them with Viktor guiding us down the trails. Worn and dirty, we ended up back at our hotel—to the obvious consternation of two hotel door guards who had to unlock the doors for us. If they knew about our escapade out of town, no one ever mentioned it.

Leningrad—A Decaying Museum of Architecture

Our last city to visit was Leningrad. It was old, tired, drab, but also noble and magnificent. My first inclination was to search for a huge brush and cans of Ajax so I could start scrubbing buildings. Later it was explained that for decades Moscow intentionally denied Leningrad funds for the city's upkeep. Competition between the two cities and citizens had been keen since the revolution. In this cultural capital of Russia, we saw magnificent museums and palaces, the interiors of which had been meticulously restored. We walked into schools without permission and were struck by their children's knowledge of English and world literature, including American authors. Nearly every neighborhood seemed to have a kindergarten. As the weather turned chilly, babushkas on the sidewalks were seen adjusting children's hats, buttoning coats, and blowing little noses, while admonishing them to take care before walking off. By now it was becoming clear to us that the children of the U.S.S.R. were their protected and "honored citizens"— and that they were everyone's responsibility.

We were shocked to see babies left on sidewalks in carriages while mothers were inside stores shopping. My American alarms went off. I asked our guide, Masha, "Is this not dangerous?" She couldn't understand my concern and remarked that if a baby whimpers, someone will come along and jiggle the carriage. My next question was, "Are babies ever taken while mothers are away?" She looked at me as if I was crazy, then said, "No, we've never heard of such a thing ... why would anyone consider taking another's baby?" I was left to ponder the many unexpected differences I was observing in our two societies.

Numbers of Leningradians were frank with us about what did not work in their country, their deep wishes to travel abroad, and their sense of how far behind the Soviet Union was compared to the outside world. Most Russians we met in Leningrad listened daily to BBC. They compared what they saw in their heavily controlled newspapers and TV programs with BBC's radio messages. Many held unrealistic images of America with golden streets and Hollywood-like people. Nothing in the U.S.S.R. could compete with their visions of American life.

It would become known many years later that on September 26, 1983, while our small group was in Leningrad, that World War III was averted by a Soviet Lieutenant Colonel, Stanislav Petrov, who was in charge at the Soviet Nuclear

*Command Center outside of Moscow. That September day, sirens and flashing
red lights went off alerting that intercontinental ballistic missiles from the U.S.
were headed toward the U.S.S.R. Petrov refused to launch. See pg 199 and 208,
and Google Stanislav Petrov.*

Meeting a Young Communist Party Member

Select Soviet party members were permitted to meet with foreigners at the Houses
of Friendship in each Soviet city. We were invited to the Leningrad chapter where we
met a young party member, Elena Sadovnikova. She was lovely, curious, and at most, 30
years old. Elena showed up at our hotel the night before we left for America. I remember
little else about that evening other than strolling down the hotel corridor with her and
talking. She moved a bit closer and quietly whispered, "If you ever come back, would
you please bring me a book that I can't get here? The title is Shambala. It is by our great
Russian mystic, Nicholas Roerich." The name meant nothing to me. She passed me her
home telephone number and was gone. Once home, I located Shambala by Roerich and
on the second trip delivered it to Elena. Over the years, Elena would play a large role in
my understanding of her country and its leadership.

A Forward Thinking Young Journalist

Toward the end of our trip, we asked Masha, the Intourist guide, to arrange discussions
for us with a young Soviet journalist. Intourist organized a meeting with Evgeny
Lukyanov at our hotel. We assumed he was a spokesperson for the Soviet government
since his English was perfect. He seemed to be intrigued with our reason for being in his
country. About 30 years old, Evgeny was different from the older generations of Soviets
we had met in official meetings. Our session with him lasted for hours. He had exciting,
open-ended responses for the tough questions we posed. On departing he gave us his
personal telephone number. We would meet this young man again over the coming years.

Piskaryovskoye Cemetery

Last our group went to Piskaryovskoye Cemetery where half a million local citizens
are buried in dozens of mass pits from the Siege of Leningrad. Two small museums
at the entry of the cemetery tell the story. The Nazi's surrounded Leningrad for 900
days between 1941 and 1944 during one of the coldest winters ever experienced in this
northern city. Temperatures dropped to 45 below zero Fahrenheit. Within one two-month
period alone, over 200,000 Leningraders perished from starvation and freezing. Photos
in the museums depict stories of unimaginable circumstances. Blow ups showed family
members dragging dead loved ones on sleds through the snow to the mass burial plots of
which Piskaryovskoye is but one around the city.

We began to grasp the enormity of the human sacrifices made by Soviet people to
stop the Nazi war machine during World War II—which had not been talked about in
America that we could remember. The U.S.S.R. lost over 26 million citizens fighting the
Nazis compared to America's 400,000. Only three percent of the young Soviet men born
in 1923 survived the war. As the young men perished, young women picked up their
weapons and continued to fight. Every Soviet with whom we had spoken in the three
cities, including Tbilisi, Georgia told of multiple family losses—which at the time of
our visit was 40 years after the war. The Great Patriotic War, as the Russians call World
War II, was still very much alive in the minds and hearts of every Soviet citizen whom
we met.

Evgeny Lukyanov: Young Soviet journalist who seemed as interested in us as we were in him. Soon he would become a weathervane for the rapid happenings going on within the archaic Soviet system. He was an early predictor of Gorbachev's rise to General Secretary. We met him first in 1983.

2010: Eugene is currently the Deputy to Ilya Klebanov, the President's Director of the vast Federal District in NW Russia, one of seven such districts across Russia.

Elena Sadovnikova on the left, was a young party member and psychologist we met at an official meeting in 1983. Other Soviets there were fronts for the government, Elena was a reformer in disguise. Later she would find ways to get up the political ladder in order to make changes. Fortunately change was increasingly in the air, so she never suffered repercussions.

Piskarovskoe cemetery, one of a number of burial grounds in St. Petersburg where Leningrad families brought dead relatives and friends during the 900 Day Siege of Leningrad. Workers excavated 186 deep pits where half a million men, women and children were buried to prevent health consequences of the living. The winter was fierce; most died of starvation and freezing. Two small museums at the entrance depict the times in photos and memorabilia. The Eternal Flame burns as visitors enter the grounds.

Departing the U.S.S.R. for America

Departing the U.S.S.R. through Leningrad was bittersweet. We experienced the chilling impact of the most devastating war the world has ever known—and the tragic consequences of a highly controlled society on its own people. But we had grown to feel empathy and admiration toward those whom we had met. Upon saying goodbyes, Masha and Vera hugged each of us while brushing away tears; they laughingly joked that we were still trying to convert them to capitalism.

Through the kaleidoscope of Soviet people we had met, none of them fit the stereotypes with which we had arrived in the U.S.S.R. Theirs was a worldview and a system under which we would never want to live, but also one that we could never again see as "enemy." All those we met with positively envied and admired Americans. Our slides captured every conceivable type of setting in which we had found ourselves in those packed three weeks. The film crew, with us in all three cities, had 40 hours of excellent broadcast quality film. Young Elena, the Gosteleradio official, had not tried to control us or the cameras. Gennadi German, at the San Francisco Consulate had lived up to his word.

Former FBI warnings of "never meeting anyone who wasn't previously set up" simply were not true. It was the official party line from agents who had no personal experience of the country with which they had chosen to work. They knew the language, had become "specialists" of sorts, and yet didn't have a clue what the actual reality was in the land of their "enemy." Our flight home was a mass group-processing event held 30,000 feet up in the air. Sleep was impossible—too many ideas were crashing around inside our heads. Before landing in New York, we had all decided that one trip to the land of the enemy was not enough.

Indeed, our work had just begun.

Back Home—Outcomes and Opportunities

Debriefing with the FBI—October 1983 and Beyond

Shortly after arriving home, a call came from the FBI. "Gerry Tracy here, we would like to debrief you regarding your trip." Having trekked up to the FBI building numerous times, we felt it fair for the two agents to come to us. We were eager to show them our photos. In early October, seven of us received the two agents for lunch and a slide show at my apartment. The images revealed impromptu circumstances—street diplomacy, inside Soviet apartments, visiting schools, interacting with teens, shopping in markets, picnicking with psychologists, visiting the Moscow Baptist Church, and much more. Both agents appeared shocked at the diverse experiences we had encountered. The less inquisitive one seemed somewhat upset, but the other, Gerry Tracy, asked intelligent questions.

From then on, Gerry Tracy conducted our debriefings. Soon our citizen diplomacy trips were frequently leaving the U.S. for the Soviet Union. Each season more Americans signed up to travel to the forbidden territory, and each time we debriefed upon return home. These sessions had become enjoyable. Gerry never discounted our experiences; she just listened.

A couple of years of debriefings passed, and I received the usual call from Gerry. This time she asked to meet, not at the FBI building, but at Louie's, a funky little restaurant that hangs out over the Pacific Ocean in San Francisco. It was a strange place for such a meeting but was fine with me. Having parked my car up the street from Louie's, I began walking down toward the ocean. A woman in maternity clothes was standing near the café door. As I got closer I was shocked to see that it was Gerry. Somehow she must have covered her condition well when we last met. We settled into a booth and began chit chat about her first pregnancy. She began the usual questioning. "With whom did I meet? Did they ask anything about the U.S. government? Did they want me to take any packages?" The answers were generally no, no, and no. She then entered into a conversation completely unrelated to our usual discussions. "My mother may not be able to come when my baby is delivered. Might I call you around that time if I need to?" It dawned on me that our relationship was changing, that Gerry trusted me, and that now we were just two women facing life's natural happenings. I agreed, of course. As I left Gerry on the sidewalk, she remarked, "Take good care of yourself. You are my only eyes and ears into that country."

In a month or so, I left for the Soviet Union again. When I returned, strangely there was no call from Gerry. After a couple of weeks, I called the familiar FBI number to check in. "Hello, may I speak with Gerry Tracy." A cool and impersonal voice said, "Sorry, we have no one by the name of Gerry Tracy working here." "Of course you do," I replied, "I just met with her a couple of months back." The same voice with the eerie tone again said, "I'm sorry we have no one by the name of Gerry Tracy working here." I protested again, and the third time got the same message and the same tone. I was stunned.

Had Gerry taken early medical leave and this was the FBI's way of handling it? Had there been a bug planted on her (of which she was not aware) when we met at Louie's? Had she begun to believe there was a story different than what she had been told at the FBI, and decided to do something different with her life? Could she have been terminated due to our developing a closer relationship? Maybe someone reading this book will know Gerry's whereabouts ... if so, please tell her I'd love to talk with her again.

A Second Meeting with the CIA—October 1983

As previously agreed, I made the follow-up call in October 1983 to the U2 pilot to tell him what we had experienced with Soviet people. We met in a San Jose cafe. He was quite interested in what Soviet society looked like on the inside. Even more he was completely stumped that ordinary American citizens like us would take on such a mission.

Before leaving the restaurant, he leveled eyes at me and cautioned, "Sharon, what you are doing is dangerous. Not only are there those in the Soviet Union who don't want this kind of unofficial activity to continue, but there are also those here in the U.S. who can't afford to let this activity succeed—and they are in high places." I protested, saying that everyone knew that we were innocent travelers. The debate continued, and at last he cautioned, "If, after this warning, you are determined to continue, there are some things you must do to protect yourself. Find a good, respected lawyer immediately. You must carry a tape recorder with you at all times to record everything you do and everyone you meet. And you must send these tapes to the lawyer every day for safe keeping." Again I protested saying I wanted no part of this kind of spy scenario. He may have thought my resistance was due to financial concerns. Next he offered to purchase the tape recorder, which I instantly refused. He continued, "You need a trail of evidence of everything you do, and others in high places need to know that this trail exists. It will be your only protection."

"Are you saying that people in my own country and government would intervene?"

"It's not called intervention; it's called national security," he replied. I left the restaurant on that sunny October day feeling as if I had been hit by a freight train. If he was right, I was definitely in some sort of unfathomable zone that I couldn't even begin to comprehend—for the first time I felt abject fear. I don't know whether his information was accurate or not, but certainly the photos of him with Fidel Castro couldn't have been faked. I never contacted or heard from him again.

Ultimately, it didn't shake my inner sense that the U.S.-U.S.S.R. standoff was so dangerous that, if it wasn't gradually resolved, a nightmare of nuclear war could result. With my mind crowded by this immediate preoccupation, I didn't have time or energy to worry about tape recorders or lawyers.

The PBS Documentary

Our big hoped-for public relations opportunity was to get our trip behind the Iron Curtain documented and broadcast on PBS. The end of November, we got a call from the video manager, Jim Small. "We are ready for you to view the first cut for half of the documentary. When can you come?" A couple of days later five of us sat in the studio waiting to see how they had juxtaposed the scenes and voices to tell our story.

Lights went off and images began to show in the dark room. Firestorm noise, stills of Lenin, hammer and sickle shots, and general chaos covered the screen. Canned B-grade footage had been used to put an "us-them" slant on our story. Part of our 40 hours of tapes was spliced into the roughly edited piece.

Ceiling lights went on. We looked at each other in disbelief. What we saw didn't represent our three-week experience in the Soviet Union. This film crew had been through the same experiences that we had. How could they turn our story into the rough cut we had just previewed? Immediately we confronted Jim who had traveled with us. He replied as a professional, "Trust us, we know what the American public will be interested in watching. We know what it will take to get this footage on PBS. They aren't interested in 'powder-puff' pieces." Arguments flew back and forth. He finally said, "Let us know within the week whether this is a go or not; we have other projects to get to."

The choice was ours. The professionals had spoken. They thought they saw a way to cut the footage so it would be acceptable to PBS audiences, never mind whether it was true or not. We were heartsick. We had paid for their trips, we had paid for the footage, and our intention was to encourage others to take up the cause of reducing tensions between the superpowers. Now all hopes were going down the drain.

We went to Sarah Seybold's home and caucused for hours. At the end we decided it was better that the footage never be used, rather than letting it become one more sensational piece that showed a few smiles from Soviet peasants while still maintaining the perennial "us-them" mentality. The next day we called Jim and gave him our decision. In addition, we told them that they would be sued if they copied and used any of our footage—and requested that it be returned to us immediately.

A month later, Jim telephoned and said he had a lull in his schedule and a bit of free time. So, if by chance we wanted him to put the story together as we saw it, he would help … but the team didn't want their names associated with the final product. The deal was that one of us would need to write the story line, select the footage, hire voiceovers, get permissions for background music, and complete all responsibilities needed for the final computerized edit. Jim would cut the sequences, mix them on his equipment, and we would pay him the final installment. We had no experience in film making, weren't technicians, and considered the entire process absolutely overwhelming. However with nothing to lose, we accepted Jim's option.

In late 1983, I carried the 40 hours of footage to Carol and Paul Hwoshinsky's Palo Alto home to take advantage of the best technology that could be used for free—and lived with the hours of images until the most important pieces were identified. The footage selected was consistent with our experience in the U.S.S.R. A professional "voice over" and music were procured.

The race against Jim's timetable required 12 and 14 hour days of working feverishly with the newly developing script and the footage. Finally, a video resulted. It had technical flaws obvious to us, but at least it told our real story.

"When the People Lead" never made it to PBS, of course. However, between 1984 and 1989, CCI trip travelers continuously used the video for presentations in cities around the U.S. During the 1988-89 "Soviets Meet Middle America!" program, the video was sent to coordinating committees in 265 American cities that hosted the program. Numerous cities showed excerpts from "When the People Lead" on local TV channels.

Founding the Center for U.S.-U.S.S.R. Initiatives

By late 1983, we realized it was necessary to have official status for our mission and activities. We had used personal monies thus far to cover operation expenses, but in order to expand the work, we needed to raise funds from the public. This required the coveted IRS tax deductible status. Within three months the status was granted and CUUI became a legitimate nonprofit organization.

Becoming Public Educators

In 1983 each of us wrote Christmas newsletters describing our new mission to friends and colleagues across the U.S. We invited both local and at-distance friends to join us in a trip to the Soviet Union—or to invite us to make slide presentations at their clubs, classrooms, and universities. Some recipients decided to travel with us, and others, school principals, university professors, civic club leaders, and church groups began contacting us to speak on U.S.-U.S.S.R. topics. We were encouraged by positive interest in most audiences. Sometimes we dealt with hecklers who labeled us unpatriotic and ridiculed those in audiences who took us seriously. Future travelers began signing up for trips as a result of these presentations.

We hadn't been able to get mainstream media attention. By the end of 1983, it seemed that stepping out with some bold action was necessary. I decided to take off the year of 1984 to work as a full-time public educator—hoping that awareness could be raised in other parts of America about the dangers of missile race and the deteriorating superpower relationship.

Have Message, Will Travel

We contacted friends in Arizona, New Mexico, Texas, and Oklahoma to learn if they could set up public speaking engagements if I came through their areas. Soon a "road trip" was in the making. A hastily created flyer explained our investigative work in the U.S.S.R. and asked readers to think of new options that might be less dangerous than 50,000 nuclear weapons on launch pads. We intended to put these flyers in the hands of as many people as possible between California to Texas—also to tape them when appropriate in restaurants, convenience stores, or gas stations along the way.

Dallas was the final destination. Due to budgetary constraints, my car became a portable office and hotel. It was loaded with newspaper articles, newsletters, and flyers. For sleep, my Subaru pulled into truck stops and parked alongside 18-wheelers. It's hard now to imagine what crusty drivers must have thought if they noticed a middle-aged lady sleeping next to their rigs.

Audiences en route were small … sometimes no more than a dozen people, but those who showed up had a visceral fear of nuclear weapons. Men and women alike poured out their anxieties. Fathers admitted to late night worries that their families could be gone by morning. Mothers shared apprehensions of hearing a boom and seeing a mushroom cloud forming on the horizon. America was awash in fear—and yet there was no venue in which to vent their helplessness and angst. By the time I arrived in Dallas, it felt like our message about the insanity of weapons on hair-trigger alert was tapping into a hot wire with ordinary Americans. Meanwhile the U.S. administration continued to build nuclear weapons, as did the Soviets in the U.S.S.R. The media of both countries continued to excoriate each other as though its own stockpiles were of no danger at all.

In Dallas—A Propitious Set of Circumstances

Vivian Castleberry, editor of the *Dallas Times Herald's* Living Section, welcomed me into her comfortable home, which became my Texas base for nearby cities. A trailblazer for over 40 years, Vivian knew how to get her readership activated. Ready with pen and pad, she began asking questions. An article publicizing the nuclear issues and CUUI's trip appeared in the Herald overnight. Her phone began ringing. I asked if she would consider going on the next trip with me. Her first answer was, "No, Russia has never been of primary interest to me." Later she would say, "I continued to listen to Sharon as she spoke to people across the country. The day she was leaving, I walked into her bedroom and handed her a down payment check for the next trip. We had three daughters in universities, my retirement was not adequate, and I had absolutely no idea how I would pay for an unexpected trip—but knew that I had to go."

Vivian's extensive following of women friends supported her U.S.S.R. trip in May of 1984. She was the ultimate citizen diplomat, exchanging ideas with officials in Peace Committee meetings, interviewing ordinary people on Soviet streets, and hugging children in schools. Little did she know that the next direction for her life was taking form. When she arrived home from the U.S.S.R. after her first trip, she began speaking and writing about her Soviet experiences.

By 1987, Vivian formed a nonprofit organization registered as Peacemakers, Incorporated, to create an international peace conference for women. In 1988,

Peacemakers held its first International Women's Conference in Dallas with over 2,000 delegates from 52 countries attending. For a week they brainstormed how to create a safer planet for the world's children. Conferees returned to their home states and countries inspired to lead their constituencies in this new direction. In 1999, a second Peacemakers Conference was held.

At the third Peacemakers Conference in 2007, 1,400 women from 45 countries passed a resolution to create a permanent Peace Institute, which would focus on educating women throughout the world to be peacemakers. In 2009, Peacemakers Incorporated unanimously agreed to name the new entity the "Castleberry Peace Institute" (CPI). It is officially affiliated with the University of North Texas, which is the only four-year university in the America's southwest that offers degrees in Peace Studies.

Introduction to Rotary International—1984

While in Texas, the Rotary Club of McKinney, Texas, asked me to speak on, "What citizens can do relative to the U.S.S.R. and nuclear weapons." This was my first opportunity to learn about Rotary International. Vaguely knowing that Rotarians were businessmen and understanding that Texas was quite a conservative state, I pondered how to approach this hot subject. The slides would tell the story, and I would have to take the consequences … whatever they were. The day came, and the slides and the story rolled into action. The room of Rotarians fell ominously silent as I tried to explain the issues without offending their conservative points of view on the superpower race. As I closed the slide show, hearty applause broke out and hands went up signaling personal questions to be answered. Following the discussion, the young McKinney club president wrote out a check for $200 and presented it to me. This was an unexpected turn of events!

The McKinney Rotary connection was the beginning of CUUI/CCI's long and remarkable history with Rotary International. As time moved forward, over 500 American Rotary Clubs would be largely responsible for the success of CCI's Productivity Enhancement Program (PEP), an adaptation of the historic Marshall Plan's Productivity Tours.

Studs Terkel—A Catalyst for an Explosion

Back in Dallas at Vivian's home, the phone rang. I answered. A booming voice was on the line, "Is this Ms. Sharon Tennison?" "Yes, this is she. Who is calling?" "This is Studs Terkel," the voice blared back. I wracked my brain. Did I know this voice or name? No, I didn't. The pause was enough to set off the voice at the other end. "Do you know who I am?" he blared out. "No, I'm afraid I don't, sir. What can do I do for you?" The voice exploded over the phone, "God, this is even better than I thought!" he yelled to someone nearby. Immediately I guessed a crackpot was on the line. Wondering whether to hang up or not, I waited. The voice settled down, "Ms. Tennison, are you the lady who went to the Soviet Union recently?" I confirmed. He continued, "I have a nationwide program in Chicago, and I'm calling to see if you will come to Chicago and be on my show!" Thankfully, I hadn't hung up! I told him I'd call back. Now I needed to find out who this Studs really was. Vivian soon came home from work and was shocked to learn that Terkel had called and that his name hadn't registered with me. She could not imagine that I didn't know that Studs Terkel was a well-known media personality and a Pulitzer prize-winning author.

A flight to Chicago was not included in my plan. I had budgeted only enough money for a 3,500 mile road trip—and that only if American homes could be used for sleeping on the way back to San Francisco. By this time, sleeping in my car at truck stops had worn thin. While deliberating what to do, a call came in the next day from our San Francisco tour agent, Marguerite Craig. She reported she was mailing her $400 airline commission check as a contribution to CUUI's work. That was how I managed to fly to Chicago to meet the famous Studs Terkel. What a character he was—at seventy-five years young, he was on fire for truth telling in politics and citizen participation in government affairs. He welcomed me to an hour of boisterous questions and answers on his Chicago program. Studs repeatedly gave out my home telephone number during the program. Call-ins came from all over America. Arriving back in San Francisco, my answering machine was chock-full. A nerve had been struck in the heart of Middle America!

A Chicago Connection—Barbara Rinnan

Before flying to Chicago, I called Asilomar conferee Dave Hardin who lived in the 'Windy City.' He belonged to a group of local CEOs who sponsored weekly TV talk shows on current events. Fascinated by our story of citizen involvement in the superpower realm, they arranged for me to be interviewed on their Sunday evening program. This unexpected opportunity brought more contacts. The most propitious Chicago meeting of all was with Dave Hardin's right-hand partner, a dignified Chicago matron named Barbara Rinnan. For years Barbara had poured out her concerns to him and all who would listen about the imminent dangers of nuclear weapons on launch pads. Dave arranged a luncheon for Barbara and me to meet at Chicago's Art Institute. From the first few minutes, it was clear that Barbara's eyes and voice mirrored my concerns. She was already trying to find a way to get to the U.S.S.R.—but just hadn't yet found the way.

Barbara went on CUUI's third Citizen Diplomacy trip and was an intrepid diplomat. She bowled over Soviet officials with her regal looks and fabulous wardrobe. She was equally accepted in tiny apartments where they had never experienced such a blonde-haired wonder. She tactfully let officials know that real differences of opinions existed, and she instinctively knew how to empathize with the least of Russian people on the streets.

Barbara came back to Chicago ready to enlist Illinois' elected officials into her concerns. She started with senior Senator Paul Simon, whom she had known for decades. Next, she formed the Mid-West Center for U.S.-U.S.S.R. Initiatives, which she ran for 10 years. It became a mirror image of the rapidly growing CUUI office in San Francisco. We worked hand-in-hand on all programs up until 2000. Barbara is a legend for many in the U.S. and across Russia. Eighty years young she is still active, and I believe she was at least partially responsible for Obama's foreign policy person emailing me to get a second opinion about the Georgia/South Ossetia/Russian war in August of 2008.

After traveling to enemy territory and finding no enemies there, we traveled around the U.S. with slide presentations that showed us in all sorts of interactions with Soviet citizens.

This provided a format to speak about the insanity of the nuclear arms race, track II diplomacy as an alternative to the Cold War, and backing away from the brink of a nuclear confrontation. American citizens were unexpectedly open to our message.

Vivian Castleberry shown with a WWII war veteran during May 9th Victory Day celebration across the U.S.S.R.

Little did Vivian know that this trip would begin a fascinating new chapter in her life.

Barbara Rinnan (left), initiator and director of MidWest CUUI in Chicago. This was Barbara's first of many trips to the U.S.S.R. Shown here with granddaughter of world famous choreographer Georgi Balanchine in Tbilisi, Georgia.

CUUI's Expansion

My three-bedroom flat had quickly become a hub of intense activity. Volunteers came all hours of the day and night. Names of future travelers with their contact information were put on waiting lists while we figured out how to set up the next trips.

With no funds in the beginning, we spent from our pockets until the amazing day when a little known donor sent in a check for $3,000. It felt like $3 million. Our greatest need was an assistant with computer skills. At the same time, Simi Cover, a Russian studies major from the University of Kentucky, contacted us by telephone. She heard about CUUI's mission from a citizen diplomacy traveler in Kentucky and wanted to apply for a job. Sight unseen, we offered her a part-time position at $1,000 a month for three months—if she paid her way west to San Francisco. Her mother provided her air ticket, and Simi joined our team as our first employee. We hoped we could raise funds for her future salary but gave no assurances. She moved into my apartment temporarily. Simi, with no relevant experience, began organizing future trips for citizen diplomats. A $300 "tack-on" fee was added to each traveler's actual cost, which began paying Simi's salary. Soon she had a full time salary and found a flat of her own. This continued the off-and-on practice of using my apartment to move CUUI forward.

Breaking Down Stereotypes—Through Personal Encounters

Meanwhile the trips were revealing that invariably, face-to-face interactions with Soviet citizens in everyday venues broke through lifetimes of entrenched stereotypes on both sides. Americans and Soviets were bewildered that politics and geography had kept our citizen populations apart for so many decades. Hearing their life stories, and experiencing their genuine responses, it was hard to believe that our lives were still jeopardized by politics and power.

The first two trips were highly experimental. They set the model for CUUI's future work.

Profiles of People and Events in the 1980s

Henry Dakin and the 3200 Block of Sacramento Street

Space was rapidly becoming a challenge for CUUI. Worse still, we didn't have an official business address. In 1984, Dr. Willis Harmon took me to meet a wealthy San Francisco iconoclast, Henry Dakin of the Dakin Toy Company. He was to become our godfather. Henry was converting a former automotive repair building on Sacramento Street into a two-story hub for innovators involved with global technology and U.S.-U.S.S.R. work. Why the latter? Perhaps because in the '70s, Henry had helped publish Samisdat, the underground press of Soviet dissidents. On principle, Henry was interested in any work that broke through social and political barriers. And he had the personal funds to support such operations. Henry owned several buildings and leased others on the 3200 block of Sacramento Street.

Soon CUUI was in a small corner of one of his buildings. Henry provided all innovators he took in with a pro-bono desk, a Mac computer, and a telephone. My home office was still in constant use. With entrance into Henry's world, we had a prestigious address in San Francisco's elite Pacific Heights and the use of his large new second-floor presentation room with a spacious deck overlooking the city. Henry's latest toy was a large white satellite dish on a deck behind the building, which picked up Soviet television 24 hours a day. Soviet news was carried over several monitors throughout his building. A Russian expatriate was hired as interpreter for non-Russian speakers. The Soviet Consulate began sending daily couriers to pick up tapes of Moscow's last 24 hours of news coverage.

A block away from Henry's building sat Picnix, a restaurant that promptly became a hangout for all of us in Henry's domain. Impromptu work meetings were held there as the "3200 block" grew exponentially. It was also rumored that FBI agents frequented Picnix to pick up the latest on U.S.-Soviet happenings. It was also rumored that more work regarding Soviet issues went on at the 3200 block than in the whole of Washington.

Soon Henry moved our rapidly growing CUUI to another house in his nest of buildings. It was the second floor of an old, unheated Victorian house. At first, we had one large room, then two. Over the next year, we took over the whole house. CUUI trips were finally making sufficient money, and we began paying full rent. Henry's goal for each micro-organization was to become economically self-sufficient within a couple of years. If not, they would vacate to make room for other innovators.

At any one time there were at least a dozen struggling nonprofits in Henry's 3200 block. Many came in and out, but a couple made it big. The largest was a tiny tele-communication startup, the brainchild of wizard, Joel Schatz, which began the first ever email link between the U.S. and the U.S.S.R. Shortly thereafter, Schatz brought the first live images of Russians and Americans to each other through his San Francisco-Moscow Teleport, Inc. His operation eventually became the Sov-Am Teleport, which had a virtual monopoly on high-speed U.S.-U.S.S.R. communications. Joel sold out in the 1990s making himself a rich man for life.

CUUI grew to be Henry's second largest and longest-running NGO in terms of both programs and financial resources. Without Henry's support and wisdom, few, if any, of us on the block would have survived during the critical period before the Soviet Union fell apart. By 1995 CCI expanded beyond the block's space capacity. We moved our operations to the historic Presidio National Park, which was being renovated to house successful non-governmental organizations in the Bay Area.

Americans of Different Persuasions

In the summer of 1984, I found myself sharing a train compartment with officers of the U.S. Consulate in Leningrad. The train was on its way to Finland. After a brief conversation about our on-ground citizen work in the U.S.S.R., I was politely told, "No doubt your activity could harm what real diplomats are trying to do." The lead officer turned back to his reading material. I felt like a compartment companion with chicken pox. Reflecting later on this interaction, I couldn't help pondering how bizarre it was. Here was a U.S. government official who didn't ask a single question about what we were learning on the streets and in Soviet apartments or how we viewed the relations between the two countries.

I could have never guessed that our quality time with the U.S. Consulate, the Moscow Embassy, and the U.S. Foreign Service community would come later— and that by 1993, they would welcome us and generously fund our work in the Russia field.

Our Journalist Friend's Prediction

The young Russian journalist, Evgeny Lukyanov, whom we met on our initial 1983 trip, remained an insider I could telephone when in Leningrad. In May 1984, I sat with Evgeny in a corner at Leningrad's huge Pribaltiskaya Hotel. Our discussion was, as always, how to constructively influence future relations between the two countries. Evgeny hunched over, with head in hands, and said quietly, "There is one younger man coming up through the ranks in the Politburo who might make it to national leadership. If he does, I believe my country stands a chance of making serious changes. His name is Gorbachev." This was the first time I had heard the name that would become famous throughout the world. To my knowledge it had not appeared in any media, but Evgeny's words and the name Gorbachev sunk in, and I fervently hoped that he might be right.

Mikhail Gorbachev's Ascension to Power in the U.S.S.R.—March 11, 1985

After a series of aged and ill Soviet leaders, Brezhnev, Andropov, and Chernenko, the world waited to see who would be promoted to Secretary General, the top office in the U.S.S.R. To the surprise of most, it was Mikhail Sergieyvich Gorbachev. He was said to be the protégé of Andropov and more reform-minded than previous Secretary Generals. Remembering the words of Evgeny Lukyanov, we at CUUI were more hopeful than most in the West that this new man would bring changes to the decaying political system of the U.S.S.R.

The 1985 Geneva Summit became the first step on the road to transforming the entire system of international relations between the United States and the Soviet Union. It didn't produce any major treaties at the time and was not seen as a breakthrough. But President Ronald Reagan stated at its conclusion, "The real report card won't come in for months or even years."

A striking photo showed up on the front page of one of the Russian newspapers. It was a wide-angle shot of Reagan and Gorbachev walking toward each other with outstretched hands. I was in the Ukraine Hotel in Moscow when someone handed me the paper. I distinctly remember standing in the middle of the room, staring unbelievingly at the photo, and saying aloud to myself, "Is it time for me to stop this work and go back home to a normal life?" At that moment, I believed that it was.

Little did I know that another woman with a mission had been meeting privately with President Reagan to prepare him for his first meeting with Secretary General Gorbachev.

Suzanne Massie—Extraordinary Influence on Events

I wish I had known that Suzanne Massie was undergoing the same angst that I was in the early 1980s. Her mission was even more impossible than mine. Author of *Land of the Firebird* and *Pavlovsk* and co-author of *Peter the Great* and *Nicholas and Alexandra,* lecturer and specialist on Russian culture, Suzanne developed an overwhelming urgency to speak directly to President Reagan prior to his first meetings with Gorbachev. Amazingly, Reagan's National Security Advisor, Bud McFarlane, was somehow contacted, and he agreed to set up a meeting with the President! The official meeting that took place didn't assure results—perhaps because so many people were present. The room was full with the President and his top advisors in addition to Suzanne. But this was the beginning of a much longer story. Shortly thereafter, Mrs. Reagan telephoned Suzanne and invited her to a private breakfast with her and the President. Over a short period, 20 more meetings ensued, wherein Suzanne spilled out to Reagan everything that she knew about the Russian people, their history, culture, and their quite understandable fears of those outside their borders. Suzanne says that Reagan absorbed it all. These 20 encounters between Suzanne, President Reagan, and Nancy were most likely responsible for the magic that occurred when these two heads of state, Reagan and Gorbachev, met. See http://www.russiaotherpointsofview.com for the full story.

Henry Dakin, Godfather of CUUI, CCI and many other non-profit organizations, was truly a unique individual. He was a quiet philanthropist and supporter of all good causes to make the world a workable place. His 3220 Sacramento Street building and the surrounding block became known as a hub for U.S.-U.S.S.R. initiatives which served as track II diplomacy during the Cold War.

Suzanne Massie, author and Russia expert, held numerous private discussions with President Reagan leading up to the crucial time prior to the Reagan/Gorbachev meetings in 1985.

Mikhail Gorbachev, last Secretary General of the U.S.S.R., and President Ronald Reagan demonstrated that there can be goodwill between Americans and Soviets. Unexpectedly, they became respected friends during the tense years in which they worked together.

The Gorbachev Era—A Windfall for Our Work

Within a couple of months after Gorbachev's coming to power, we felt a loosening among Soviet citizens. Apartment meetings were on the increase. Soviet citizens were becoming indifferent to senseless regulations and were less concerned about the KGB. One young friend reported that a KGB person called her to come in to discuss her relationship with me. She told him, "I'll have time to talk with you after the group leaves Moscow." This incident was shared with a hint of pride and new confidence. Experimental CUUI programs were spun into existence without interference. Some Soviets were still suspicious of us, but nevertheless, our work produced a cornucopia of new ideas that turned into projects during the 1980s.

Branching out to Exotic Soviet Cities

As more travelers scheduled trips in 1985, we began exploring far-out Soviet cities to get diverse cultural experiences and to test citizen diplomacy with other ethnic populations. All CUUI travelers visited Moscow and Leningrad after which they traveled to two additional regions. Early groups went to Kiev, Tbilisi, Riga, Tallin, Vilnius, Yerevan, and Baku. By 1986 we were adding exotic cities like Bukhara, Samarkand, Mahachkala, Tashkent and Alma Ati. Informal CUUI offices were started in Moscow, Leningrad, Kiev, Tbilisi, Minsk, Vilnius, and Yerevan. Local Soviet people who we met in the streets of these places became our CUUI coordinators. They were paid "under the table" based on the number of Americans for whom they set up home visits and private excursions to schools, hospitals, and institutes.

CUUI Moscow Coordinator—Mikhail (Misha) Malkov

We first met Misha on a frigid Leningrad Street one night in 1983. Later we learned that he was a 40-year-old hermit, who only went out at night ostensibly to avoid the disdain of his housemates and former fellow workers. His tragic story follows.

Ten years earlier Mikhail's career was rising in the Soviet system. He worked in radio research and production. His wife and children considered that they had the good life although neither were Communist Party members. They had a roomy flat in north Moscow and the accepted conveniences of Soviet life. Quite unexpectedly, Mikhail began noticing that fellow peers were ignoring him at work; they didn't speak or acknowledge his presence. Soon afterward, he was demoted with no explanation. When he questioned why, he got vague answers. At last, he was laid off and couldn't get a job elsewhere. Finally, he became a "faceless" person in the U.S.S.R., and even friends outside of work stopped dropping by. Meanwhile his wife, Tamara, was a young professional with high standing in the Brezhnev government. She was the favored interpreter for Middle East specialist and Politburo member, Evgeny Primakov. Despite Misha's isolation, Tamara still accompanied Primakov when he needed to travel on diplomatic missions.

Misha was obviously a brilliant man; his English was impeccable. Meanwhile, Tamara shared Misha's confusion and sadness, but neither of them felt that they had any recourse but to accept his fate. "Someone above" had given an order, for what reason neither of them knew. Since Misha spoke perfect English, he was relieved to run into Americans in the streets who offered some diversion to his otherwise bleak life. In 1985, we invited Misha to become CUUI's Moscow coordinator.

Gorbachev began opening up the U.S.S.R.'s secret archives a couple of years after he came to power. At last, ordinary Soviets could get into the files and look at their past records. Misha was eager to know the story of his defamation. Eventually he found his file and among other incidentals, it revealed that a fellow employee with whom he was competing for a promotion had given utterly false reports to their boss regarding Misha's character and morals. The other employee got the coveted position. The rest was history. So it was in the U.S.S.R. during those years—any Soviet could become an informer and, on occasion, did to their own personal advantages. Consequently, no Russian outside of family members and the closest of friends could be trusted.

CUUI's Newly Contracted Soviet Coordinators

Kiev, Ukraine: We met Natasha Gruzhenskaya in 1985 on the street in Kiev and were immediately invited to her tiny apartment. She was a feisty, black-haired young woman who spoke perfect English and walked a tight rope—that of being an English teacher by day and somewhat of an underground hippy and social agitator after hours. Fortunately for us, her address book was stuffed-full of teachers, school directors, scientists, artists, and musicians. After we made a few more visits to Kiev, Natasha was inviting crowds to mix and mingle with her newly found American friends. Her Ukrainian friends seemed to feed on her vibrancy. In 1986, we asked Natasha to advertise and organize the first AA meeting on Soviet soil.

Yerevan, Armenia: We ran into a covey of bright-eyed and upbeat young Armenian men and women on the streets in Yerevan. The proactive group was headed by Andrei Hovhannisyan. They appeared to be in their twenties and had excellent English skills. A couple of years earlier, they organized an English Club. Members were proud to be Armenians, they supported the Soviet system, and their foreign friendships didn't seem to concern Armenian officials. From them we learned of Armenia's tragic history with the Turks when they took us to their Armenian Genocide Memorial. From '86 forward, Andrei and the club coordinated CUUI travelers' visits to Armenia.

Tbilisi, Georgia: Quite a few Georgians spoke fairly good English. In 1985, a 40-year-old man, Gizo Grdzelidze, became our coordinator. CUUI travelers were invited to parties in Tbilisi that lasted most of the night and featured tables sumptuously heaped with every kind of food and drink imaginable. Georgia's casual style was a relief to the stiffness we found further north.

Leningrad, Russia: In April 1986, we met Volodya Shestakov. He was perfectly suited for coordinating groups of American travelers, since he was a natural born networker and had hundreds of willing and ready friends who were eager to meet with foreigners. Before we met, he translated Hedrick Smith's controversial book, *The Russians*, into the Russian language. This book was widely read in the west and confiscated at Soviet borders when it was found in suitcases. Earlier Volodya was involved with the Samisdat dissident press that was stridently anti-Soviet. Trained as a "soil specialist," he had a day job that was not demanding, so he spent his free time trying to meet English-speaking people.

Volodya remained our employee until the CCI St. Petersburg office closed in 2008. During the ensuing years, he traveled throughout Russia with me as interpreter for PEP evaluations and performed various functions in CCI's

Volodya Shestakov, Leningrad citizen diplomacy coordinator, environmentalist, my interpreter, CUUI/CCI worker in many different programs and projects throughout 23 years.

Natasha Gruzhenskaya (standing), CCI's Coordinator, had a large following, particularly among students and young professionals. Somehow Soviet officials left her alone, and we profited from her quick intelligence and the never ending variety of contacts that she provided.

Tennison with Gizo Grdzelidze, Tbilisi, Georgia Coordinator.

Andrei Hovhannisiyan, Yerevan Coordinator.

Left: Remis Bistrikas, enviromentalist, philosopher, and Lithuania Coordinator.

several Leningrad and St. Petersburg offices. He continues to help Americans visiting his city, and is a premier networker. Volodya can be reached at Volodyashestakov@gmail.com if you wish services when visiting St. Petersburg.

An Uncanny Evening with Gorbachev's Right-Hand Man

By mid-year 1985, the U.S.S.R. was at the beginning of a massive transition that was yet to be acknowledged or understood by Soviet or American officialdom. My relationship with young party member, Elena Sadovnikova, had been warmed by the delivery of a much-cherished book in 1984. Elena had recently moved from Leningrad to Moscow and had wasted no time getting up the party ladder. To my amazement, she arranged for the two of us to have dinner with Dr. Evgeny Velikhov, the Vice President of the U.S.S.R.'s prestigious Academy of Sciences, and President Gorbachev's right-hand man in advancing glasnost and perestroika.

We showed up at Velikhov's spacious but simple home one evening, where we were seated at the family's large oval dining table with his wife and children. The casualness of the evening allowed me to informally question this preeminent Soviet official. He was enthusiastic, even bubbly, about his new opportunities to help loosen the Soviet system. He and Gorbachev were ushering in ideas and reforms that a year earlier were completely unthinkable. As he discussed the mind-bending changes beginning to occur in Moscow, I mentioned that Leningraders weren't so fortunate, and told him about two master art teachers who were "sent to the streets" after permitting our American travelers to visit art classes at their governmental-supported art school.

Unknowingly I had hit Evgeny's two hot interests: children and art. He wanted to hear more. The story poured out. Elena and I both had allied with these two art teachers during their expulsion from the state school. Around the dining table, Evgeny, Elena, and I designed a project to save the teachers. We would hold an international summer art camp in Leningrad where CUUI would bring a group of children artists from America. Evgeny would come from Moscow to be the project's patron saint and assure media coverage. The summer camp would be such a success that the two art teachers would be exonerated, and Leningrad authorities would shrink into the woodwork. This outcome was predictable in those days, since Moscow authorities ruled absolutely over Leningrad and all other authorities in the U.S.S.R. Velikhov's presence would assure success. It sounded great and without a doubt would work on the Soviet side.

But on the American side, I didn't have a single contact with children's private art schools and didn't even know whether any existed. Somehow a group had to be quickly found or organized. I went back to California to search for children artists. As with other impossible ideas in those days, a solution appeared nearly overnight. Stephanie Tschuida, a CCI staffer, knew of a private art school in Southern California. We immediately contacted them regarding the exchange idea and were able to convince the parents to let their kids travel to Russia and to pay for all of their expenses. Within a couple of months, the American children departed for Leningrad.

The International Art Camp—August 1985

Together with Dr. Evgeny Velikhov, Consul General Richard Miles of the Leningrad U.S. Consulate and his wife Sharon, became co-sponsors of the International Art Camp held outside of Leningrad. American and Russian children designed and painted for two

"21st Century Through the Eyes of Children" mural created by eight children under the guidance of Natalie Gulyaeva, a master art teacher. Her professional life was at stake because she allowed citizen diplomats to visit their old Soviet school which wasn't on the approved list. Photo in 1984.

Evgeny Velikhov, Gorbachev's right hand reformer and Vice President of the U.S.S.R. Academy of Sciences. Upon hearing about two artists who were losing their jobs due to Leningrad bureaucrats, Evgny became part of solution to save them.

Younger artists at work in Natalie's and Sergei Katin's Pioneer House (afternoon school). When sufficiently skilled they could begin to work on avant-garde group murals, reproductions of old masters' works, or whatever they chose. Their work under Natalie and Sergei was highly creative compared to Soviet state art schools.

Budding American and Russian artists working together on ideas to incorporate in a group mural. Later Russian children artists traveled to California to create art and stay in the homes of those they hosted in Leningrad.

wonderful weeks in Northwest Russia's forests. Their final creation was a 25-foot-long mural. The left half displayed the symbols of Russia and the U.S.S.R.—domed churches, ships, and famous historic figures leaning toward the mural's mid-section. On the right, California children painted palm trees, skyscrapers, automobiles, and people—all leaning toward their counterpart's side of the mural. The camp was widely acclaimed in Soviet media thus drawing attention to master art teachers, Natalie Gulyaeva and Sergei Katin who had been dismissed earlier from the state art school. Leningrad authorities were boxed in. Without further ado, the teachers were reinstated in their school. In 1986, a second art camp was held in Los Angeles with the same children attending, thanks to the parents of the American kids who had come to Leningrad for the original exchange.

Women's Leadership Delegation—April 28, 1986

During the mid-1980s, CUUI leaders would occasionally lead two or three delegations of travelers back-to-back. This was the case in April 1986. First I co-led the initial AA trip to the U.S.S.R. in early April; then on April 25, completed the second group and headed back to Helsinki to pick up the third group, "Women in Leadership." This was a much larger delegation comprised of 50 outstanding women leaders from the United States. We were traveling at the invitation of the Soviet Women's Committee which had requested "bring us your women" to meet face-to-face with outstanding Russian women. Vivian Castleberry helped select and invite the American participants and traveled with the group.

I arrived in Helsinki just before dinner and had only a short time for an update on this group before going to bed exhausted. Early the next morning I went downstairs to begin briefing the group only to find our women in a state of considerable agitation. They had just learned from Finnish TV that an alarming situation was in process. The details weren't known, but a high level of radiation was being released from somewhere in the U.S.S.R., and it was already drifting into Finland.

Chernobyl Reactor Meltdown—April 26, 1986

Facts were confirmed that radiation was coming from somewhere in Ukraine or Byelorussia. Getting through to the American Embassy or the Soviet Embassy was impossible—phone lines were jammed. Instead of the usual citizen diplomacy training in Finland, our 50 VIP women spent the day in tense caucasing about what to do. Should we cancel our trip into the Soviet space? Should we take a chance on the unknown and continue our journey? Should some of us return to the U.S.? Late in the evening one of our travelers, a Native American college administrator stood and said, "I don't know about the rest of you, but I am going in. Our Soviet sisters need us now more than ever." With that 48 of the women signed on to continue the journey into the U.S.S.R. We sent home one young woman in her first trimester of pregnancy and an older woman with a heart condition.

Bit by bit we learned what had happened. Chernobyl in the Republic of Ukraine had suffered a major nuclear disaster. We flew on to Moscow where I went to the authorities and explained that we would have to cancel our scheduled trip to Minsk; it was too near Chernobyl. We negotiated to stay in Moscow for the next nine days. Fortunately, our numerous Moscow contacts and the countless streets and metros of that vast city offered unending opportunities to experiment with citizen diplomacy. We called friends in Kiev and Minsk who knew little more than we did, but were scrambling to get their children out of contaminated zones. Within 24 hours some of them showed up at our Moscow hotel on Red Square. A few had children with them; others had already dropped them off with friends or families in the capitol city.

Nine emotion-packed days later, we left for Leningrad to the north. There, the disbelief and horror was the same as in Moscow. Leningraders questioned, "Why us— why does our country always bear the brunt of international catastrophes?" During this angst, a large group of American and Leningrad citizens came together in a room only half big enough to hold us all. One person after another spoke poignant words of grief, empathy, and fear. One Russian man of about 35 years spoke with greater ecological understanding than others. As the meeting ended, this man and I waded across the sea of bodies toward each other and exchanged contact information before he disappeared in the crowd. I lost the crumpled paper with his coordinates. Before the next trip, I began a search and located him. This is how we first met Vladimir (Volodya) Shestakov.

Meanwhile, the world was aghast at the enormity of the Chernobyl meltdown Gorbachev's right hand man, Evgeny Velikhov, the patron of CUUI's International Art Camp, was flying over Chernobyl several times a day in a helicopter, directing the extinguishing of fires. Later he would oversee the cleanup. It was assumed that his life expectancy would be gravely impacted.

As of 2010, Dr. Velkhov is head of the Public Chamber of Russia, is a member of the Russian Academy of Sciences, and appears to be in good health.

Thousands of Russian firefighters and troops were brought into Ukraine to work at ground level—numbers of whom died within a few weeks. CUUI's Kiev coordinator, Natasha Gruzhenskaya, became a volunteer at Chernobyl. We watched as Russian, Ukrainian, and Byelorussian citizens hunkered in facing the dangers of radiation—they quietly went about doing what had to be done.Enduring against grave odds seems to be embedded in Slavic genes.

Speaking to Naval Officers and Meeting Don Chapman—June 1986

I was in San Diego for a presentation at a Naval Officers' meeting. Walking into an all white room with my Kodak projector, I wondered how this crusty bunch of military officers would take to my message. The officer in charge introduced himself. He seemed nice enough, but appeared to be a bit apprehensive. Soon I was facing a roomful of rather stiff naval men wearing white officers' shirts with epaulettes and white slacks. Their outfits were completed with white round-brimmed naval hats. It was morning. The blinds were drawn, and I began my slide presentation. Reasons for the 1917 revolution were covered along with the U.S.S.R.'s devastation from WWII, the Siege of Leningrad, and the downside of communism and totalitarianism. This was followed by slides of home meetings, churches, schools, and interviews with ordinary and VIP Soviet citizens.

I shared my conviction that with sufficient softer technologies including large amounts of citizen diplomacy, the two superpowers could be pulled back from the brink of nuclear annihilation. Last I asked why we should be creating more nuclear weapons when there were already enough to destroy the world ten times over. By the end, the officers were curious enough to begin asking intelligent questions.

After several officers made statements or asked questions, one tall, serious man stood up. He was convinced that my comments were ungrounded and began enumerating his concerns. I had nothing but personal experience and slides to buttress my comments, so I replied, "Well, sir, if you don't believe me, consider taking a trip with us and exploring the Soviet Union for yourself." With that, he quieted. Later I learned that he was Commander Don Chapman. He had not been informed that I was on the docket as speaker until he had arrived that morning. With spicy language, he apparently registered immediate complaints about my appearance and demanded to know who was responsible for the decision. He settled down only after learning that his superior had approved my presence—but he was not happy. Fortunately, he held his peace, at least with me, until the question period ended. I was ushered out, relieved to be finished with that group.

That evening Don Chapman went home and said to his wife, Julie, "What would you think of switching our trip to China next year and going to the Soviet Union instead?" She was open to the idea. Don called CUUI's office in San Francisco, and we put the two of them on a trip in 1987.

As a knee-jerk, communist-fearing Navy fighter pilot who had flown and survived 199 missions against Russian MIGs over Vietnam, Don was entrenched in a fixed anti-Russian position. His training and experience had convinced him that Russia was America's mortal enemy. However, he had a passion for examining all sides of any issue.

On his first trip to the U.S.S.R., he sought out every learning opportunity possible. He debated bureaucrats in official meetings, discussed issues with young teenagers on streets, and met with Soviet scientists. He was shocked at how materially backward the U.S.S.R. was compared to America, and he began to question within himself whether the Soviets would be a threat if the politics between the two countries could change. Returning to the States, Don began his research to determine how better relations could be encouraged between the two superpowers. Don and Julie signed up for every exchange program that CCI offered from 1987 on. He became a board member of CUUI. Meanwhile, he paid monthly stipends to Soviet nuclear scientists to keep them from going abroad with their secrets and loaned money to young Russian entrepreneurs who were starting businesses. He became Kiwanis International's expert on all things Soviet and Russian. Don eventually retired from the Navy and became a captain for Delta Airlines. As of 2012, he still serves on CCI's board of directors.

Meeting a Weapons Analyst—June 1986

A small jet took off from San Diego. I was headed east for more presentations regarding U.S.-Soviet relations and the nuclear missile build up. To my right, a slender, attractive woman was settling in. We exchanged travel chitchat. Her comments were more interesting than most, so I asked about her career. "I'm an artist … my studio is in my home," she replied. She asked about my interests. Careful not to distance this San Diego matron, I briefly mentioned my concern over the thousands of nuclear weapons on launch pads with half of them poised at American cities.

Her eyes instantly took on a look of disbelief. "You wouldn't believe what my husband does." "What?" "He's a nuclear weapons analyst for General Dynamics in San Diego." We started exchanging concerns ping-pong style. By the time the plane landed, my seat companion remarked, "I'd like to bring my husband to San Francisco to meet you." We pulled out our calendars and penciled in a date. A week later my phone rang, "Sharon, Roberta Duffy here, Jack and I can be in San Francisco on August 31. Is this date still open for you?" I was in shock registering that this woman would actually fly a weapons analyst all the way from San Diego to talk with me. What could I say to this specialist? Would he try to show me how ridiculous my concerns are? We made plans to meet at Greens Restaurant.

Walking into Greens that evening in August, I spotted Roberta. A wave of the hand, and I was quickly seated at their table. Roberta led the conversation adroitly so as not to put either Jack or me on the defensive. We slowly explored our two work interests. Jack was a fairly open man and soon began asking good questions about what Soviet citizens think of the Cold War, my impressions of the U S S R and Gorbachev, and the Soviet Union's relative poverty compared to the U.S. I began to feel less a fool or a featherhead when it was clear he took my answers seriously. Roberta's mood shifted to her reason for getting us together. I learned that she had been wrestling with these issues around Jack's profession for years, and only now had she found a potential outlet for her apprehensions.

I invited them both to participate in a delegation of Soviet citizens coming to several American cities, one being in San Diego, their home town. Roberta signed them up. Shortly it surfaced that General Dynamics did not receive this news lightly. After numbers of General Dynamics' meetings with both Roberta and Jack, it was decided that Jack could not participate in any of the San Diego events—not even a beach outing at the ocean. However, in my ever-working mind, there would be other such options in the immediate future.

"Roberta, this is Sharon." My enthusiasm must have reverberated over the phone. "We have the perfect travel group to the U.S.S.R. for you to join! It's our September trip. Can you get permission to travel?" She exclaimed, "They won't let Jack go because of his security clearance, but I don't do missiles, I paint! Why should they care? Great idea, I'll talk it over with Jack and get back to you."

Thus began a long and tortuous road for this delightful couple in their late 40s. Jack could see nothing wrong with his wife traveling to the Soviet Union. His General Dynamics bosses disagreed. Roberta, he reminded them, was an artist who had never been interested in his work. The FBI was brought in. Interview after interview took place, each concurring that the wife of a weapons' analyst of Jack's level couldn't travel to any enemy country. After all, she might be kidnapped, held for ransom, or God knows what else.

Roberta countered that she was a free citizen who loved her country. Further that she had every right to travel wherever she chose, simply because she was an American with rights guaranteed by the Constitution. Jack was beginning to consider that Roberta had a point, and that Americans should have more first-hand information about any enemy country rather than relying on potentially manipulated intelligence. The two of them decided she would go despite official warnings.

In September CUUI travelers from across America landed in JFK and met at the Finnair counter. Roberta, loaded down with video equipment and looking like the quintessential American tourist, was ready to get images from the backside of the Iron

Curtain for her husband. Circumspect and intelligent, she sized up everyone in the delegation and became a terrific asset during group sessions. Nothing missed her shrewd artist's eye. Three weeks later Roberta had rolls of video tapes and hundreds of stills. On return home, she dove into editing film and putting together her own video of "the enemy" to be shown at General Dynamics and in other venues.

Meanwhile, Jack was undergoing increased surveillance and suspicion. Actions were threatened and then eventually taken. In the end Jack lost his esteemed U.S. security clearance and was terminated from his lucrative high-level position at General Dynamics.

Starting at the Air Force Academy and working his way up through the channels, this brilliant young man was promoted to near the top. When he retired from the Air Force, he immediately went to work in the private sector for General Dynamics, one of the world's top defense contractors.

At age 48, Jack had no other profession. With his security clearance denied, there was no place for him to go. It was a devastating blow. Following that the couple underwent three depressing long years of unemployment. Finally Jack landed a job—the U.S.-Russia Mir Space Ship Program hired him. Roberta and Jack moved from their California home to Anniston, Alabama, where he worked until retirement. Today the couple owns an artists' haven in the Hill Country of Central Texas, where Roberta still paints and Jack manages the holdings.

The San Francisco-Leningrad Sister City Project—1988

The 1980s exploded with innovations like Ground Zero, which created Sister City relationships between American and Soviet cities. We tried to make a sister link between San Francisco and Leningrad. I met with Anatoly Sobchak, Leningrad's popular reformist mayor. He was ebullient at the thought of linking Leningrad with San Francisco. Next I met with San Francisco's Mayor, Art Agnos, who also was quite favorably inclined toward the idea. Soon I learned that the San Francisco Bay Area Council on Jewry blocked the sister relationship possibility. Their goal was to stop any form of cooperation between Americans and Soviets until Soviet Jews were allowed to emigrate freely from the U.S.S.R. We understood their rationale; but at the same time believed that opening up the relationship and educating Soviets on the necessity of emigration would work better than resistance. Eventually, the Sister City project between San Francisco and Leningrad was dropped because of this counteraction. Shortly thereafter, Los Angeles' Mayor and Mayor Sobchak of Leningrad signed an agreement to twin their two cities.

I had been somewhat involved with the Jewish immigration issues since 1983 and was doing what I could to address this grinding problem by educating both sides and at the same time pushing immigration as a must with Soviet officials, when I chanced to meet with them.

Our Council on Soviet Jewry work intensified. My chief contact in the local Jewish community was a modern day saint by the name of Mariam Levy. This respected elderly Jewish lady understood both sides of the issues and was a godsend to me in dealing with the more radicalized younger people. I offered to bring all Soviet delegates coming to the

Discussing the pairing of Leningrad with San Francisco with Mayor Sobchak. He was delighted with the possibility.

Don Chapman in civilian clothes, speaking in behalf of CCI. Switching from being totally suspicious of our work, this daring war hero turned into one of CUUI/CCI's strongest supporters. Don and wife Julie hosted numbers of delegations down the time track, and he has served on CCI's Board of Directors off and on for two decades.

Bay Area to meet with the Council so the former could be educated on the issues facing those who apply to emigrate. Mariam attended these meetings. Generally the Soviets weren't educated on these topics and were aghast by the anger they encountered. Thank God emigration began to flow in the late '80s.

> *History: Anti-Semitism in Russia was centuries old. In Tsarist times, Jews with few exceptions had to occupy areas outside the economic and cultural centers. Their children were denied higher education. However, the Bolshevik Revolution of 1917 occurred with Jews on the forefront of it.*

> *Yakov Sverdlov, a brilliant Jew, was the U.S.S.R.'s first president. At last, Jews hoped for fair treatment in their homeland including the ability to live in cities and educate their children. They indeed did move to the major cities, and their children began to get higher education, even before the Slavs made consistent efforts to get their children into schools of note. The consequence of this, from the Soviet point of view, was that by the time the Slavs woke up to the necessity of education, Jewish children were already getting disproportionate numbers of the coveted university seats—and there were only so many seats to go around. Quotas were established based on the population of ethnic groups. Since the Jews were a smaller minority, they got fewer seats than they previously enjoyed.*

> *As more Jews planned to emigrate, Soviet officials made it even more difficult for their children to get higher education. The authorities saw allotting precious university seats to Jews as a lost investment, since their education would be used in a western country. The situation worsened on both sides. Soviets prevented Jews from getting into good schools, and Jews increased their anti-Soviet stances and demands to emigrate.*

> *Observing the changes in the U.S.S.R. under Gorbachev, and knowing how much he wanted rapprochement with the West, I became convinced that this hot issue would be addressed sooner rather than later. In 1987, I made a public prediction that massive emigration of Jews would be freely allowed before the end of the century. To me it was a mathematical certainty that it would happen; it was just a matter of when. Others dismissed the prediction as deluded. It was even reported that Natan Sharansky, the chief Jewish spokesperson of that era, heard the prediction and declared I was insane. However, it came true, but a decade earlier than I predicted. Fortunately, by 1989/90 Jews were leaving the U.S.S.R. in a mass exodus.*

American Foundation Directors' Trip to the U.S.S.R.—1986-1990

In the late 1980s, we organized three trips for American foundation executives under the auspices of America's Council on Foundations. This was highly advantageous for CUUI because we needed to expand programs during the Gorbachev thaw but had no funds to implement them. These CEOs represented the largest foundations in America. Among them, they had enough money to run the original Marshall Plan if they chose. I was considerably concerned about traveling with these dignitaries, since our CUUI work had focused on average business and professional Americans.

The second of the three foundation delegations was the most prestigious. I carefully studied the biographies and photos that arrived in the mail, trying to figure out what we would have to offer these people. During the lead-up to the trip, I took a call from Flint, Michigan, from a Mr. William S. White. He was president of the huge Charles Stewart Mott Foundation, which was launched with General Motors money. The voice on the other end of the line was loud and powerful. I remember nothing about the conversation except the voice—it was enough to intimidate me. A day or so later a package arrived with Mr. White's bio and photo. His face, covering the whole page and staring back at me, was more intense and fearsome than I could have ever imagined. With increased anxiety, I vowed to stay far away from this man while working with the delegation.

The big day arrived; I left San Francisco and flew to JFK to meet the group. Mr. White was spotted immediately. He was the tallest, boldest, and had the most booming voice of any member of the delegation. It was not difficult for me to keep my distance since he was easily observed at all times. As we boarded the plane to Moscow, we discovered that one CEO had forgotten her passport and had to remain at JFK while it was being FedExed to New York. I went back to my economy class seat. Some of the foundation delegates had to take seats in the economy section, since first class filled before they got reservations. Settling into the economy area, I began getting acquainted with delegates in my part of the plane.

Leeta Marting from the Whitney Foundation came back to my row and whispered, "Remember the passport situation? There's an empty seat in the front of the plane. None of us in economy class want to volunteer for it, so we thought it would be good to give it to you! By the way, it is 1B. Mr. White from the Mott Foundation is sitting in 1A. We spoke with him, and he says it's fine for you to take the seat." I almost fainted. I had never sat in the front of a plane before, and was aghast at the prospect of doing so for this trip. However, it couldn't be turned down, since Mr. White had already been brought into the decision making.

Taking my trusted laptop and inexpensive coat with me, I reluctantly trudged to the front of the huge plane. As I was buckling in, Mr. White started asking questions. How long had I been at this? Why? What's needed in the U.S.S.R. today? Is Gorbachev for real? How might American foundations play a role in whatever Russia becomes in the future? We became engaged in the topics that meant the most to me and our mission. The face and voice no longer mattered. Bill White and I talked all of the way to Moscow.

The trip was by all counts extremely successful. Foundation executives were excited at the idea of funding aspects of the social and political revolution happening in the U.S.S.R., and some delegates offered and became CUUI board members. By the trip's end, big Bill White turned to me and said, "Send me a proposal." Shocked, I asked what it should be about. He replied that he didn't care what it was about—just something that would do some good for our organization or for Russia. He asked what I needed most; I replied someone to help me with the workload. He belted out, "Then write the proposal on a brown paper bag and ask for money for an assistant!"

A New Home in Leningrad

In 1989 Volodya Shestakov got in touch, "Come quickly, we have opportunity to make an apartment for CUUI! Our two art teachers have been given a 50-year lease

William S. White, President of the Charles Stewart Mott Foundation, and member of the Council on Foundations' delegation. His Foundation has been the largest non-governmental funder of CCI programs throughout our existence.

Tennison, Dale Needles, former VP of CCI, and Shannon Lawder, a Mott Program Officer, with President Bill White.

Gennady Alferenko, dancer, choreographer, owner of a business long before they were permitted in the U.S.S.R., explaining to the Council on Foundations delegation the facts about Russia and how American foundations could help as his country experiments with glasnost and perestroika. He mentioned the need for "civil society" to develop in Russia—it was the first time some of us had ever heard the two words used together.

to build an art school in a historic three-story building—it's the left wing of the Sheremetyevski Palace on Fontanka Canal! They want to create an apartment for you in the building." I packed and was soon on my way. Arriving in Leningrad, I was taken to 34 Fontanka. The location was stunning. Looking from the third-floor window, the Fontanka canal below flowed past several palaces and crossed Nevsky Prospect in the distance. From that vantage point above Leningrad, it was also clear that the entire city below had gotten virtually no care in the past 75 years. The buildings still stood, thanks only to their original construction of one-meter thick brick exterior and interior walls.

The Fontanka house was sturdy, but post-1917 workers had literally wrecked the interiors. They chopped up elegant performing halls to create rabbit warrens in which to house incarcerated laborers working on canals and metros. Parquets had been stripped from the floors showing bare boards placed over beams. I couldn't conceive how two artists could ever renovate this space. Natalie and Sergei vowed if I could give them $5,000, they would build a small three-bedroom, one-bath apartment for me and CUUI people visiting the city ... with the provision that when we weren't in Leningrad, they could use the apartment for select "paying guests" whose rent would then support the renovation of other floors. Margo Peck, CUUI board member, and I contributed the $5,000, and left it to the artists to repair the ravaged space.

By the time Natalie and Sergei were finished renovating the little apartment it looked like a mini-palace. Doing most of the physical labor themselves, they plastered walls, mixed gypsum in an old bathtub, created intricate moldings, and even found aging parquet which they carefully laid and applied layers of lacquer. Tapestry appeared from nowhere (probably palaces) and covered the walls. Students painted copies of Russian and European masters that were hung around the small apartment. Natalie requested $836 to purchase 18 pieces of furniture. Sight unseen, I gave her the money. Settees, chairs, tables, and beds were made by their friends—these were palace artisans who were unemployed due to the collapse of the Soviet state. Later I learned that palace wood and bronze was used for the furniture. This is how Russia's palace workers survived at the end of the '80s and the early '90s when the state was unable to pay their salaries. A palace bronze worker came to live in the Fontanka house where he set up shop and created molds for chandeliers under the house's large marble stairwell. To continue his work, he brought from the palaces, long, thick bars of bronze and all the essentials necessary for his trade. Chandeliers were finished by friends at a local foundry and sold if he could find a buyer.

Much later in 2005, the art school was taken over by the Russian Ministry of Education, and the third floor apartment dismantled. I went to the school to see what was happening and inquired about the furniture. They showed me to a small locked room where beds, chairs, tables, and settees were piled on top of each other to near the ceiling. I insisted on the right to take the furniture and within days it was transported to my half-renovated apartment. Today, 20 years later, my Petersburg place is furnished with these refurbished pieces of furniture. A chandelier purchased in 1991 from the bronze worker hangs in my San Francisco flat.

Establishment of CUUI's Headquarters in Leningrad—Late 1980s

As the Soviet system fell apart at the end of the 1980s, we were increasingly glad that we headquartered in Leningrad/St. Petersburg. It was smaller, less expensive, and less dangerous to operate there. Further, we loved the city's great architecture, music, and ballet. CUUI's first legitimate office at the historic Smolny Institute was a temporary gift from Vladimir Yakunin, then a young banker at Bank Rossiya (and today the president of Russia's railroads). Knowing the Smolny space would be relatively short term, we began scouting for other business sites. Generally, we would rent one space two or three years before someone would purchase the building, at which time we would need to search for another location.

> *In 1996, we negotiated a ten-year, rent-free lease for a badly damaged old 19th century building on Tchaikovsky Street, which we agreed to renovate in exchange for rent over the next decade. Looking back, it is unimaginable how we had the nerve to tackle such projects. We never had any experience of this sort. The second floor of this old monstrosity sagged so badly, that it couldn't be walked on. Carpenters simply covered up the sagging floor and put new metal beams above the old second floor. For the new first floor, they lowered the ceiling and put metal beams below the sag. Fortunately, St. Petersburg ceilings are usually at least 12 feet from the floor, so they accommodate nicely to such alterations. We designed the inner space and hired one set of workers after another, until the building was finally completed. We stayed there for ten years paying only for the renovation costs—which in those years was not expensive at all. Leningraders were glad to get any kind of work. When the ten-year lease was up, a buyer was ready to purchase the building and remodel it again. After the U.S.S.R. fell apart, nearly every St. Petersburg building had to be rebuilt. Many were made habitable with the same "lease for repairs" option that we used.*

The Berlin Wall Comes Down—November 9, 1989

Amid shouts and excitement, the western world and East Germans celebrated the Wall coming down, and joyously hoped that the planet would be safe from 1989 forward. Prior to the Wall's removal, President Reagan assured Secretary General Gorbachev that if he would support bringing down the Wall separating East and West Berlin, NATO would not move a "finger's width" closer to Russia than East Germany's border. With this assurance Gorbachev gladly signed on.

Little could he, or the world have guessed that this promise would soon be broken during the next administration—and that the redeveloping distrust between the two countries would threaten to become a second Cold War, due to NATO's expansion up to Russia's borders.

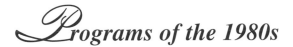

Programs of the 1980s

Summary of Major Programs

CUUI's programs in the 1980s were created to break down dangerous stereotypes between Americans and Soviets and to bring citizens together to create mutually beneficial programs and relationships. The following were carried out to meet those objectives:

Citizen Diplomacy Travel Program
Creating a Sober World
Soviets Meet Middle America
Environmental Initiative
Economic Development Program

You have read about some of these programs earlier but inside stories shared here will give you the human dimensions of each of them and their numbers. The programs grew quickly. Some were terminated near the end of the '80s; others grew into mega programs, which in the '90s were funded by large foundations and the American government.

Citizen Diplomacy Travel Program—1983-1989

Some extra details will be mentioned here. Usually delegations had about 20 to 25 travelers from across the U.S. Travelers signed up with us to have a "non-tourist" experience wherein they could get to know Soviet citizens. Tourist sites were a secondary interest. During their three-week trips they visited three to five Soviet cities.

Every imaginable profession and interest group wanted to go to the Soviet Union during the mid-'80s. The feared and closed society was slowly opening up to the outside world. Meanwhile CUUI was fast gaining a trendy reputation for "creating your own adventure" inside the formerly forbidden country.

Our basic diplomacy delegations continued and others like the Foundation Excutives and Kellogg Fellows needed exposure to specific Soviet activities. U.S. educators partnered with Soviet schools. Environmental delegations and AA groups developed long-term objectives. Bob Sturdivant from the initial group led city planner delegations, which began inner city planning projects with Moscow and other Soviet cities. Kate Brophy led Bay Area police delegations that started long-term relationships with Moscow and Leningrad. Mayors, business owners, judges, lawyers, former military officers, and even former intelligence officers made their way to the U.S.S.R. under our auspices.

We led up to 20 delegations a year until early 1990. Many of the travelers became the backbone volunteers of CCI programs in the 1990s and the 2000s.

CUUI's Two Experimental Trips

The first trip was described earlier. A second experimental trip took off in May of 1984 with twenty-three Americans aboard. A highlight of the trip was David Ellzey—a young American mime. Soviet streets were full of glum faces and colorless clothing. Picture a mime—in white face, black hair, red nose, red and white striped shirt, and black trousers on a Soviet street! Local citizens were shocked—David must have looked like a Martian parachuting in for a visit. A quick-change artist, he went into action in any location to perform his magic. Always on the lookout for human encounters he could use as a tool for goodwill, he communicated countless emotions—mirth, sorrow, interest, and surprise. Crowds gathered, some following him up the streets. At first Soviets stared; then smiles began to crack on their stoic faces.

> *David's most spectacular performance occurred when a young Soviet man was scowling beside his stalled aging car. With puzzled expressions and body movements, David expressed concern and empathy with the fellow's predicament. He walked over to the car and then, in mime, pretended to figure out the problem and a way to resolve it. A crowd began to gather. The frustrated driver slowly got into the spirit. David mimed that the man should lift up the hood, which he did. Together they peered at the engine. The crowd grew larger and spilled into the street.*

> *A police officer came along and blew his whistle to indicate that the crowd should disperse, but then he noted what was going on and lingered. David motioned that the driver should help him lift the engine out of the car. Together, with much heaving and tugging, they mimed the engine out and carefully set it on the sidewalk—all of this without a word spoken. David appeared to tinker and patted the imaginary engine while "working" on it. A few minutes later he indicated to the driver that it was time to put the engine back in the car and put the hood down. Then he motioned the man to get in the driver's seat, which he did. David went around to the front of the car—and began cranking as if the car was an old-fashioned Model T Ford. After much cranking, he motioned the driver to turn the key in the ignition. All of us heard the motor repeatedly grinding away. Then ... Lo and behold, the old engine sputtered and started! Amazed bystanders, including the police officer, broke into spontaneous applause. The driver pulled into the street and drove slowly off grinning and waving back at the crowd.*

A Visit to Georgia

The second trip's "party to end all parties" happened in Tbilisi. A local Georgian physician learned that Americans were in town and invited us all to his spacious home. Dinner started with toasts and ended with toasts, with all sorts of libations—Georgian wine, champagne, cognac, and several types of home brew made from local fruits. Georgian men toasted everything from the "fairer sex," to brave men, joyful children, departed relatives, the noble souls of both countries, on and on endlessly. Glasses were filled and refilled by Georgian women who sat nearby at small tables.

We urged the women to come sit at the big table with us. They demurred. We insisted. The Georgian men finally explained to us that it wasn't permitted for women to eat at the main table. They served but didn't enter into toasting, conversation, or merrymaking, which made us quite uncomfortable. Midway in the long evening a half dozen guitarists crawled through the window behind the host and began serenading us with Georgian folk songs. For the first time that evening we heard the touching Georgian melody "Suliko." It was sung with such haunting voices and enchanting tones that it still remains in my memory as the world's sweetest song. No doubt, a bit of Georgian wine helped seal this indelible experience. If you are ever in Tbilisi, ask at your hotel for Doctor Dato!

Vivian and Lily Golden's First Meeting

On this trip Vivian Castleberry and Lily Golden met and found they were sisters-in-spirit. Who would have thought that these women would share a common vision? One, a white Texan from America's South, and the other, a Black Soviet woman of Jewish and American heritage. By the end of their first meeting, they were planning ways to connect women to build peace between their two nations. This wasn't just travel talk—they were serious. Vivian had a second agenda—to find Lily's long-lost American relatives. Born in Uzbekistan and the Soviet Union where everyone treasures family, Lily had no family except for her young daughter, Elena, after her parents died.

Upon getting back to Texas, Vivian began her search for Lily's family by checking the telephone directory of Clarksdale, Mississippi. She found three Golden families listed. Sitting at her kitchen table in Dallas, she began making calls. The first two who answered were vague and non-committal; the third, a woman, answered the phone. She passed to her husband. The black male voice was cryptic, interrupting Vivian's explanation about her search for her Russian friend's Golden descendants, " Ain't no Commies in my family!" he responded and slammed the receiver down. She didn't give up the cause, but it did go on the backburner.

Lessons Learned From CCI's Two Experimental Trips
- Learn by doing: Never wait until a good idea has been totally thought through. We simply started with the need, experimented, and refined our approach as we moved forward. The idea or project or program took shape in the process.
- Be proactive, even if at first, local people look disinterested and distant.
- Introductory cards: 3x5 cards in simple Russian language were critical to introduce ourselves and our mission to local people. Most of our early Soviet contacts were made in this manner.

David in mime outfit which was unheard of on Soviet streets! Even a policeman, who came to disburse the developing crowd, became amused and began to watch the happening. Fortunately the young man was

friendly enough to go along with David's instructions. The two of them created wonderful street theatre for all who watched.

Roberta Duffy in rapt conversation with a young Kiev man who got invited to an apartment to hold discussions with Americans.

Serious about her mission to get information to take home to her weapons' analyst husband, she never lost an opportunity to interview Soviets of all ages.

Bob Sturdivant (bottom left) meeting with City Planning specialists in Moscow. He has developed several projects with Russian planners over the past two decades and has traveled there numerous times since his first trip in 1983.

Kate Brophy, a high school teacher, has been a strong contributor to CCI since the beginning. Her most exciting endeavor was to introduce American and Soviet police officers in 1989, 1990 and 1991.

This photo was taken of the first delegation of American Police Officers to the U.S.S.R. Later,

several projects were initiated by Soviet and American officers themselves. Some of the relationships continued for several years.

The "Women in Leadership" delegation of 52 women traveled to the U.S.S.R. at the invitation of the Soviet Peace Committee. The delegation was complicated by the Chernobyl catastrophe but still spawned numerous actions down the time track.

- Hitchhiking: Thanks to Vladimir Pozner, we learned how to get around in Soviet cities: he recommended us to lightly extend the hand to indicate a car is needed. Any driver going your direction would take you to your destination.
- Trip regulations and rules: Most travelers had genuine hopes for bettering U.S.-U.S.S.R. relations. A few had other agendas. We found it necessary to create rules and to exact serious penalties for aberrant behaviors, since one mistake could affect CUUI getting visas for future trips.
- Soliciting new contacts and guarding information: Each traveler was tasked with making new street contacts to add to the CUUI database. Personal data of Soviet citizens was scrupulously guarded. By the time the U.S.S.R. dissolved, CUUI was reputed to have the largest database of ordinary Soviet contacts in the U.S.

By mid-1989, glasnost and perestroika had unleashed such radical changes that political unrest, food shortages, chaos, and societal disintegration were increasing across the vast country. Most Americans were fearful to travel to a society in such profound crisis. CUUI's Travel Program was terminated in 1990.

Today, it still isn't clear how we succeeded with a travel program. Lacking travel experience, background in Russian culture, and contacts in the U.S.S.R., we had no discernable assets in the beginning. What kept us out of trouble must have been friendliness, transparency, and an absolute conviction that someone had to do something to build sane relationships with the other superpower.

"Creating A Sober World" (CASW)—1985-1992

CUUI's second program really began in January of 1985 when Sarah Seybold and I visited Max and his handicapped wife in their Leningrad apartment. From that night on, we knew we would do something for alcoholics—we just didn't know what. A few days later I jotted down some notes of the evening.

Icy snow pricked the train window as we departed Leningrad. Sarah and I had just come from a tiny, sparsely furnished Russian apartment where a middle-aged man poured out a confession. It was as though we'd been confidants for a lifetime. Max had met us on Leningrad's Theatre Square one frigid evening in 1984. We were looking for the "Max's" of the U.S.S.R.—those bold enough to test the system and risk talking with foreigners. Before moving off in another direction that night, he quietly scribbled his telephone number with the request to call anytime we come back to visit Leningrad. Then he and his friend Mikhail Malkov from Moscow sprinted away on foot, disappearing into the dark night.

Here Sarah and I were, over a year later, in Max' two-room apartment drinking hot tea and getting to know Natasha, his crippled wife, and their 11-year-old daughter, Olga. To our surprise, Max inquired, "Do you in the West have any treatment for alcoholics?" We explained the little we knew of AA and the Alcoholics Anonymous' "Big Book." "Please bring me this book if you come again—I must quit alcohol. I'm the only livelihood for the three of us, and I'm trying everything I know of to stay sober. Right now I'm reading a Bible another

*American gave me, but it is an hourly struggle." Max's utter sincerity, the tone
in his voice, and watching the little family of three caught up in their hope for
survival, swept Sarah and me up into their dilemma. Departing their apartment,
we promised to bring AA's Big Book when we returned.*

Dashing back to Pulkovskaya Hotel for luggage, we barely made it to the midnight
train to Finland. As the train pulled away from the station, our only concern was what we
could do for Max and others in the U.S.S.R. whose lives were being wrecked by alcohol.
An impossible idea passed between us: wonder if Alcoholics Anonymous (AA) could
be eventually started in the U.S.S.R.? It was totally unthinkable since anonymous group
meetings of any kind had not been permitted for decades. The most we could do would
be to hide AA books in our luggage and distribute them to Russian friends.

Alcoholism was rampant in the early 1980s. Workplace drinking was said to be
prevalent. Paddy wagons drove around the cities looking for fallen drunks, after which
they patiently delivered them to their tiny apartments. There was societal acceptance,
co-dependency and protections for alcoholics up to the point of diagnosis, at which time
they became stigmatized. Treatment was primitive in "drying out" institutions where
abrasive injections and other "cold turkey" treatments were common. The largest such
institution was Moscow's Hospital #17, which was rumored to keep 5,000 beds full at
any given time.

Synchronicity—AA to the U.S.S.R.—1985

Back in San Francisco the telephone rang. "We hear that you girls take Americans
to the U.S.S.R. Could you take some of us from Southern California to the Soviet
Union? We are an AA group. We hope to do something special by April 16, 1986, to
celebrate the 50th Anniversary of Bill Wilson's starting AA in 1936. We would like to
hold the 'first-ever' AA meeting on Soviet soil to commemorate the anniversary." Our
first response was, "Well, to date anonymous meetings aren't permitted on Soviet soil!"
We were stunned by this totally unexpected but timely request and began caucusing
immediately.

We began to realize, that if we were really determined to work with Russia's alcohol
problem, we had no choice but to risk going directly to Soviet officials, to be upfront,
and to explain in good faith AA's record with alcoholism in the West. We had no contacts
at the U.S.S.R. Ministry of Health, but since alcohol was so destructive to the country's
productivity, we felt maybe Ministry officials would see the wisdom of permitting at
least one experimental AA meeting. By this time we had become somewhat accustomed
to unexpected breakthroughs, so perhaps another might occur.

Back in Moscow the next month, we found the U.S.S.R. Ministry of Health. In the
interim we had absorbed as much about AA as possible and had some written materials
in tow. With no introductions, we nervously walked up the steps of this prestigious Soviet
institution. Surprisingly, lower level bureaucrats didn't turn us away.

We found ourselves in a dark paneled room talking over a polished table with
two middle-aged officials, a woman who was the spokesperson and a younger male.
They were fairly pleasant and non-committal but heard us out. Our AA materials in
English were received with polite "thank you's." Then they requested the materials to be
translated into Russian language in the event non-English speaking researchers wished

to review them. We departed feeling at least they hadn't flatly turned us down. By late spring we were back at the Ministry to drop off the Russian translations. During another visit in the autumn, we handed over additional materials they requested. It felt we were getting a little closer to having the idea accepted. As we conducted our meetings at the Ministry, other unexpected but important developments in Soviet society were taking place. Mikhail Gorbachev had just ascended to power, and unknown to most, he was deeply concerned about the country's out-of-control alcohol consumption.

In December of 1985, Faith S., who had the original vision for the 50th Anniversary being held in the Soviet Union, accompanied us to Moscow. A striking, white-haired lady, Faith was a crowning example of the power of AA recovery. She had been sober for over 20 years. We entered the Ministry Building, this time with Faith at our side. It was her moment to convince these officials, as only an alcohol survivor could, how important AA is to a hopeless alcoholic. Buttressed by a sense of mission, she appeared ready. The same two officials entered the paneled room. This time they began asking Faith about the program, sobriety, hospitalizations, meetings, and the rates of recidivism. She answered openly and convincingly.

By the end of their questioning, the woman official offered quite seriously, "We have taken this AA program and its results to the highest level—our new Secretary General says that our problems with alcohol are so great that we can't afford to ignore any answer that the West has found successful. We hereby give permission to hold anonymous AA meetings in Moscow and elsewhere in the country." With a look of shock, Faith's white head fell to the table with a cry of relief. Recovering speedily, she thanked the officials. Goodwill and hope pervaded the room that had earlier felt so sterile and non-committal.

We decided to hold the first AA meeting in Kiev as a dress rehearsal before going to Moscow. The date was set for April 10, 1986. Natasha Gruzhenskaya in Kiev was alerted. Her friend, a school director, agreed to provide an auditorium. Information began going out by word-of-mouth in Kiev.

Back in Southern California, a delegation of 20 AA's from all walks of life were being selected. A local artisan designed a large yellow lapel button with the phrase, "Step by Step," printed in Russian language.

The First AA Meeting on Soviet Soil—April 10, 1986

With bright yellow buttons on their lapels, the group of American AA members caught public buses to the school. We expected a small turnout due to the shame connected with admitting that alcoholism was within the family. The American AA's weren't concerned about numbers; even a half a dozen would have been fine for them.

Upon arrival at the aging school building, we saw a few Soviets walking toward the doors. By starting time, some 150 Kiev residents packed into the auditorium. Few seemed to know each other. For the most part they sat silently waiting for clues regarding what to do for themselves, their spouses, fathers, brothers, or adult children.

Twenty American AA's sat on the stage facing the audience, each ready to share his/her personal story with alcoholism and their degradations. Natasha interpreted for the event. She explained that the meeting would be held like AA meetings over the world. Excerpts from the "Big Book" were read. A white-haired, healthy-looking American woman quietly stood up, looked across the audience and said, "Hi, My name is Faith,

I'm an alcoholic. I want to share my story about how AA saved my life." She described in detail starting as a social drinker, then the spiral down into despair, losing respect from colleagues, friends, and finally family members. Kievans sat in stony silence, unable to grasp that anyone would ever make such personal disclosures about themselves in public.

Following Faith, AA's spoke one after another, each with a completely different but painful story to tell. Charles, a handsome, black-haired Hollywood-type of about 35 years, told about coming to Los Angeles to break into movies. His multiple rejections for roles were handled with alcohol, then drugs, until he bottomed out in despair and learned about AA, where he eventually got sober through the program's teachings of a "Higher Power."

Last, a modest young 19-year-old fellow stood up, "Hi, my name is Billy. My parents were both alcoholics. I began drinking regularly at the age of nine years, and my parents never noticed. This affected my school grades and friendships. I became a loner, depending more and more on alcohol to ease my pain. Soon alcohol wasn't enough. I tried street drugs. They made me feel important. But I needed more and more drugs. I started selling uppers, downers, cocaine, and heroine to people on the street and to children in schools. When there wasn't enough money to satisfy my habit, I began selling my body to strange men to get my next fix. I passed beyond every barrier of decency. I had nothing to live for. Eventually I overdosed and was left for dead in an alley. An AA member came by and picked me up. He arranged for medical help and took me to his home. Had it not been for him, and the AA program, I'd be dead and not here to tell you my story tonight. By the power of AA, I have been alcohol and drug free for two years."

Women and men in the audience were reaching for handkerchiefs, dabbing their eyes, sniffing, and whispering to one another. These people in a closed society were accustomed to guarding their personal lives and sharing secrets only with the closest of relatives or a dear friend. They couldn't believe what they had just heard—in particular, young Billy's personal story had broken their hearts.

The school needed to close, but no one wanted to leave. The director ushered the audience out of the building and locked the doors. Soviets hovered around different AA's in the school yard with Natasha's English-speaking friends helped with interpretation. Slowly small clusters ambled down the sidewalks together—none wanting to catch buses back to their homes or hotel rooms. Gradually, they walked through the dark night back to the Kiev hotel—where they sat locked in intense discussions on the asphalt parking lot until after midnight. The first AA meeting on Soviet soil had been an over-the-top success, and Ukraine's first AA group was later formed as result of that historic evening.

The next day, with informal Ukrainian interpreters along, AA members took to the streets with hard-to-miss yellow buttons on lapels. They began quiet conversations with weaving drunks on sidewalks and in the metros. Possible at-risk youth on the streets were also targeted. Impromptu meetings were held day or night if a drinker was interested.

Charles, the Hollywood type, ran into a small group of youths on a central Kiev street near the end of the trip. Their dyed black hair and funky clothing was a dead giveaway to him. He suspected alcohol if not worse. Hours later he was taken to an apartment where a brother and sister, both teens with modest English capabilities, showed him their home-rigged equipment for distilling poppies and two multi-use syringes.

He shared his AA story with them, hoping they would heed his personal disclosures and decide to leave the drug scene. Describing his experiences with the "Higher Power,"

Charles related praying with these two kids, at which time he claimed they felt a very strong connection with each other. By the end of their encounter, the siblings said they wanted to leave the drug scene and understand more about the Higher Power's ability to help them lead new lives. In their new found fervor they smashed their syringes, and Charles gave them each a yellow button before reluctantly leaving them.

Charles came back to our hotel sharing information about being with these two kids. Our response was not all that supportive—we had many concerns. What would they do when the rigors of withdrawal began after we left Kiev? What might have been a different alternative? Charles was convinced that the siblings would make it. Sarah and I left Kiev wondering what would happen to these kids after the group departed.

Moscow's First AA Meeting

Three days later on April 13, 1986, the first AA meeting for Soviet citizens was held in Moscow. It was carried on a huge outdoor tele-screen that attracted a lot of attention. Many contacts were made as Muscovites began to learn that there were alternatives to incarcerations in Moscow's Hospital #17. However, the first Kiev AA meeting will remain etched in our memories forever as the miracle that we never thought could happen when we first walked up the steps to the Ministry of Health the previous year.

During the process of working together for the first meeting, we learned that AA doesn't permit the use of their name, Alcoholics Anonymous or AA, in association with other organizations. Since CUUI was organizing these groups and had an active role in pushing the program further along, we needed another name for the organization-sponsored delegations. "Creating a Sober World (CASW)" became the official CUUI program name thereafter.

> The seventh or eighth delegation of CASW AAs landed in Moscow a couple of years later. The latest group was walking down a central Moscow street with the yellow buttons on their lapels. An unknown young Russian woman rushed toward them. Touching their flashy buttons, she urgently requested, "Take me to your leader!" Her story poured out. She and her brother had met Charles in Kiev two years earlier. After that encounter, the two of them had stayed sober and had recently moved to Moscow.

> However, they had not known of any AA groups in Moscow, since Soviet groups didn't advertise themselves in the early days. She yearned to be with these American AA's. When asked how she and her brother had maintained sobriety without group support, she replied that they stayed sober through contact through their "Higher Power"—which she explained ... was Charles.

> Over the next seven years, CUUI/CCI ran the Creating a Sober World (CASW) program under the direction of "Brother Leo," a member of the Christian Brothers Order, who moved to Kiev and Moscow to live as an alcohol counselor for four years. In San Francisco, "Camille" directed CASW's work with the help of CUUI/CCI's veteran non-AA volunteers, Sarah Seybold, Barbara O'Reilly, Peg Smith, and others. CASW 12-Step travelers introduced AA concepts throughout eight former Soviet republics over the next few years. By 1995, ten years after

meeting with Max and his little family, AA travelers had sufficient experience to move out from under CCI's umbrella. Many delegations continued to travel in the late '90s, during which additional cities across Russia and the former Soviet Union were introduced to the AA program. In 2006, Russian AA's held their 20th Anniversary in Moscow. See page 68.

"Soviets Meet Middle America" (SMMA)—1988-1989

The SMMA program was barrier breaking. Ordinary Soviet citizens had never been permitted out of the Soviet Union. At a time when very few Americans had traveled to the U.S.S.R., some 400 Soviet citizens in small groups of four persons were brought to 265 American cities over a two-year period. This first-ever program happened in the following way:

In 1987 a call came from Craig Comstock, a partner of Bay Area philanthropist, Don Carlson. He requested a meeting. We had barely sat down for brunch at Mama's Café in Oakland when Craig threw out a question, "What is the most effective action that CUUI could organize next year to ease tensions between the two superpowers?" Stunned at the question and guessing that money was probably behind it, my mind reeled. I picked up a pen and a paper table napkin and began sketching a map of the two superpowers with the ocean between them. The pen swiftly made paths going between the two countries—this time not of missiles but of Soviet citizens coming to the U.S. to meet American citizens in hundreds of cities and towns from East to West. I envisioned them sleeping in American homes, visiting businesses, civic clubs, schools, hospitals, and being interviewed by the U.S. media. The Soviets would be non-party people selected by CUUI, and they would show American citizens that really good, genuine people live in the other superpower. And in this rapidly evolving scenario, Soviets would take a chunk of goodwill and the American dream back home when they returned to the U.S.S.R.

The vision rolled out on the napkin in a minute or so, but there was a huge challenge. The Communist Party elite in the U.S.S.R. would never allow ordinary Soviets "from the streets" to travel abroad. Only carefully selected party members had this privilege. After explaining this to Craig, he still offered $50,000 for CUUI to push this first-ever project into existence.

My overwhelming concern was how to find a crack in the Soviet concrete to make this vision possible. How could it possibly happen? Upon hearing about this latest improbable prospect, CUUI volunteers weren't skeptical—they began gearing up for our next big experiment. Their logic was simple ... if Soviet rules were set aside for AA, then anything was possible. We went to work with no clue about how the project would materialize—just with faith that it would. Barbara O'Reilly purchased a large U.S. map. Twenty of us met at the Montara California Lighthouse hostel for the weekend where we set goals for this project that would bring our Soviet "street" friends to America. Our modus operandi during those heady days was: Dream big, work hard, and something great will happen!

An idea occurred to offer one Soviet bureaucrat to travel for every four of our Soviet street friends. We would later reduce the ratio of bureaucrats and increase the number of our friends for future trips. Back in Moscow and Leningrad for a quick trip, our street friends scoffed at the idea! "Don't kid yourselves, they will NEVER allow any of us to travel!" "They may agree, but in the end, they won't permit it." "You naïve Americans!!!"

Russians and Americans on way to AA meeting in Leningrad.

*AA worldwide gathering of 47,000 AA's from 70 countries
rose to give a standing ovation when, for the first time,
Russian participants presented the Russian flag in 1993.*

CCI volunteers in 1987 with a newly purchased map to track all SMMA Soviet travelers as they migrate across America. We had only Don's money, no volunteers other than ourselves, and no idea how it would all come together.

Don Carlson, original funder of the SMMA idea, and Craig Comstock, his partner in philanthropy.

First SMMA delegation is greeted with balloons as they start their first visit to the USA. ABC-TV cameras recorded the event for the 10 PM news.

Steve Wozniak (better known as Woz) was responsible for making the Soviets Meet Middle America! (SMMA) happen. There were no other funders available to support this kind of "get to know each other" program—however, in both countries it was the talk of ordinary people. The supposed enemies met each other and thoroughly enjoyed one another!

SMMA would have never been possible without Gennady Alferenko. Had Gorbachev not had the wisdom to bring him to Moscow and turn him loose to innovate, we would have never been able to get exit visas for our Soviet invitees. It was as though Providence was moving impossible happenings into place.

SMMA's Soviet guests experienced the most colorful and culturally delightful events in America.

Soviet SMMA delegate Igor Tipans of Riga answers questions from students at Hyde Junior High School in Cupertino, California. Soviet visitors on the first SMMA delegation made contact with some 3,500 students while in American cities.

I approached the only official Soviet group who could make this happen, the Moscow Soviet Peace Committee. They listened, seemed interested, and finally agreed that they would participate as full partners with CUUI. I was determined to get Lily Golden on the first SMMA delegation, so I started early with the Peace Committee officials. They were adamant they couldn't allow Lily to go to America, since they feared she would become the victim of racial discrimination. We promised to take full responsibility for her.

We outlined to the Soviet Peace Committee that the delegations would be composed of 20 Soviets, 16 of our street friends and four of their bureaucrats. In New York they would subdivide into five groups of four persons each and take five routes across the U.S. where each sub-group would stop for visits in four or five American cities. The sub-groups would all meet back in New York and return to Moscow together. Our list of 16 street friends to be invited for the first trip was given to the Peace Committee. They agreed. All seemed to be in order.

With the Soviet agreements nailed down, we needed to recruit American cities to take the first delegations. I had recently taken a delegation of highly respected young Kellogg Fellows to several Soviet cities. The Fellows were energetic, well-connected professionals who lived in numerous states throughout America. We asked if they could host our Soviet delegates, and their instant response was Yes!

Travel plans were finalized, and the Peace Committee was informed to organize the delegation. We pressed for names of Soviet participants to travel, but got none. I telephoned to stress that we expected our personal selections of delegates to be on the plane. Yes, they would be—I was assured. The first delegation arrived at JFK Airport in New York with not a single delegate of our choice on board. Outraged, I turned to plan B. It was midnight in Moscow. I telephoned their home numbers and demanded that some of our choices be sent on the plane the next day—or we would report this fiasco to the American press and cancel the Peace Committee's participation in the program. I hung up.

A call came back within hours saying that two of our personal contacts, Slava Kuznetsov and Valentina Frantseva, would arrive the next day. No mention of Lily Golden. They sent Kuznetsov and Frantseva … too few, too late … but at least, we had two invitees of our own on the first delegation. So it went—pushing, pulling, embarrassing, and dragging our Soviet street friends to America, one by one for the next four or five delegations—the numbers were not even close to what we negotiated. What was to be done?

Lily came on the second delegation as a token friend of CUUI. As expected when she finally was able to travel, she was welcomed wherever she went across America. As the delegation ended, we applied to the San Francisco Soviet Consulate to extend her visa, which they did. Lily flew to Dallas where Vivian Castleberry arranged meetings for her—then she flew to Clarksdale, Mississippi, where her father, Oliver, had grown up. The mayor of Clarksdale met her in a white stretch limousine and gave her a tour of the city. She spoke at Tuskegee, where her father had both graduated and taught. But her Black relatives in the South and her Jewish family in New York still eluded her.

Much later in 1995, Mike Wallace interviewed Lily from Moscow on "60 Minutes." During the show Lily held up a photo of her father and asked if anyone in America knew anything about him or his living relatives. The family floodgates opened! Shortly after the show ended, the 60 Minutes' telephones were ringing off the hook. Both sides of Lily's relatives from the South, New York, and Chicago called; some had an identical photo in their homes. Their joyous reunions can be found in Lily's book, "My Long Journey Home." For several years Lily lived in Chicago where she taught at Chicago State University. Lily returned to live in Moscow with her married daughter and her young granddaughter. She passed away quietly in November of 2010.

A Miracle Breakthrough in Soviet Exit Visas—May 1988

Unknown to us, a breakthrough in exit visas was in the making in early 1988. Gorbachev's latest initiative to reduce Soviet barriers included creating an "informal" way to grant the much-coveted exit visas to ordinary Soviets. Vigorously opposed by all high-level bureaucrats, Gorbachev prevailed. He chose a young Siberian, Gennady Alferenko, as his "point person" for exit visas and other never-before-tried, radical experiments. We met Gennady shortly after his arrival in Moscow. Small, nimble and outlandish, this young Russian was utterly fearless among the archaic Soviet structures in the capital city.

Gennady's personal story was intriguing. He grew up in a Siberian orphanage as a charming little boy whose avant-garde inclinations were irrepressible. Eventually as an adult, Gennady created and operated his own private Siberian dance company that hunted down talent, hired and trained dancers, designed costumes, gave performances when and where he chose, and charged fees for performances.

His operation flew in the face of Soviet laws, but nobody in Siberia cared. They were far away from Moscow, and, besides, they were enjoying Gennady's talents too much to report him to authorities. The rumor was that Gorbachev heard about Gennady's innovations and ordered, "Send this young man to Moscow!" He, thereupon, incorporated Gennady into his new plan to shake up the Soviet system. Gennady's first assignment was to begin granting the highly valued exit visas. This was a first-ever happening in the Soviet Union. The only catch was that Soviet citizens had no contact with foreigners—and they needed an invitation from a foreign national or a foreign organization to travel abroad.

Gennady and I met and quickly realized that we were the perfect combination for each other's work. He immediately agreed to take SMMA under his wing.

Next it seemed important to tell the Peace Committee we had found a new partner. A meeting was scheduled with the full board in Moscow. I explained to them that CUUI was withdrawing our partnership since agreements made with them in the beginning had not been honored; further, that exit visas for our Soviet friends would now be granted through a special dispensation initiated by Gorbachev. They were utterly shocked at this news! From April 1988 forward, SMMA delegations consisted only of our Soviet street friends—and frequently we were able to send them to the cities and towns where American friends who traveled as citizen diplomats coordinated their delegations. These wonderful Soviets, who considered themselves as "nobody's," were traveling abroad for the first time ever. The completely impossible idea two years earlier suddenly became reality.

Dwindling Funds—Meeting Woz

The exit visa problem was solved at the very time we were running out of Don Carlson's money to operate this program. A SMMA delegation traveling across America had landed in Los Gatos, 50 miles south of San Francisco. Eager to attend the "welcome party," I scurried down to Los Gatos. Upon entering the large hall, a friend pulled me aside and whispered, "You will never guess who is in this room." I didn't have the slightest idea. "Steve Wozniak (Apple Computer's technical genius) is over there," he said, pointing to his right. I looked and didn't see a notable person anywhere. He murmured, "He's the one in the shorts and running shoes." Other guests were clad in summer casual to very dressy, so Steve was then easy to spot. The room was abuzz with eager and joyful conversation passing between Americans and first-time-traveling English-speaking Soviets, but I was obsessed with the immediate possibility in front of me.

Steve Wozniak looked like a university student! I quietly walked up and introduced myself by inquiring about his recent work funding U.S.-Soviet TV spacebridges. I began telling him about SMMA and what it could accomplish. Steve was easy to talk with. The party was going on, but I was in some sort of a bubble trying to get this fellow interested in our SMMA dream.

The next week I was sitting in Steve's office. He looked over the two-year SMMA plan, and just before parting asked how much money was needed. I mentioned that "$100,000 would help greatly." He thought for a moment and said, "I think you will need more, perhaps $200,000. He grinned like a happy teenager and casually remarked, "My assistant will give you a check." With this and other such unexpected happenings, I began to wonder if we had a special muse temporarily riding on our shoulders.

Steve's generosity was sufficient to underwrite the entire SMMA program. I walked out of his office in a daze. Thanks to his help, between mid-1988 and the end of 1989 we brought an additional 350 ordinary Soviet citizens to about 230 American cities where they stayed in over 900 Americans homes, and broke bread with many thousands of Americans at potluck dinners in banquet rooms, gymnasiums, and parks. First-ever ordinary Soviets in American cities caused a media blitz. Over a two-year period they were featured in more than 1,000 newspaper articles in addition to TV and radio interviews. They went back to the U.S.S.R. as America's finest ambassadors—and they became missionaries for open borders, market economy principles, and democracy within their own country.

CUUI Environmental Initiative—1987

Our first environmental initiative came as a result of a plea from Leningrad's scruffy ecologists. Leningrad officials had a dream of building a dam in the middle of the Neva River and were ready to implement the project. Local ecologists knew the dam would turn the Neva into a cesspool due to upstream pollution coming from pulp and paper mills near Lake Ladoga. Having never stood up to authorities, the fledgling environmentalists urged us to give them training so they could learn how to stop the dam project. Leaders of CUUI alerted U.S. ecologists and foundation directors. Within a couple of months, the U.S. Council on Foundations delegation landed in Leningrad and assessed the situation. By the trip's end, they delivered recommendations to the young Soviet environmentalists. The Charles Stewart Mott Foundation was the first American foundation to award a grant to support Russia's nascent environmental movement. The Leningrad dam project was defeated. Our involvement in the Soviet environmental sphere afterward brought about a myriad of eco-related projects, which American foundations funded, the story of which will be covered later under programs of the 1990s.

The Economic Development Program (EDP)—1989

Early in 1989 three unknown young Soviet entrepreneurs appeared at CUUI's Leningrad Office. One of them spoke up, "Your organization has created many other programs, now we need a program to teach us business." Another continued, "Gorbachev has let us develop "cooperatives," (the first stage of private business since the 1920s), but we have no history of how to run a business; worse still, we don't even have a business textbook in the country."

We could see that there was a huge void to be filled if this vast country ever developed toward a market economy. I returned to San Francisco with another impossible dream for our next big endeavor—a business training program for Soviet entrepreneurs. But who were we to run a business-training program for these eager entrepreneurs? We weren't a business, we were a non-profit organization. But ideas began coming. Finally we realized we didn't have to train the entrepreneurs in business matters; Americans who own successful businesses could do that. We just needed to organize and run the program.

"How-to" ideas began bombarding the brain cells, the best of which seemed to be to match bold young English-speaking Soviet entrepreneurs with American entrepreneurs who owned businesses parallel to the Soviets' small businesses. English was a necessity since interpreters were quite expensive. We hoped that the Soviet English speakers would cascade the business information down to non-English speakers after returning from the U.S. training.

The EDP scheme was for the Soviet entrepreneur to shadow the American in all business activities for a month. In doing so, the Soviet would absorb ideas, instincts, and "American know how" to take back home to his/her micro-businesses. The Americans would train and house the Soviet entrepreneurs. The Soviets would pay all transportation costs to the American city. CUUI would design the program, search for the business trainers, oversee logistics, and raise money for operating expenses.

Up to this point, the Economic Development Program was sheer "make believe" in the head and on sheets of paper. We had only three Russian entrepreneurs with requests for business information and hadn't contacted a single American business owner to ask if they would participate in this unorthodox undertaking. And we had no funders big enough to consider such a project.

Our seasoned Soviet friends were convinced these young English–speaking entrepreneurs would use the EDP program as a springboard to immigrate to America. This could have daunted us, but so many impossible schemes had become reality by this time, that we weren't afraid to try another one.

Alexei Krupin, an architect from Moscow, was selected as our first EDP pilot entrepreneur. Young and enterprising, Alexei had created a tiny architectural firm and had begun drawing plans for buildings and charging fees. By the time we met him, he had registered his cooperative and talked his institute into renting a small corner of their building for his start-up business. Next, we needed to find an American architect with a small but successful architectural firm. Mike Falkner of Ventura, California, a friend of a friend, became Alexei's mentor in the first EDP experiment. Mike had a highly successful small architectural firm with 12 employees. He thought it was a super idea to train a Russian architect. For a month, Alexei shadowed Mike, accompanying him everywhere while learning the private architecture business from the bottom up. By the end of the month, both architects declared the intensive training to have been a superb success. Alexei went back to Moscow pumped up with new confidence and American "know how," and Mike felt great believing that he might have made a big difference in Alexei's future. We sent a message to our Moscow coordinator Mikhail Malkov to spread the word that CUUI had a new business training program in the offing and to get ready for first stage interviewing.

> We didn't keep up with Alexei Krupin after his internship. Eager to know if our first delegate had made it or fizzled, we began searching for Alexei. Finally in 1992, we located him, and he agreed to come for an interview. At the appointed time, Alexei raced into the room, pulled out his brochures and told his story. He owned five companies, including the original architectural firm, a door and window sash company, an electric company, a plumbing company, and a porcelain company for making light fixtures. He employed 500 full-time workers and added 300 more during summer seasons. What was the most important thing he learned from his American training? That architectural companies are not just about drawing plans for structures, but also about building or buying companies to provide products needed by their clients!

R̸eflections: Looking Back on the 1980s

Looking back to 1983 when we first arrived in the U.S.S.R., we really didn't understand what we were seeing. The world outside our bus windows was a step back into a reality that we had never before experienced. We wondered how this weathered, gray country could have happened to a society which, less than a hundred years earlier, had placed so much emphasis on beauty in public architecture, residential buildings, boulevards, churches, gardens, and the classical arts. This was a nation that had imported the finest of architects and craftsmen from all over Europe to satisfy their penchant for esthetics. In just a few decades it all had devolved into decaying structures and massive gray block houses. There was nothing of quality any place we looked—except inside the museums.

However, we increasingly found quality in the people—those we first chanced to run into in the streets or parks. They were intelligent and warm hearted, modest and surprisingly cultured. They were a magnet for us. We couldn't understand how to connect the decaying society at large with these fascinating and deeply philosophical human beings who were trapped within it. They accepted much that we couldn't have accepted—they had more patience, more endurance, and more willingness to hunt down what they needed for daily life than we could have mustered. And obviously they didn't need nearly as many consumer goods as Americans were accustomed to. But it was their intellect that so took us by surprise, their love of languages even though they never expected to be able to travel, and their respect and enjoyment of the classical arts.

They had devised so many small ways to squeeze enjoyment out of their limited lives, and so many means to get around the system in which they lived. It seemed defeating the system in small ways or getting around it was accomplishment and pleasure in itself.

Even though they didn't trust Gorbachev when he arrived on the scene, they immediately began taking advantage of the small changes in glasnost he was ushering in. Perhaps it was their well-honed minds from school and university classes that made it natural to move to the next step—at least at the philosophical level. They relished the relaxing of structures, opening up to foreigners, and being able to write the truth of what they felt to the newspapers.

I remember the "Bank of Ideas," a bold Gorbachev initiative that invited any Soviet to write to the Komsomolskaya Pravda newspaper their ideas for changing the society. I was there when the mail trucks delivered letters one day. They had no place to put the latest deluge of mail from Soviet citizens and finally dumped them into an old bathtub until they could be sorted out. Wonderful solutions were pouring in, and many ideas were used.

Next Gorbachev invited them to open up the repressed chapters of tragedies during the Stalin era. Painful stories were chronicled daily in Moscow and regional newspapers. Soviet people were finally able to share their hidden grief after so many years of carrying it stoically. But this freedom had its downsides.

Pain and angst was now free floating throughout Soviet society, which seemed to me to strip away any remaining vestige of self worth or national pride that Soviet citizens once had. Being a people who had deep and strong loyalties and pride in their country and their cities, and to see it all crumbling from continuous newspaper revelations, was more trauma than they could deal with.

Too Much, Too Quickly

My sense looking back is that all this was too much change too quickly—too much catharsis for one generation to bear. And yet as the decade ended, the Soviets were careening toward yet another set of traumas in the 1990s that would exhaust their remaining coping mechanisms.

Their society was rapidly moving into profound political, economic, social, and psychological chaos. Gorbachev unleashed glasnost and perestroika (voicing and restructuring) but hadn't factored in the degree of destabilization that both would bring about. The Soviet Union's economic situation was complicated by the earlier collapse of world oil prices in 1986. Oil and gas revenues were critical to maintain the country and its empire. It became increasingly difficult to pay salaries for bureaucracies, institutes, enterprises, and state farms where ordinary Soviets were employed. People scrambled to find other work and yet there was none to be had.

The system could no longer support itself; but three and a half generations of people had been deeply conditioned by the heavy mind print of top-down, authoritarian communism. Soviets were restless for more freedom—but for 70 years the population hadn't been allowed to think independently or to develop the bottom-up skills needed to create new economic structures.

The stage was set for the disintegration of Soviet society in the 1990s.

Part II

1990-1999

Overview of the 1990s

The Tragedy of Russia's 1990s

It is nearly impossible to summarize the degeneration of the U.S.S.R. and Russia, its successor state, as the 1990s began. Gorbachev's reforms unleashed forces across the vast region that couldn't be controlled. The planet's largest nation was undergoing a massive 180-degree upheaval, the likes of which hadn't been dealt with before.

A hundred or more nationalities, including the Russians, were thrown into a situation that they had no idea how to handle. None of their instinctive assumptions, ways of life, or security mechanisms worked in this devolving new world. Some 250 million people were severely impacted by these events.

No sooner had the Soviet Union imploded when young Russians (former Komsomol youth of the Communist party who previously shuffled party bosses' monies), were creating get-rich-quick schemes to siphon the U.S.S.R.'s huge financial assets for themselves. These soon-to-be-called "oligarchs" grabbed Russia's largest industries, which previously had provided salaries and social safety nets for Soviet citizens. The revenues were deposited to their private accounts in offshore banks beyond the reaches of legality and taxation.

Crime exploded in this new lawless environment. An extra-legal "mafia" class quickly developed across eleven time zones. Former KGB, black market operatives, and other assorted high-risk takers learned to rake off profits from Russia's struggling new small businesses. By the end of the '90s, the craven excesses of Russia's new super wealthy class, along with cash hungry bureaucrats and mismanagement of Russia's post-Soviet banking system, left the country flat on its back. But let us return to the early '90s.

Americans' Perspective on the New Russia

Russia's 1990s were seen by most Westerners through rose-tinted glasses. Americans looked on with relief and excitement. The deeply feared U.S.S.R. had vanished; communism had imploded; the loathed Berlin Wall had fallen; Eastern bloc countries were free; and Russians and Soviet block peoples, at last, could vote and elect real leaders, speak their minds and travel freely—or so we thought. We Americans were sure that Russians would rise up quickly, take hold of their lives ... and become "free like us." Our assumption was that if people were given freedom, they would automatically have the "know how" to handle their new reality. Russians were much more circumspect about their frightening new situation.

On the grounds of the Leningrad Seismic Laboratory in 1991, I sat with a group of highly educated young scientists. The discussion was how to stimulate the local economy by developing new small businesses. Optimistic that this could be done over a relatively short period, I suggested numerous ways they could get started.

Tatiana Kochetova, a 40-year-old English-speaking Russian scientist, questioned my optimism. "Sharon," she said emphatically, "We are not like Americans. We don't have the natural instincts your people have cultivated for generations. We have another set of instincts, another mentality. It will take us a very long time ... and it will be a very painful process for us to learn a new mentality. First, we will be flat on our stomachs for probably seven years, then we will have to hobble on our knees for probably seven more years, then maybe we will get on our feet in the next seven years. We don't know—we can't see what is ahead at the end of this black tunnel. It is a totally unknown future we are walking into."

Tatiana's words were incomprehensible to me at the time. From my American perspective, people identified their problems, developed plans to deal with them, and began to forge ahead. But Soviet people had not been allowed to develop plans, organize initiatives, or forge ahead for over three generations—if not scores of generations. These instincts may be encoded in Americans' DNA, but the same instincts may not yet exist on Russians' DNA—and they may need to be developed as Russian people move forward slowly under new conditions.

Only after years of working closely at Russia's grassroots with very bright and educated Russians across eleven time zones, did I realize that Tatiana had understood their grave situation far better than I. My optimism that Russians would rise out of this chaos in half a decade, gradually gave way to reality—along with a whole host of other penetrating realizations about how differences in the histories of countries impact human beings' instincts and capabilities—regardless of their basic intelligence and classical educations.

CUUI's Obsession—To Provide the Missing "Know-How"

CUUI's driving obsession during the '90s was to provide practical education and western methodologies to former Soviet citizens. We hoped this would help them fill the voids left by the failed Soviet economic experiment. Secondarily, we hoped to find

Survival mechanisms were developed in the early 1990s. At every train stop local people were selling whatever they produced.

At this stop near Kazan, a Soviet glass factory paid workers in products (not rubles—they were worthless). Glass makers "worked the tracks" to sell to train passengers coming through. Some of the stemware was quite lovely.

Tatiana Kochetkova, a scientist at the Leningrad Seismic Laboratory in the outskirts of the city, understood instinctively that the way ahead for Russians would be extremely difficult. Her sense was that Russia's past was so radically different from where it would need to go in the future that Russian people would be unable to make the necessary changes in the short term.

However, some young Russians were ingenious. This young man knew that oyster mushrooms grew on wood, so he acquired an old beer boiler, steamed wood scraps to make porous wood squares and began seeding them with oyster mushroom spores. His friends made metal frames to hold the squares. This new business was housed in the basement of a large Soviet enterprise's bomb shelter, several floors below ground. Soon Mikhail was selling his product to local restaurants all across the city. We had the pleasure of taking U.S. Congress members to the bomb shelter that grew benign little oyster mushrooms. Mikhail is an alumnus of CCI's Economic Development Program (EDP). Photo taken in 1992.

ways to short circuit the devastating social upheaval unleashed across Russia. Most of our former Soviet friends were now out of work, and the whole nation was falling into the same predicament. When CUUI's travel program terminated in 1990, we began to concentrate on basic life support programs for the new Russia.

Surviving During the Difficult Years

Citizen diplomacy organizations that had blossomed in the 1980s soon faded out of existence as the difficult years set in. What worked earlier was no longer relevant under the harsh new conditions. Totally new objectives had to be thought through. Somehow or another, one step at a time, we at CUUI managed to get through this shaky transition to a new type of organization. Fortunately, in the '80s we learned how to get things done without bribes or dishonesty and had begun to somewhat understand Russian mentality, which was quite different from American mentality.

We developed instincts for what would work, what wouldn't work, whom to trust and whom not to trust. Probably most importantly, we had become a trusted partner to all with whom we had dealt. This reputation held us in good stead during the entire decade—during a time when Russians didn't trust anyone else. We spent money sparingly, developed quality programs, and kept funders and constituents informed of our progress and Russia's transition.

Consequently, we were a magnet for American foundations and U.S. government funding. During the '90s, thanks to these funders, we expanded CUUI's Economic Development Program and Environmental Initiative, and we started CUUI's Agricultural Initiative. Our Russian Initiative for Self Employment (RISE) for unemployed Russian women and its micro incubator program were thrust into action practically overnight. Russian people saw CUUI programs as a life raft to a better future for themselves and their families.

Events and People — 1990s

The Attempted Coup … and Its Aftermath — August 1991

At 7:00 AM on the morning of August 19, 1991, CUUI's Vice President, Dale Needles, telephoned me at home urging that I turn on the TV immediately. A Soviet coup was taking place, tanks were headed toward downtown Moscow, and citizens were building barricades to prevent the putsch organizers from getting to the Russian "White House." I threw on clothes and raced to the office. Within an hour NBC, ABC, CNN, and CBS reporters were filling the narrow stairwell leading to our second floor CUUI offices. They bantered with one another good naturedly while waiting in line to get interviews.

I could believe easily enough that the coup was happening, but I could not believe, in a million years, that it would hold. The Muscovites and Leningraders we had come to know over the past decade would not back down. It was impossible to think that the courage unleashed by Gorbachev since 1985 would slither away without a revolution. Moreover, it was beyond belief in 1991 that young Russian soldiers would open fire on their own people.

A CNN reporter with a camera asked me if I had a prediction. Responding from somewhere deep inside, I blurted out, "I do! This coup won't last a week! It's a mathematical certainty. Russians' pent-up hope for freedom can't be forced back in the bottle." The one phrase, "This coup won't last a week," was carried around the world by CNN. Interestingly, my face and few words were sandwiched between the Hoover Institute's Sovietologist, Robert Conquest, and another older academic, both of whom reported that the coup would hold and that "the U.S.S.R. would be eclipsed for another 25 years."

The August 19 coup was over in three days, but the country was rapidly deteriorating into social chaos and economic collapse. Elderly populations, ordinary workers, and marginal people were hardest hit. Soon state employee salaries went unpaid; doctors left hospitals to use their personal autos as taxis, and many teachers had to abandon classrooms to seek revenues elsewhere, while others who could, continued to teach without compensation.

So went the first half of the '90s for most of Russia's population; they performed any kind of task to make a few rubles. Many educated brains with English skills and portable careers fled Russia as soon as they could find ways to get to other countries.

By the end of 1991, the Center for U.S.-U.S.S.R. Initiatives as a name, was no longer relevant—since the U.S.S.R. no longer existed. We huddled in the front room of our San Francisco Victorian office trying to figure out what to call ourselves from then forward. Not knowing what the new region would be called, we finally renamed ourselves the Center for Citizen Initiatives (CCI).

Emergency Food Lifts—1990-1991

Soviet farms broke up and farmers left to search for quick rubles elsewhere. Food distribution links disintegrated. Vast fields lay unattended. Products disappeared from grocery shelves; long lines formed on street corners for food products that were brought in from neighboring regions or countries. For our Russian friends in the two large cities, the daily search for food items became top priority.

We decided to do an emergency food lift. We sent out an SOS. CCI volunteers from around America sent checks to our San Francisco office for friends they had met earlier on Soviet streets or in the SMMA program. We purchased survival foods and appealed to cheese and sausage makers to contribute products to the cause. Emergency foods were boxed up in Henry Dakin's big basement and sent in 40-foot Maersk shipping containers to the Port of Leningrad. From there the boxes were trucked to friends in the Leningrad and Moscow regions.

A few months later a different type of lift was carried out—a "cash lift." The food boxes helped, but better still American dollars could be stretched to purchase local buckwheat and other inexpensive food staples that were still available on Russian shelves. Again following a newsletter request for funds, checks poured in from American friends for Russian families. Checks were converted to cash. We couldn't send the money, so we had to travel with the cash on our bodies. U.S. Customs required that Americans could carry only $10,000 cash out of the country, so for every $10,000 donated, another CCI person had to be added to the travel list. Each designated Russian family received from $50 to $100, which amounted to quite a bit of help since dollars at that time could still be exchanged for rubles at a favorable rate.

Original traveler Barbara O'Reilly brushed up her sewing skills and created "money carriers" for CCI men and me. They were thin undergarments with narrow pockets sewn precisely to hold multiples of $100 bills. The men's garments were T-shirts with pockets on the undersides. Barbara found a filmy consignment store nightgown for me. She cut off the bottom and made underneath pockets for the top to carry the bills. Looking like stuffed robins, each with $10,000 in our pockets, we sailed without a glitch through American, then Finnish checkpoints, then through Russian customs' guards. Shortly we were in Leningrad's Pulkovskaya Hotel calling Russian friends to come for quick pickups. We were no longer worried about using phones since the whole intelligence system had collapsed. Russians were stunned to learn that an American friend whom they had met previously had sent them cash. For some, it was their first time to hold dollars in their hands.

Urban Gardens for Inner City Russians

With state farms falling apart, food scarcity was severe and time was short. How could Russian city dwellers produce their own food in one growing season? Some of us remembered America's World War II Victory Gardens. We began to talk about planting vegetables at ground level in public spaces. Russian friends were shocked saying that ground-level gardens would be robbed at harvest, and the physical effort would have been in vain. But even more dangerous, we learned that the city soil was heavily contaminated by lead from truck diesel exhaust that had spewed out at ground level for decades.

We took American urban gardeners to Russia to demonstrate how to use every square meter of soil for food production. Soon vegetable gardens were being planted in "safe" spaces such as large upper-floor decks of institutes—with soil that had been trucked in from the countryside. Even at Leningrad's massive Kritski Prison, inmates grew vegetables with CCI seeds and planting instructions. After the first growing season, Kritski officials reported that prisoners who tended vegetables during the hot summer months didn't riot as usual—an unexpected benefit that neither they nor we had anticipated.

A Different Type of Soviet Bureaucrat—1991

In late 1991, we hoped to begin a project that required permission from St. Petersburg's Marienski Administration (City Hall). Entering the former palace through a small side door, Volodya Shestakov and I found ourselves in a tiny unimpressive room. Behind the desk, sat a trim and seemingly reserved man of about 40 years. After impersonal greetings, he began to ask specific questions: What was our proposal? Why? How would it work? Who would it benefit? Where would the money come from? Each additional question was related directly to the last answer given. Not accustomed to pragmatic questions from such people, I became aware of this bureaucrat's impersonal focus.

By this time, I'd had my fill of Soviet public officials. They always had personal agendas … they wanted a trip to America, a trip for one of their relatives or friends "to see what you are describing in person." Or they wanted to subsume CCI projects hoping to get some tangible gain for themselves or their relatives. My retort was always that CCI's projects were for the good of Russia, not individuals, hoping to enlist their support without directly saying, "No," to their personal agendas. Much of the time it didn't work, in which case I took pride that I'd never given personal favors or bribes to any of them. I hoped the word would get around that CCI operated solely on "merit," not on "connections"—which was quite unusual in Russia.

After an hour of grilling, the information gathering was over. Everything that could have been known about our project had been questioned. Indications were that he was interested in our proposal. Now was the "traditional" time for him to assess what he could "get" for giving his official permission. He patiently explained that what we proposed

Left, August 19, 1991, Mayor Anatoly Sobchak, speaks to Leningrad crowd saying the city will not capitulate to coup leaders. He immediately began organizing resistance to the putsch. Meanwhile Yeltsin was leading resisters in Moscow. We were in touch with Vladimir Shestakov via e-mail and were keeping up with hour-by-hour happenings of this soon to be defeated coup. Below, crowds gathered on the Dvortsovaja square in support of Sobchak's decision.

We received emails from St. Petersburg and Moscow saying that foodstuffs of all types, even grains, were disappearing from shelves. A quick group e-mail was sent to our CCI trippers which brought an instant response of checks. Emergency foods were purchased, and Henry Dakin cleared his large parking garage to permit scores of Bay Area volunteers to set up lines to pack the foods. The boxes were shipped post-haste in Maersk Line containers to St. Petersburg where some of us were on site to assure that the shipment was intact and that the boxes got to their desired destinations. Photo of CCI volunteers in 1991.

Some high-risk planters chose to grow summer gardens at ground level in the cities.This young mother was photographed showing Sasha Gavrilov, CCI's Petersburg agricultural director, the lush greens she had planted with American seeds. By spring of 1992 CCI distributed massive amounts of vegetable seeds not only to individuals but also to small private farmers, thanks to the generosity of several American seed companies.

was a really good idea but that, at that time, it wasn't within legal boundaries. That was all. It was an immediate let down for me; I assumed that he had liked the idea and would provide the official stamps to make it happen. But, no, it wasn't possible.

However, to his credit, he carefully considered the project and had taken us seriously. I remember walking out the door and onto the sidewalk saying to Volodya, "At least we have been heard by one ex-Soviet bureaucrat who didn't ask us for anything." I had not heard his name previously. The business card I took away gave his full name as Vladimir Vladimirovich Putin.

In late 1999, I saw a reference in The New York Times regarding President Yeltsin's grooming of his latest in a string of Prime Ministers to be the next president of Russia—his name was Vladimir Putin. Surely not the Putin I'd met! The next day, the photo of one and the same Vladimir Putin appeared in the Times.

"Egad," I exclaimed to friends, "I've met this character; he's not presidential material at all! He's too intellectual and too introverted. He could NEVER lead Russia out of the pit the country is in!" I was hoping someone strong would emerge and clean house in the Kremlin, so this news was disastrous for me.

I remember telling my American friends, "For Russia to succeed, whoever takes Yeltsin's place must do two things: 1) Wrench the oligarchs out of the Kremlin and politics; and 2) Find a way to take Russia's 89 corrupt regional governors out of power"—both of which I felt would be totally impossible for this new Prime Minister to accomplish.

Russia's Early Grassroots Economy—1990–1995

Able-bodied, educated Russians were scurrying about trying to find niches from which to earn food money for their families. Legally they were able to develop micro-businesses, but there were no laws or business structures to assist them. Young engineers, physicists and military officers were the first to succeed as business experimenters in the '90s. Why I wondered? It appeared that people from these three backgrounds were somewhat better able to initiate, plan, and organize than those from other backgrounds. But even they had to totally reinvent themselves as they dove into any service niche available. They often ended up with businesses that had nothing to do with their formal educations. Physicists became construction company owners, engineers became plastics manufacturers, and military officers built wholesale foods companies and so on. In each city we visited, we found this "reinvention of career paths" going on at the grassroots level. Men worked 100-hour weeks; wives became bookkeepers; and sons and daughters helped out wherever they could to support and learn the family businesses.

It was a highly creative time for the brightest and most diligent Russians—but it was disastrous for those who had worked on assembly lines in large enterprises. They didn't have the innate instincts to create a new or become entrepreneurial. The top-down Soviet system of "give orders or take orders" hadn't allowed the development of skills for creating, problem solving, or thinking outside of the box. This left a major swath of people in the country who were helpless under the sweeping new conditions.

Other unexpected changes were taking place. By 1992 former Soviet price controls were lifted. Bread and other staples were sold for whatever the seller asked. This was devastating to elderly and disadvantaged Russians who were accustomed to heavily subsidized prices for inexpensive foods. Russia's infamous "voucher program" was unleashed. Unfortunately, the program ended with many former Soviet bosses getting most of their companies' assets—which meant that the enterprises continued to be "Soviet" managed and lacked controls regarding how company monies were spent. Rubles were being printed around the clock. Hyperinflation rose to 2,600 percent.

Bartering for Survival

Throughout the Soviet years, the ruble wasn't taken all too seriously—it seemed to us that rubles were looked at more like monopoly money—in that they were handled and borrowed rather loosely compared to our experience with U.S. dollars. In addition, many workers seemed to use the state enterprises to their own advantages. It wasn't uncommon to get state products, foods, or equipment parts from one's place of employment and then exchange items among friends with no rubles changing hands.

It was natural that during the early 1990s, barter activity, a moneyless economy, quickly developed throughout Russian society. The ruble had lost 35 percent of its value, and the essentials for daily living doubled in price—making the ruble practically worthless and not an option for most families. By the mid 1990s barter had replaced the ruble as a means of exchange for getting what one needed or wanted. To us this looked undependable and murky. Deals were struck behind closed doors; no one disclosed what was being given or received. The mafia couldn't determine what percentages to take, so they demanded a higher take, just in case. Tax authorities had no way to track the barter business. Unfortunately, barter added yet another layer of distrust among Russian citizens since nothing was transparent and all dealings were suspect.

Big enterprises also used this non-monetary form of exchange to keep their businesses afloat. We were fascinated by how small businesses managed to survive under these conditions. Down at the street level, ingenious bartering loops were being created, which required significant amounts of skill and trust among those intimately involved.

Interviewing a Barter Organizer

I was in Volgograd interviewing candidates for CCI's Economic Development Program. Sitting in front of me was a Volgograd man who was applying for business training in an American financial company. He didn't have a name for his business; he had no title for himself nor could he give a description of his business. He said he wasn't sure what kind of American company could help him but probably a firm that understood numbers and could assist him to come up with a new financial system, perhaps even a computerized one. When he learned he wouldn't be eligible for the program without more definitive information, he finally spilled out his current unorthodox career.

This mathematician-turned-entrepreneur explained that he was the central brain in the middle of several bartering loops. His task was to organize these loops and to be sure that each participating company was fairly compensated for its contribution of products or services. Also his responsibility was to determine the real worth of products given or received, and then pay each company in-kind with bartered products. He described the enormous amount of work involved in dealing fairly with each company in the loop. He wanted to consult with an American to learn how he might better manage these loops for small and mid-sized regional businesses.

One loop he described was a hospital needing sugar and medical garments for which in exchange they could provide medical services; a tire company that needed vehicles and sales and could provide tires; a sewing operation that needed fabrics and clients and could produce apparel; and a sugar beet operation that needed equipment and clients and could provide sugar. Somehow the interviewee had arranged to get most of these major business needs met within these bartering loops, either directly or indirectly. He would then get a share of the goods or services being exchanged and would sell them on the local market for his personal remuneration. These companies were keeping their businesses alive without money during a time when the ruble was all but worthless. At last, through this mathematician's disclosures, I was allowed to see how barter worked in Russia's turbulent 1990s. It gave me considerable respect for Russians' ingenuity.

Barter transactions in Russia during the mid '90s accounted for an astonishing 50 percent of activity for midsize enterprises and 75 percent for large enterprises. No one bothered to calculate the percentage for small businesses, but I suspect it was near 100 percent.

Three Types of Russian Business People during the 1990s

Oligarchs: These outrageously wealthy men became super-rich from being unscrupulous and in the right place at the right time when the U.S.S.R. fell apart. Quite a few were young communist party-affiliated Komsomols (members of the communist youth organization) during the 1980s. Others were high-risk takers on the fringe of corrupt Soviet leaders. They were eager to get their hands on big money as the U.S.S.R. imploded. Many got their mega money making enterprises during the so-called "Loans-for-Shares" auctions. Yeltsin supporters acquired major parts of Russia's energy, metallurgical, and telecommunications sectors for a fraction of their worth. Their money got Yeltsin elected again in 1996 but at a gargantuan price to the new Russia. They became the political power within the Kremlin and were able to wield immense influence over public policy to benefit themselves and their ill-gotten holdings. The country was now run by an oligarchy that had no concern for ordinary Russian people.

Bootstrap and Grassroots Entrepreneurs: This category was comprised of well-educated, entrepreneurial younger men and women primarily from Soviet institutes and the military. They were quick learners and desperate to find ways to survive in the crashing world around them. Their range of businesses was about the same as those in America—private construction, apparel making, food production, wholesale operations, legal services, transportation, retail outlets, printing, and a host of other products and services needed to grow a private sector. We watched as these businesses began to take off, particularly for those owners who had trained in American companies under CCI programs.

Mafia: Simultaneously with the operations of the oligarchs and entrepreneurs, a sinister business was becoming more powerful and infiltrating both small businesses and the upper echelon of Russia's massive trans-regional enterprises. The breakdown of Russian society, coupled with high unemployment, brought about a criminal element that hadn't previously existed. Jobless KGB operatives and former black market operators in every city found their new niches—they could extract money from struggling new business owners under the pretext of "protection services." Policemen, with little to no salary, were readily subsumed into this racket also. Mafia simply walked into the new businesses and announced, "We are here to protect you. If you don't like this arrangement, we have ways to take your business down." The fastest way was to "torch" the business and leave a heap of burning embers to intimidate others.

We experienced the mafia first hand. In the early '90s, we were interviewing a CCI participant when a stranger in black leather walked into his office where we sat. Oblivious to us, he announced to the owner that he was there to protect this business and needed a few minutes alone with him to go over details. The owner scribbled something on a piece of paper and handed it to him. The "visitor" looked at it and walked out. Later we learned that the EDP entrepreneur we were interviewing had already made a deal with another such mafia character, so he referred the intruder to talk with his current mafia man. His attitude was that they could fight it out if they wished.

All of our Russian EDP alumni had to have protection if they wanted to continue running their businesses. These protection thugs were called "roofs." They were also carving up Russian cities by geographic sectors and production. Guns were plentiful. With the Soviet military breaking up, small weapons of all sorts were for sale by whoever had keys to the storehouse and sold to any who had money to purchase them. Roofs didn't hesitate to use guns, particularly on each other. The mafia grew rapidly as small and large businesses got more successful. It was a despicable alliance. When the mafia knew that the entrepreneurs' businesses were selling more products, they increased their percentage. So new businesses could never get ahead.

What in the beginning were small criminal groups soon became blood-spattered operations as the mafia got more vicious and entrepreneurs got more desperate. Arkady Ivanov, an EDP alumnus in Penza, shared a shocking story as we sat in his restaurant. A local roof had been "servicing" his business for a couple of years. Time came when the roof wanted to take ownership of his restaurant and let Arkady manage it for him. Arkady had worked diligently to build this business, which fed his family, and he wasn't about to give it up. We were sitting in his restaurant and it was clear he still owned it, so I asked how this situation was resolved. He calmly replied, "I took him out." Not being sure what this meant, I phrased the question another way. Arkady replied, "It was either him or me. I decided it would be him and not me." Then he added, "And no roof has approached me since."

Closer to home for CCI was the day in 1995 when three young guys sporting guns walked into our St. Petersburg RISE office saying that they were there to become our new protection. Fortunately, our Russian managers were on site. They told them that RISE already had a "roof." They wanted proof and the managers had none. The three were asked to return the next day. In the interim, the managers quickly called several EDP alumni and found one who was willing to share his roof with CCI. He brought his business cards and his roof's contact information. The thugs appeared the next day, took the information and were never seen again.

By early 1996, Russia's entrepreneurs began reporting that the mafia was beginning to shrink. It wasn't clear to us why this was happening. They still needed money, and businesses were still easy targets. Then we began hearing that being a roof was becoming a "lethal business." In addition, quite a few mafia had made enough money to start their own businesses with extorted money. Soon the explanation was reduced to an unofficial formula: 25 percent of the Mafioso got killed while carving up territories; 50 percent took their ill-gotten money, left the racket world, and became small business owners; and 25 percent went "upstairs" to big businesses where the money was much better—but the mortality rate was much higher. At least one criminal aspect of Russia's wild 1990s was fading away!

By late 1997 roofs, the original street mafia in Russia, had all but disappeared. There were, of course, those who became bodyguards, intimidators, and contract killers for the super wealthy, but after 1997 they didn't focus on average Russian entrepreneurs, our target population.

However by this time, another group of predators had begun to live off of Russia's young entrepreneurs. Petty public bureaucrats in official offices in every city had begun to extort ever-larger bribes from local business owners. Business owners all needed official documents with which to register their businesses, renovate, expand, and to start second businesses. Starting with small bribes in the early '90s, local officials grew greedier by the year. Entrepreneurs began calling these local officials "the institutionalized mafia."

A New Philanthropist for CCI—1992

I was told that a philanthropist was interested in Russia and CCI's work, and he was watching us from the periphery. His name was Arthur Schultz. Being a capitalist, Arthur was intrigued by our Russian entrepreneurs but not in funding our training programs. Finally, I got to meet him. His first interest was helping Russia's young businessmen learn accounting. He brought a Harvard accounting book to us for translation into Russian. Soon we had it translated, printed, and then distributed to Russia's new entrepreneurs. Next he asked if CCI could develop handbooks for Russia's fledgling business owners that included the topics of the "ABCs of Creating Businesses" and "Micro Business Accounting." We hired a sharp English-speaking Ukrainian businessman, Boris Khersonski, to help write these books. Printed in Moscow, they were distributed by CCI to Russian entrepreneurs in the Moscow region and in Northwest Russia. Arthur came up with other ingenious ideas to be covered later. His full story about "why Russia" came out only years later after he had funded a number of CCI projects.

Arthur Schultz was a teenager in Norway's partisan movement during World War II. The Nazis had already taken over his country. He and other youngsters met in Norway's forests with ham radio sets where they tuned into the war's "front" all across Russia. They believed that if the Russian soldiers could turn back the Nazi war machine, Norway would one day be freed from Nazi occupation. They followed each geographic location where Russian troops were pitted against German forces. The Russians had grossly inferior equipment and training compared with the Nazi's—yet, they fought with every ounce of their blood to save their Motherland. Young Norwegians listened to radios and rooted for the Russians with all their hearts. Later Arthur would remember, "We cheered when the Soviet forces began to overtake the Nazis—and today I feel a very deep debt to Russia and to the Russian people. Whatever I am doing now, is repaying that debt in some small way."

Arthur made his money the hard way; he came to the U.S. as an uneducated 20-year-old with $250 in his pocket. Landing in Los Angeles, he worked hard, put himself through university, and eventually became a CPA. Los Angeles was in a huge economic boom in those days. Arthur was a financial whiz who was trusted by large company owners. He handled their finances well and began to build his own fortune by buying shares in companies on the rise. Fortunately, we intersected with Arthur when he was searching for ways to "give back" to Russia.

Learning the Ropes in Washington, D.C.—1992

So much needed to be accomplished on ground in Russia in the '90s. Our programs needed to be greatly expanded since they were far too small to make much difference in the overall Russian situation. On a plane en route to Washington, D.C., CCI board member, Anthony Garret, leaned over and quietly said, "I have committed myself to raise $1,000,000 for CCI within the next year." I thought he was joking—but soon it became clear that he wasn't. Over the next three days we crisscrossed Capitol Hill dozens of times meeting with a dizzying array of Congressional members on Appropriations Committees in both the House and the Senate—18 agenda-packed meetings in all. These committees determine where U.S. government spends its money. This was a very propitious trip for CCI.

1992 Presidential Elections
EDP Funded by USAID—1993

William J. Clinton won the 1992 U.S. Presidential election. With his appointees fresh in their new seats and Russia high on Clinton's agenda, Anthony and I made a second trip to Washington. We hoped that CCI's four years of training Soviet entrepreneurs would give us an edge over other competitors regarding funding for Russia programs.

We ended up securing an appointment with USAID's new Russia Director, Greg Hugar. Sitting in his handsomely appointed office in D.C., I explained CCI's history with its Economic Development Program and tried to persuade Greg how important it would be if USAID could expand EDP. He listened carefully, asked good questions, and then inquired how much CCI would need to significantly expand our operations. Explaining that we operated CCI on a slim budget, I suggested that we could get a lot of work accomplished with $100,000. A strange silence fell over Greg and his colleagues. Then he quietly replied, "Sharon, we don't do $100,000. What could you do if we gave you $10,000,000?

I was speechless! I had, of course, daydreamed about what could be done with lots of funding but never allowed myself to entertain it seriously. Recovering fairly quickly, the "what to do's" came rushing out: 1) Dramatically increase the volume of training for Russia's regional entrepreneurs, 2) Create business centers in several important regions, 3) Bring American business consultants to Russia's regional cities to consult with Russia's non-English speaking entrepreneurs who weren't eligible for EDP training in the U.S., 4) Provide business education through regional media, and 5) Teach business courses to the next generation coming into the new market. This must have satisfied him and his colleagues. He said, "Okay, go back home and write the proposal."

Greg then brought up a caveat: The grant monies could only be used in Russia, not in the former Soviet republics, which had become independent states. I balked at this since we had excellent informal offices in several newly recognized states. He explained, "If Russia makes it, then most likely the other smaller states also will; if Russia doesn't make it, then all of them will be in grave trouble." It made sense.

A White House Appointment—1993

Returning from Russia in mid-1993, I stopped in Washington, D.C. to give a progress report to USAID. Walking down a State Department corridor, I met a well-placed Clinton appointee who quietly said, "Sharon, we have recommended you for a White House appointment—to serve as a director on the new Russian-American Enterprise Fund's Board." The Fund was news to me. He continued, "This fund is meant to support the development of small businesses across Russia. We submitted your name since we know you will speak up if something goes awry."

Thirteen of us sat on the RAEF Board, including several well known Wall Street investment bankers. I was the one most disappointed in the direction that the Fund took. The investment bankers considered a small loan to be in the range of $10 million; I knew for Russia, they should be $25,000 or less. The last straw for me was learning that RAEF had spent $11 million of the fund's money to renovate RAEF headquarters in Moscow. I registered my discontent to those who had recommended me for this appointment and to the two or three non-Wall Street bankers on the Board whom I trusted. Soon the Fund was pushed to change course—or to close and restart as another entity. RAEF ceased to exist in the mid 1990s. It was reorganized as The U.S. Russia Investment Fund (TUSRIF), and later reorganized again as the Delta Private Equity Fund. Pat Cloherty, a brilliant and tough fund manager, became the guiding light of this latest and successful incarnation of what started as the misguided RAEF.

Angry U.S. Congress Members—1994

My phone rang. "Sharon, Jack Gosnell here." Jack was U.S. Consul General at the American Consulate in St. Petersburg. "I need some help. Can you drop by as soon as possible—like today?" This was an unusual request, so within a couple of hours I was at the Consulate residence.

"Fourteen key Congressional members will arrive here in three days, and they are mad as hell! They are in Moscow investigating how U.S. taxpayers' dollars are being spent and are furious at the waste they've found. I need you to brief them on CCI's U.S. government programs and let them know that something is working with U.S. tax dollars. Also I need you to give them your perspective on ground in the Russian cities where CCI works."

Jack and I brainstormed a final evening event for the Congress members: a first-ever, sure-fire way to give these VIPs something to talk about when they got back to Washington.

We would introduce them to CCI's entrepreneurs who had trained in American companies, then split them up in pairs and send them to different apartments for dinner and discussions. Each VIP would be transported from the Grand Europa Hotel to the entrepreneurs' small apartments, not in limousines but in not-too-comfortable, and often old Russian cars. They would have a real Russian evening in addition to enlightening discussions. On hearing about this scheme, State Department officials were adamantly opposed to it. They gave endless reasons why it wouldn't work, why it should be done another way, and why it would be dangerous for these VIPs. We didn't give them heed.

Meanwhile, we were feverishly telephoning CCI's St. Petersburg entrepreneurs. Not a single Russian business owner turned us down. Pairings were made on paper. Jack

Arthur Schultz was a self-made multi-millionaire who wanted to repay Russians for winning the war against the Nazis. But he wanted to do it his own way.

CCI is deeply grateful to Arthur for allowing us to work along side him with a number of project ideas that he created.

U.S. Consul General, Jack Gosnell, admits to being non-traditional in order to accomplish unusual results. His idea to take Congress members to ordinary Russian entrepreneurs' homes was brilliant; however, it set some of his bureaucracy on their ears. To his credit, 14 Congress members raved about their first-ever experiences in Russian homes and are still talking about their impressions years later.

Democratic Congressional Leader, Richard Gephardt and Republican House Leader, Robert Michel questioning a CCI alumnus at a home visit about how America might help Russians as they attempt to build a private sector.

Meanwhile, twelve other Congress Members were spread across St. Petersburg. Congressman Newt Gingrich shown here with Sergei Baranov, advertising businessman, Irina Ivanitskaya (l), electrical company chief, and Marianne Gingrich.

described the personalities of Congressional leaders Dick Gephardt, Bob Michel. and the others. We matched them with CCI entrepreneurs according to personalities. Gephardt and Michel would go to two sophisticated business partners at a home in Pushkin. Newt Gingrich was paired with energetic Irina Ivanitskaya, a fiery woman entrepreneur with a great future and Sergei Baranov, an innovative wholesaler. All others were matched accordingly.

Briefing U.S. Congress Members and a New Ambassador

We barely got the evening event organized before it was time for me to show up at the U.S. Consulate for a noon luncheon. As I stood at the Consulate residence door, it dawned upon me that in a few minutes I'd be meeting these Washington VIPs without a single thought about how to speak intelligently to them. I wished the granite steps would open up and I could vanish.

Jack, in professional attire, welcomed me at the door. Our VIP guests were milling around the magnificent guest room with glasses of wine and hors d'oeuvres in hand. The tallest man in the room immediately strolled my way and said in a southern drawl, "Little lady, I'm Bob Livingston from Louisiana. We hear you know more about Russia than any American in this country. We need to talk with you!" I was taken back at his remark and began wondering how Jack had explained who I was. Taking a low-key position, I explained to Congressman Livingston that we work at Russia's grassroots with start-up entrepreneurs but that this was the limit of my experience. One after another, VIPs began introducing themselves. They seemed open to me, an ordinary American citizen in their midst. A bell rang, and we were invited into another big room with a long, long table with chairs on each side. I was ushered to the middle of the table on one side and noted that Dick Gephardt, Newt Gingrich, and Thomas Pickering, America's incoming Ambassador to Russia, were seated directly across from me. A priority of seating was fast becoming obvious. What did this mean? I was soon to find out. Jack reintroduced me, made some exaggerated remarks and turned the luncheon over to me to "brief" this distinguished group of Congress members and the new ambassador to Russia. I could have dropped dead at the prospect!

Fortunately, I had been so immersed in Russia's development over the previous few years that I must have rattled on like an automaton giving the history of ordinary Russian citizens' attempts to develop Russia's first-ever, bottom-up private sector and what was needed to build a viable economy across the country. When I ended, first Dick Gephardt and then Newt Gingrich began grilling me with one question after another. Newt's questions were suspicious. With each plausible answer, he fired back with yet another tough question. On and on the interaction continued. It felt like a game of high-stakes poker or mental tennis. In the process I realized I knew more than I had assumed. Ending the session, we explained the evening plan for them to go to different apartments of CCI alumni for open-ended discussions. Here they could learn about what Russia's entrepreneurs need to succeed and how to avoid wasting American's tax dollars. They appeared to greatly appreciate this unorthodox experiment, rather than attending the usual Congressional meetings with talking heads.

Photo taken in December 1993. Ten years before in 1983 we had two FBI agents watching our every move. With the White House appointment, we thankfully had come full cycle.

Newt Gingrich's no-nonsense prediction regarding the PEP proposal: "If you want it done, CCI will have to do it." But he offered that he and Leader Gephardt would take the proposal to the White House if CCI would agree to implement it.

U.S. Ambassador to Russia, Thomas Pickering and wife, visiting CCI's Volgograd office which was the first CCI-EDP office to be establised.

Soon EDP was funded by USAID, we established a full service business center and library in Volgograd, then began to branch out in other Russian cities for CCI's next five offices.

We were fortunate that the Russian Directors we hired were perfect representatives for our mission. They remained with us from 1994/5 through 2008. Some continue to operate local business centers in their regions up to the present time.

Congressional VIPs Visit Homes of Russian Entrepreneurs

At 6:30 PM we met the Congress members in the elegantly renovated foyer of the Grand Europa Hotel, just off of Nevsky Prospect. State Department officers stood by silently as their charges were swept off to unknown Russian apartments. Our advice to the Congressional members: When you enter the apartment, loosen your tie, trade your shoes for Russian "tapochki" (house slippers), and be prepared for down-home discussions about anything you wish to ask. Our advice to the entrepreneurs: Welcome your guests like you would your school friends, don't consider them as "big bosses or authorities," give them house slippers, answer their questions honestly, and feel free to ask them whatever you wish.

The ice was quickly broken across St. Petersburg that evening. I was with leaders Gephardt and Michel and their wives at a home near Pushkin. The aroma of Russian food welcomed us as we entered the door. Introductions were loud and joyful. Ties were loosened, house shoes were donned, and an appropriate amount of vodka was offered. Questions and answers continued until late in the evening.

A van came to Pushkin to take us back to the Europa. On the way to their hotel, Leader Gephardt and others behind me in the van began peppering me with questions about what more could be done to assist Russia's attempts toward private sector development. Turning around in the seat and resting on my knees, I explained the vision of what should be done next: It was an adaptation of the historic Marshall Plan's "Productivity Tours" of the 1950s. I explained this should be a nationwide program that would bring delegations of "non-English speaking" Russian entrepreneurs (with two interpreters per delegation) to American companies of the same industry sector in which the Russians were building their new businesses. As we said our goodbyes, Dick Gephardt, Newt Gingrich, Bob Livingston, Nita Lowery, and Tom Lantos asked me to get in touch when I was next in Washington.

The Conception of CCI's Productivity Enhancement Program (PEP)

That evening was really the impetus for the largest and most intensive business training program ever undertaken for Russia's entrepreneurs. It was based on the Marshall Plan's Productivity Tours, which brought 24,000 foreigners to American plants and companies after WWII. A few months earlier, I'd read the "Analysis of the Marshall Plan Tours for Post-Socialist Countries," written by Jim Silverman and Charles Heldt. I found Silverman, the architect of the original Marshall Tours, in Maryland. He was still very much alive and in his 80's. He was able to tell me in detail how the original "Tours" were organized and carried out. Previous to our phone discussions, I had absorbed every page of the Silverman/Heldt analysis—underlining, highlighting, and making notes in the margins of nearly every paragraph. This 90-page analysis for me was like bread to a hungry person. It was precisely what Russia needed to convert to a market economy. This was all in my mind when Dick Gephardt asked, "What needs to be done next?"

PEP Proposal Requested

A month later, I was in the Washington offices of Dick Gephardt and Newt Gingrich. Both asked for a proposal showing how the historic Productivity Tours could be adapted for Russia in the 1990s.

It was clear to me that this mega-program needed to be run by the U.S. government, as was the original Marshall Plan. The projected cost would be about $50 million dollars over a five-year period for 10,000 Russian entrepreneurs to be trained in American companies at a cost of $5,000 per Russian.

"If You Want it Done … "

Back in Washington with the proposal in hand, Newt pronounced, "It looks great; only one thing is wrong with it. The U.S. government will never do this—and besides the American people today would never trust the government to do it. If you want it done, CCI will have to do it. Do you want Dick and me to take this proposal to the White House to assure support for it?" Again I was stunned. I'd never considered that CCI could run this program. We were still a relatively small organization, and we were already implementing EDP with a three-year, $7.3 million USAID grant. Finally, convinced by Gephardt and Gingrich that the Marshall "variant" would never see the light of day if the U.S. government was expected to do it, I began to consider that CCI would have to take it on—but on a much more modest scale than $50,000,000.

Richard Morningstar, Clinton's New Tsar for Russia

I'm not sure how I ended up in Dick Morningstar's office with the PEP proposal. But I do remember that he had hardly warmed his seat as Clinton's new Tsar for Russia. Morningstar had a long and successful business career behind him—thus providing him a business sense about what would work and what wouldn't. He introduced himself unpretentiously. His to-the-point questions made for quick and easy answers. I remember that he balked at the proposal line that assumed that Rotary and other civic clubs would provide pro bono sponsorship and accommodations and identify business trainers for this new program. He found this unbelievable from a business perspective—it took serious convincing before he could grasp that civic clubs might actually provide the support pro bono. Minutes later he put his pen down and casually said, "From which government agency would you like this to be funded?"—as though funding was a foregone conclusion. It felt like some sort of reality warp … where all it took was showing how a program could be implemented—and funding followed naturally. Together we quickly decided a direct State Department grant for CCI would be best. Thus, CCI's first $5 million contract for PEP was awarded. This was at the turn of 1996.

Bank Rolling the U.S. Government

The Republicans took the House of Representatives in January of 1996, and Gingrich had shut down the U.S. government just as PEP was supposed to start. Little did we know that CCI's grant monies would be withheld for months. With assurances from the State Department that funds would eventually come through, we started the huge program and began spending down CCI's general reserves for monthly expenses. PEP delegations began coming. January, February, and March passed with our reserve funds dwindling precariously. I had already begun discussions with President Bill White at the Mott Foundation about borrowing money until the standoff was broken. Finally, in April the logjam broke—in May, State Department funds began to roll into PEP's bank account.

The Dream of a School of Management (SOM) in St. Petersburg

CCI became involved with yet another type of activity with Arthur Schultz. Early in the 1990s, Russia's oldest higher education institution, the St. Petersburg State University, paired with the University of Berkeley's Haas School of Management to begin developing a world-class School of Management within the St. Petersburg State University system. Teams of professors and students from Berkeley and St. Petersburg began to exchange information between each other's campuses with the dream of a new MBA school for Russia. A dilapidated Soviet structure temporarily housed the university's first class of 34 graduate students.

John Pepper, the just retired CEO of Procter & Gamble, became chair of the advisory board and spearheaded the new effort. Susanne Campbell, a long-time Russia specialist, became director of the project. I was invited to sit on the board of advisors.

In 1995 the city of St. Petersburg gave the university two severely damaged, co-joined Yakovlev palaces on the Neva Embankment for the proposed School of Management (SOM). The stipulation was that those interested in using the palaces for the new school must raise funds to restore them to their former splendor. Creative ways would be required to integrate administrative offices, classrooms, lecture halls, a library, and computer laboratories without compromising the palaces' architectural and artistic integrity. Artisans and project managers agreed it could be accomplished.

Susanne Campbell went to Arthur Schultz, a potential donor. Art saw the long-term value of this project. He made a challenge grant of $1,000,000 to jumpstart fundraising for the new school. Feeling reasonably sure that the rest of the funds could be raised, John Pepper instituted a donor drive.

Soon afterward, it became obvious that an American nonprofit 501(c)(3) was needed to receive tax-deductible donations and disburse funds for this non commercial project. CCI was asked to take on this responsibility.

Throughout the arduous development campaign, major funders came forth—George Soros, John Pepper, U.S. corporations including Procter & Gamble, American and European foundations, USAID, Russian business leaders, and many others contributed. The project attracted and spent over $4,000,000 in contributions for the renovation of the two palaces.

CCI received funds and paid expenses, watched over project managers, withheld funds when necessary, and kept an eye on the renovation itself. Surviving numerous challenges with construction companies, project managers, official agencies, and climatic conditions, the project finally reached its grand goal, and students began classes in September of 2003. What an honor it was to be there for the celebration—and what a pleasure it is today to see the quality of students and education in the new Graduate School of Management on the Neva Embankment. For the full story, check it out on Internet.

The Graduate School of Management (GSOM), one of the 22 Faculties of St. Petersburg State University, was founded in 1993 in partnership with Haas School of Business, University of California, Berkeley (USA).

*Arthur Schultz made a million dollar pledge to begin St. Peterburg's School of
Management (SOM); John Pepper, Chair of the Board, oversaw the mission and
the fundraising campaign. Susanne Campbell was the Director and CCI managed
contributions, expenditures, and oversaw project managers.*

*The decaying old palaces became a splendid example of how exquisite architecture
of the past can retain its historic ambience and still be useful in today's world. The
space now has numerous classrooms, extensive computer labs, presentation halls, a
modern library, elegant receiving rooms, and administration offices. Today, faculty
and students take excellent care of these palaces.*

*John Pepper, retired CEO of Procter
& Gamble and Chair of the SOM
Board, did a masterful job of raising
matching funds from international
corporations and individuals to
complete the restoration of the SOM
buildings.*

*One of the project managers (l) in the
newly finished northeast wing of SOM.*

Today GSOM is the leading Russian university-based business school with strong international recognition proven by prestigious accreditations AMBA (Executive MBA) and EPAS (Bachelor), and membership in global alliances of top international business schools (PIM, CEMS, EFMD, AACSB, EABIS, and GMAC). It participates in exchange programs with over 40 leading universities and business schools from Europe, America, Asia, and Australia.

The Eduniversal Ranking has named GSOM #1 business school in Russia (2008, 2009) and one of the three best business schools in Eastern Europe (2009).

Currently the School has around 1,200 students at degree programs (bachelor, master, EMBA, doctoral), as well as a well-established executive education center.

In 2006 the School became a part of the Russian Government National Priority Project in Education with a mission of establishing a world-class business school in Russia. St. Petersburg State University was given a group of historic palaces 30 kilometers south of St. Petersburg for the development of GSOM's new southern campus.

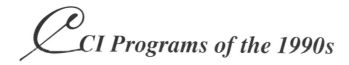

CCI Programs of the 1990s

Economic Development Program (EDP)

Between 1990 and 1993, CCI's business management training program, EDP, provided the first ever out-of-country business training for entrepreneurs from Russia, Belorussia, Ukraine, Georgia, Uzbekistan, Armenia, Latvia, Estonia, and Lithuania. Their internships were one month, generally in the same company. Companies ranged from private apparel making, architecture firms, bakeries, banks, construction, dental clinics, farms, schools, legal services, medical clinics, poultry operations, retail, wholesale operations, and more. The business owners' ages were from 21 to 45 years. They had higher education and were strongly motivated. These entrepreneurs went to all corners of America where they were usually home-hosted by the families of the American business owners who trained them.

In Part I, readers learned about the first experimental EDP Fellow, Alexei Krupin, the architect, and Mikhail (Misha) Malkov, our Moscow Coordinator of EDP.

Prior to EDP's startup phase, Misha was extremely negative about the program. He was convinced that it would be a tool that Russians would use to stay in the United States. I had to coax him to sit in on the first day's candidate interviews with me. After his ordeal with defamation in the 1970s, Misha couldn't trust any fellow Russian. It took interviewing eight EDP candidates for him to realize that there had been only one candidate whom he had distrusted. He understood that the other candidates genuinely needed information that they couldn't get in Russia. Thereafter, Misha and I consulted with each other after each candidate left the interview room. His insights were perceptive, and he often picked up on nuances that I didn't. To his credit he seemed unbiased in his assessments. After several months of interviewing candidates, Misha's cynicism began to dissipate.

One candidate, out of the eight we interviewed the first day, greatly impressed Misha. His name was Evgeny Gontmakher, a serious young man who claimed he needed to get to America to learn how to address social issues within newly privatized large industries in the far north of Russia. As far as I could tell, we had nothing in the U.S. that could be of help to Evgeny, and told him so. He had already researched American agencies himself and provided me with a California company's name and contact information. Back in the states, we contacted the agency. To my surprise, they were willing to take in this young Russian sight unseen for a month of training. It ended up being a highly successful internship.

Evgeny brought a trunk of information back to Russia—it was precisely what he needed for his self-appointed task in the new Russia—that of watching over the social concerns of the population as the country struggled to learn how privatized monolithic enterprises could meet the social needs of their workers.

Evgeny's story is a long one, but suffice it to say that almost immediately he rose to prominence in the newly forming Russia. He became a voice in the government who was looking out for the social welfare of ordinary people during the wild '90s. Working around the clock at the end of the Gorbachev administration and then in the new Yeltsin administration, he admitted to sleeping in his office due to workload. Evgeny gave his self-devised recommendations to the print media—to goad officials. His newspaper articles tried to get attention directed toward his concerns as Russia continued to fall apart. I visited with him on and off throughout those years. He was going against the political tide and taking issue with social problems that were being ignored or mishandled. And he still is. I continue to wonder when those in power will tire of his goading. Currently, Evgeny is a respected consultant to the Medvedev government as a board member of INSOR at website, www.riocenter.ru/en/. He is still railing and still being listened to—even if not always heeded. Earlier he credited his ability to advise and to get attention at the highest of levels to the trunk of materials from his EDP training in 1990.

Development of CCI's Regional Russian Offices and Funding from USAID–1993

The new EDP grant from USAID required huge expansion of CCI. Among the most important tasks was the need to identify Russia's regional cities, which would become hot economic spots where we could place CCI offices. Determined to work outside of Moscow, we selected St. Petersburg, Volgograd, Yekaterinburg, Voronezh, Rostov on Don, and a Northwest Moscow Oblast regional office in Dubna. We went to these outlying areas to interview local people to run the new CCI offices. Like a magnet, our mission was able to attract a cadre of future local leaders all of whom we have worked since 1993.

Evgeny Gontmakher, an EDP delegate, (second from right) was a leading thinker in Russia's 1990s.

Evgeny in 2011 is Management Board Member for the Institute of Contemporary Development, (INSOR) said to be Medvedev's think tank.

Left bottom to right

Evgenia Terekhova, Director Vladivostok CCI Office

Olga Kriakova, Director, Volgograd CCI Office

Lena Novomeiskaya, Director, Ekaterinburg CCI Office

Nelli Schukina, Director, Voronezh CCI Office

Andrei Skorik, Director, Rostov on Don CCI Office

Madina Bikbulatova, Director, Moscow region Office

Olga Chubarova, Director, St. Petersburg Office

Nonna Barkhatova, Director, Novosibirsk Office

Irina Berezhnaya, CCI's Moscow Embassy Liaison and Coordinator of all delegations

CCI's complex programs could have never been accomplished without these committed Russian Directors: Olga Kriyakova (deceased) CCI Volgograd; Lena Novomeiskaya, CCI Ekaterinburg; Nelli Schukina, CCI Voronoezh; Madina Bikbulovota, CCI Dubna in the NW Moscow region; Olga Chubarova, CCI St. Petersburg; and Andrei Skorik, CCI Rostov on Don. Most were the Russian directors of EDP and the PEP program. In 1997 Evgenia Terekhova, CCI Vladivostok, joined our group, and in 2006 Nonna Barkhotova from Novosibirsk became part of our team. In 1997 when CCI's USAID grant expired, our Russian Partner offices were forced to become financially independent, since there were no remaining grant monies to support them. A program for their sustainability was developed.

EDP and PEP in Transition—1996-97

In 1996 CCI began operating EDP and PEP simultaneously—with the goal to phase out EDP in 1997 and to expand PEP to be the largest every business management training program for Russian entrepreneurs. The phase-out happened over a two-year period. The most challenging aspect was transitioning our Russian regional offices into fully independent, self-sustaining non-commercial (nonprofit) organizations, which we completed successfully. By December 1997, EDP was closed—and over the next years PEP rapidly grew into the program we projected.

During EDP's eight-year program, it trained, mentored, and provided consultations for thousands of Russia's regional entrepreneurs. Once-struggling EDP start-up companies are now successful mid-sized firms, which are helping to build civil society throughout Russia's cities.

The Arthur B. Schultz Equipment Award Program—1995-2000

Arthur's history and earlier contributions to CCI's efforts were covered previously. By 1995 he was brewing yet another bold concept. Arthur wanted to promote a "philanthropic impulse" among Russia's newly developing business owners, thus hoping to create a philanthropic mentality where none had existed before. He puzzled how to do this. His first grantee, Alexander Lubyanoi, was brought into the initial planning process.

The new Arthur B. Schultz Award Program began giving equipment loans of $25,000 to carefully selected CCI entrepreneurs who agreed to pay the loans back by giving an equivalent amount of service or products to unknown disadvantaged persons in their local communities. The entrepreneurs had to search out populations of needy people, design plans for providing them goods or services, create schedules for repayment, and record all contributions week-by-week. Over a five-year period, CCI's staff carefully monitored the recording and distribution of all of these charitable contributions to indigent Russians in St. Petersburg, Volgograd, Voronezh, and Ekaterinburg. We visited organizations and recipients and watched with delight as Russia's veterans' homes, orphanages, facilities for disabled adults and children, single mothers, and elderly populations routinely received free dental care, medical care, food, clothing, and other services.

Grantees of the Schultz Awards confirm that participating in this program made them life-long contributors to the less fortunate in their communities, where previously they had not given a thought to their needs. Arthur Schultz now operates this same model of financial grants to worthy entrepreneurs in Vietnam, Palestine, Kenya, Ghana, and Nicaragua. For more information check website: www.absfoundation.org.

CCI's Environmental Initiative—1990 to 1997

Our environmental work that began in 1987 was seminal, but it wasn't until 1990 that the impact of Russia's ecological devastation and the ability to speak out across the country would result in dramatic programs. CCI Board member, Fran Macy, our senior environmentalist, along with CCI managers, Michael Passoff, Mark Chao, Hank Burnbaum, and Will Easton, analyzed the regions continuously to determine where to best put CCI energies. During that time they worked with Bill Davoren to get the Aral Sea program up and running. This fourth largest sea in the world had been rendered useless by diverting the two rivers that fed it in order to grow cotton in nearby Uzbekistan, leaving behind a dry, salt-filled seabed that could no longer sustain life for local peoples. Meeting with young scientists and protesters in different areas of the vast country, CCI staff and volunteers began to focus the organization's energy. CCI's first huge program was to work toward restoring the Lake Baikal area.

The Rehabilitation of Lake Baikal

This "Blue Pearl of Siberia" is the oldest, deepest, and most voluminous freshwater lake in the world—and it is surrounded by a huge basin. Careless development and industrial pollution during the Soviet years had seriously damaged its pristine waters and unique ecology, thereby eroding the lake's ability to protect itself.

Requests from Siberian environmentalists resulted in a combined CCI-Earth Island Institute scout trip of environmental specialists to Lake Baikal in 1991. This group included noted environmentalist Dave Brower and 35 environmental experts in national park management, eco-tourism, environment law, and even organic agriculture. A second investigative trip was made in 1992.

Drawn to work in this spectacular region of mountains, pristine forests, and startling deep blue waters, our American volunteer specialists began setting their goals to completely restore the entire Baikal basin. CCI Project Director George Davis and a team of experts from the U.S., Russia, and Mongolia labored to create a comprehensive land-use plan and policy for the 25,000,000 hectare Baikal watershed. Proposals were presented to Russian policy makers and USAID in March of 1993. Nine model projects for the Lake Baikal Basin were devised and funded to promote sound ecological and economic development. The Baikal land use plan itself certainly turned out to be a provocative document, one that helped local environmentalists and government representatives understand what needed to be done to protect the great lake.

The projects included creating an anthropological reserve in Buryatia and reviving traditional Buryat agricultural practices that languished during the Soviet era. Breeding stocks of yak, reindeer, and Mongolian cattle were restored to the land, and other land use practices were developed. USAID gave a major grant to CCI in 1994 to carry out additional projects under the Lake Baikal Project. George Davis and his team of East Coast professionals later took over implementing the rehabilitation of the Baikal basin and the work in Mongolia.

To assure cooperation, CCI and Earth Island Institute hosted regional governors and other key leaders from the regions around Lake Baikal. Governor Salganov of Buryatia went back to the region and created the new Tunka National Park, more or less by fiat, using recommendations gleaned from the discussions to expand the park system at the lake.

> *Tunka Park, just south of Baikal, has since become a fortuitous addition to protect areas around the lake. It turned out that one of the newly projected massive oil pipelines of the 2000s were slated to run just south of Baikal and would have had to run through Tunka Park. This kind of pipeline in a national park is illegal according to Russian law. Local environmentalists protested vigorously that the oil project had to be moved north out of the Baikal watershed—meaning that the Tunka Park created by Governor Salganov most likely saved Lake Baikal. In April 2006 President Putin signed the decree to move the pipeline to avoid endangering Lake Baikal.*

The Nuclear Watchdog Partnership

The U.S.S.R.'s nuclear weapons program produced unprecedented nuclear pollution in cities scattered across the Ural mountain areas and throughout Siberia. Activists from Moscow and more remote Russian regions met with CCI leaders to develop work strategies to address these problems. One of the most rewarding aspects was working with Russian activists—primarily women scientists, who were cleaning up local weapons sites to protect their children's future health.

Lydia Popova, who would become a heroine in the Russian environmental movement, became CCI's chief guide on nuclear issues and cleanup. With equipment provided by CCI, Popova exposed high levels of nuclear contamination in one weapon site after another. In Chelyabinsk nuclear contamination levels reached 2,700 times the acceptable limits.

Funds were raised to bring activist groups from America to Russia to partner with local leaders. Activists from Three Mile Island in Pennsylvania, Hanford in Washington State, and Livermore in California partnered with Russian environmentalists to draw attention to these contaminated sites and to begin cleanup operations. Numerous American foundations made grants to CCI to carry out this important work. Voiceless for decades, Russian ecologists finally had help to investigate the trauma of nuclear pollution to their cities and regions. Several organizational spin-offs of projects occurred as the work progressed.

Fran Macy and Enid Schriebman, former CCI board members, created the Center for Safe Energy, which continues to support partnerships among environmental activists in Ukraine, Kazakhstan, and Kyrgyzstan. A special thanks to John Knox and Gary Cook of Earth Island Institute and Edward Nute for their strong collaboration on all of CCI's environmental projects.

Francis (Fran) Macy, Director of CCI's Environmental Program, 24-year CCI Board Member, worked in the U.S./Soviet field since the 1970s. Fran's expertise was used in every CCI program. He instinctively knew where to move next and did so with a measure of grace and understanding that his Russian colleagues treasured. He was active developing programs until his final day on the planet. Fran Macy—1927-2009

At one of the many edges of the spectacular Lake Baikal, which is considered the "spiritual home" of Russia.

It is the world's oldest and deepest lake, being 30 million years of age with an average depth of 744 meters. It is the most voluminous freshwater lake in the world containing roughly 20% of the world's unfrozen surface fresh water. Baikal is 1,642 meters at its deepest.

It is home to more than 1,700 species of animals and plants, two thirds of which can't be found elsewhere in the world. It was declared a UNESCO World Heritage Site in 1996.

Lydia Popova, Russia's hero of ecologists, focused on exposure and cleanup of nuclear weapons sites in her later years. She was photographed near Chelyabinsk, Russia using a CCI-provided monitoring device which revealed levels of contamination 2,700 times higher than acceptable limits.

Lydia was a researcher at Russia's Ministry of Atomic Power, where at great personal risk, she became a whistle-blower. In 1999 she was awarded the internationally prestigious Nuclear Free Future Award in Los Alamos, USA. Lydia passed away in 2008.

CCI's Agricultural Initiative—1990-1997

The year was 1990. Soviet agriculture was failing. It had been built on "factory farms" that mono-cropped huge swaths of land—most of them far removed from major cities. To avoid spoilage, trains carried unripe vegetables and fruits over vast territories. With the U.S.S.R.'s agricultural system collapsing, only small dacha plots were left to feed people living in the cities.

Searching for new ways to grow food for Russia's city-bound people, we learned of Dr. Martin L. Price. Martin was rumored to be the world's top specialist in "rooftop gardening." We finally located him and persuaded him to go to Russia as a pro bono consultant. Once in St. Petersburg, Martin climbed up a rickety ladder to the roof of a seven-story Soviet apartment building. Like all Soviet residential houses, it had a flat, steel-reinforced concrete roof.

Looking out across the city's thousands of large apartment buildings, Martin was stunned. Never before had he seen so much potential for growing food above a city. He declared that Leningrad could become a "net exporter" of vegetables if most of Leningrad's rooftops were planted with vegetables the following spring.

Martin's photos showed us that all vegetables including carrots and potatoes could be grown in large, quite shallow open containers with soil no deeper than five inches. Soon soil was being carted up elevators; hoses for irrigation were attached to apartment water lines; and shallow containers began to be planted with seeds and sprouts. Thanks to St. Petersburg's White Nights during the summer, within weeks rooftop gardens on multi-story houses were growing greens high above the city.

A steady source of organic fertilizer was needed. Martin educated us on "vermicomposting," which produces the world's richest soil fertilizer. The source of the fertilizer happened to be a little critter close to our home—the California red worm. These worms, when put in a tray of vegetable scraps mixed with newspapers, will digest everything and immediately begin turning out fabulous "castings," which provide an abundance of nitrogen, phosphorus, potassium, and calcium to reinvigorate any soil. CCI travelers began carrying small containers of California red worms to Russia concealed within their personal clothing. Apartment dwellers collected leftovers for the constantly hungry worms. Soon eaves and basements were full of even more shallow trays of rapidly multiplying red worms. Babushkas grew tomatoes, cucumbers, squash, onions, radishes, and even carrots and potatoes according to Martin's guidelines. Berry bush grafts in buckets occupied some of the space on the rooftops. Micro-businesses of berry-bush grafts and seedlings became revenue generators for the babushkas.

One Russian grandmother, Alla Sokol, became the driving force behind Russia's "Gardens in the Sky." Alla appeared on Russian television and radio, and her story was covered in magazines and newspapers. St. Petersburg's rooftop gardens are still flourishing, fertilized by descendants of the original California red worms. The worms are protected by eaves in the summer and spend Russia's cold winters down in the basements of the Soviet block houses. Red worms, too, have become micro businesses for the babushkas.

Seed Lifts for Private Farmers

It became obvious in 1991 that seeds would be needed in large quantities for Russia's 1992 growing season. We called Barbara Rinnan, CCI's Chicago-Midwest Director.

Natalia Andreeva

Sylvia and Walter Ehrhardt

Above center: Dan Dippery, Director of CCI's Agriculture Initiative (AI) conferring with young Russian agronomists. Below, Dan leading a conference on small-scale agriculture. Left: Natalia Andreeva, CCI Russian Director of AI and developer of the Extension Service model across Russia. Right: Sylvia and Walter Ehrhardt, experts in organic, small-scale agriculture who volunteered their time and expertise to CCI, AI, and Natalia for over a dozen years.

Dr. Martin Price (r), world expert on rooftop gardening for developing nations, strolling ground level dacha gardens in St. Petersburg.

Professor Keith Kennedy from Cornell University's School of Agriculture being offered salt and bread, Russia's traditional welcoming ceremony from centuries back. Keith was a great asset to CCI's Agricultural program.

Alla Sokol, Russia's queen of rooftop gardening, squats with children as she teaches them her passion for growing food in "sky gardens."

Barbara Rinnan called the George J. Ball Seed Company and got an appointment on the following day. The Ball Company had a diversity of cold climate seeds from wheat to vegetables. Lo, another miracle! They had an extra load of seed in a German harbor. It was diverted to the port of Leningrad.

Soon we were at the Russian port overseeing a huge seed shipment that was dispensed by citizens to a local warehouse, then trucked and distributed to dachas and small farm growers in various parts of Northwest Russia up to Murmansk, north of the Artic circle.

Once we figured out how to get seed shipments donated, the process became routine. By 1992 we were shipping vegetable and grain seed down into Russia's black soil region, where state farms were being broken up and handed over to local farmers. Over a three-year period, CCI shipped and distributed more than 300 tons of top-quality, cold-clime vegetable and wheat seed, donated by the George J. Ball, Burpee Seed, and Asgrow Seed companies. In our "closed loop" operation, we were on the ground to oversee the distribution of each shipment to keep the seeds from being diverted for personal profit.

CCI Begins Working with the All Russian Agricultural College

In 1993 following a flurry of food-sufficiency efforts, we agreed to start working directly with the All Russian Agricultural College in Sergiev Posad, which managed 345 agricultural colleges throughout Russia. The director and affiliate managers were eager to teach American practical know how in their colleges. Delegations of Russians interested in alternative agricultural techniques were sent to America to learn the latest practices from U.S. state university extension service specialists. We ourselves learned how important the U.S. Extension Service was to America's rural farmers in its early years—and how important the extension program is even today to American farmers. The concept was a perfect fit for Russia's rural needs in the 1990s.

> *The U.S. Agricultural Extension Service has roots back to the Hatch Act of 1887, which established a system of agricultural experimental stations in conjunction with state universities that were supported by the U.S. government. It is a system which assists farm people through providing educational materials and hands-on consulting to improve farming methods and techniques. These services increase both food production and income and provide better life styles for farmers, thereby lifting social and educational standards for rural areas.*

Cornell University's Support for CCI's Agricultural Program

In 1993 Cornell University's former Dean of the School of Agriculture, Keith Kennedy, began a pro bono consulting relationship with CCI. Keith traveled to Russia with us, and at age 80 he was still climbing wobbly ladders to get to rooftop gardens. He was vitally interested in helping the new Russia redevelop private agriculture. Soon Cornell's extension materials were translated into the Russian language for use in all 345 agricultural teaching institutions. Developing a Russia-based extension service was on the minds of all Russians who studied those materials. American extension consultants and Russian agronomists traveled back and forth to share details related to setting up Russia's own extension service mechanism.

New Director of U.S. Extension Service for Russia

Natalie Andreeva, a bright young instructor at the central Agricultural College in Sergiev Posad, was hired by CCI. We gave her the task of modifying an experimental extension project for Russia—she was intrigued by extension concepts and expanded them to also focus on organic growing. CCI received a three-year grant from USAID to design and implement the U.S. extension model throughout seven of Russia's agricultural regions. While earning her Ph.D. from Moscow State University, Natalie ran this effort for the entire three years of the grant period.

The Extension concept worked so well with Russian consultants and farmers that in 1997, CCI requested USAID to expand the Extension model grant to 11 more of Russia's regions. Unfortunately, U.S. advisors were consolidating their Russia agricultural portfolio, and we learned that CCI's independent grant would not be renewed. We pled our case in several Washington offices, but were turned down. CCI's Agriculture Initiative was terminated in 1998 when our effort was only half completed.

By this time, Natalie Andreeva had gained quite a reputation across Russia's regions. The Russian Ministry of Agriculture decided to create a new program, Extension Services at the Ministry of Agriculture, and hired Natalie to begin working as its new director. Sixty-nine of Russia's 89 regions were placed under Natalie's supervision for extension development. Special kudos to Sylvia and Walter Erhardt, CCI's volunteer specialists in small farm and organic methodologies, for their contributions to this program over the number of years that we operated it in Russia.

RISE—Russian Initiative for Self Employment—1993 through 2008

In 1993 four of St. Petersburg's unemployed professional women came to CCI to ask if we could help them learn how to develop livelihoods. They were single mothers with no income to support their children. And they had one skill in common—sewing, as did many Russian women who were unemployed. Hence, everything produced with a "needle" became the defining focus of our Russian Initiative for Self Employment (RISE) program, which assisted Russian women to become self-sustaining.

We borrowed aspects of Muhammed Yunas' Grameen Program in Bangladesh and appealed to President Bill White of the Mott Foundation with a proposal for $100,000 to provide start-up capital for our micro-enterprise program. After studying the RISE proposal, Bill offered $200,000 saying it would take at least that much to do the work listed on our proposal. By this time he knew us well and understood that we would cram every possible action into a proposal and then stretch our resources thin to make them all happen.

Within four months, Leesa Wilson, a young CCI program officer, arrived in St. Petersburg to start RISE's first component—the "ABCs of Business Training" for Russian women's micro-businesses. In 1994 the Mott Foundation provided an additional $200,000 for a micro-loan program. In 1995 USAID offered CCI a $1.6 million, 3-year grant to develop a full-fledged micro-business incubator in the heart of St. Petersburg. Philanthropist Arthur Schultz provided dozens of new state-of-the-art Juki sewing machines. With this new level of activity, RISE needed serious expertise.

Nancy Glaser, a CCI board member, had management experience in the U.S. apparel industry. We enticed her to go to St. Petersburg to build the new apparel-related

Nancy Glaser, Director of the apparel incubator of the Russian Initiative for Self Employment (RISE) program. Photo taken 1995.

The RISE Fashion Library and Training Center was a magnet for young Russian women who hoped to design, make clothing, and work in the apparel industry.

RISE LOGO

Designing patterns was done on long commercial tables with newly acquired professional equipment. The young women encouraged and helped each other during their difficult learning periods.

RISE's production room was equipped with commercial Juki sewing machines, which were purchased with grant funds from the Arthur B. Schultz Foundation.

CARGO was born in 1997 when the USAID RISE grant was terminated. RISE employees decided to keep their team together and to create a private apparel company—which they did and named it CARGO. For 11 years they focused on youth clothing—a fabulous decision!

incubator. Leasing a battered old three-story building, we built dividing walls, applied gallons of white paint, and Nancy hung Gap and Esprit fashion posters everywhere. A 72-hour course in business development was required before admission to the incubator. Soon 19 apparel-making micro-business start-ups filled the newly built cubicles. Schultz's Juki sewing machines whirred day and night in the incubator's common production workspace. St. Petersburg's young designers got their first chance to begin serial manufacturing. RISE bootstrap loans enabled them to purchase bulk fabrics and other design essentials. A critical component of the program was to bring over, through USAID programs, expert volunteers who brought industry expertise that was so badly needed in Russia. These specialists held workshops for not only our clients, but also for students at the universities and St. Petersburg's large established but struggling apparel companies.

A RISE Fashion Library was quickly set up with donations from the best of the world's apparel industry. Nancy's friends in the New York design industry donated top of the line international fashion forecast materials, videos, color swatches, and literature to the library annually. Teeming with newly energized Russian women, the RISE incubator became the apparel industry standard and an exciting place to work in St. Petersburg. Throughout the years that the incubator was in operation, it averaged graduating a business a month to the outside market place. In addition, hundreds of businesses attended our industry-focused workshops.

In 1998 much to our distress, USAID decided to discontinue funding all incubators in Russia. USAID, Eurasia Foundation, and IREX provided closeout grants to help CCI push RISE into a private self-sustaining operation.

A "for profit" apparel production company was created from the "non-profit" RISE operation. Employees and the sewing equipment from earlier grants were of inestimable value to the new startup operation. Young RISE designers began to roll out a new "youth line" that produced high-quality, trendy street wear under the trademark of CARGO. Young Russians flocked to stores that sold this line. By 2002 CARGO labels were even sited in Paris' Orly airport. During its privatized period, CARGO Production Company funded the non-profit RISE Training Center and the Fashion Library.

During the critical market transition of Russia in the mid-to-late 1990s, the RISE incubator and training center sparkled with talent, energy, and hope. In the late 1990s, we were funded by the Eurasia Foundation to "train the trainers" throughout Russia who wanted to start up their local business incubators to support fledgling businesses. We also contributed to the creation of the Russian National Business Incubator Association.

Finally in 2009, the global financial crisis brought down the 16-year-old RISE/ CARGO operation. The RISE Fashion Library was donated to the St. Petersburg University of Technology where it remains open for young designers up to the present. RISE became history with us knowing that the industry know-how, business training, and "can do" spirit of RISE had become an integral part of the lives of the many Russian women who had walked through our doors over the years. RISE accomplished both its short and long-term goals.

CCI's Small Programs in the 1990s

The Non-Profit Management Program—1993-95 and Beyond: In 1993 CCI created a program to support Russia's "not-for-profit" organizations. Patterned after CCI's Economic Development Program, it included U.S.-based internships, training programs in Russia, conferences, and small grants to Russian citizens to expand their charity works. Managers of orphanages, schools for deaf and blind children, and organizations assisting disenfranchised Russians participated.

This program was more difficult to fund than CCI's business programs since Russian non-profit organizers and participants couldn't afford to contribute to program costs, as did Russia's for-profit entrepreneurs. The Non-Profit Management program was spun off from CCI's umbrella in 1996 and continued its mission under Dale Needles at the Fund for International Nonprofit Development (FIND) until 2008.

The Presidents' Management Training Initiative (PMTI)—1997-1998: CCI cooperated with the U.S. Department of State to develop a Yeltsin-Clinton Initiative designed to give management training to young Russians professionals with business interests. PMTI was basically an EDP format for English-speaking Russians. CCI's PEP work became so demanding by 1998 that it was necessary to forego running the Presidents' Management Training Initiative program to concentrate on CCI's ever expanding programs.

Consulting Services for Regional Entrepreneurs (CSRE)—1997-1998: We cooperated with USIA in 1997-1998 to send American business consultants to Russian regions under the CSRE program where they provided on-site business planning and other consulting activities for Russian company owners. This program was directed by Evan Donahey and was essentially the same as CCI's EDP consulting model. USIA funding for this activity ceased after two years of operation.

Productivity Enhancement Program (PEP)—1996-2008

Aspects of PEP were addressed previously in "Events and People—1990s" and more will be covered in Part III.

The Productivity Enhancement Program (PEP) burst upon the scene in the '90s with excitement and brilliance. Quickly it became CCI's all-time flagship program. It was perfectly timed to meet Russia's greatest need in the mid-1990s—and was the first to offer management training in U.S. companies for non-English speaking delegations of Russian business owners.

PEP delegations were intentionally composed of Russian entrepreneurs from seven or more different Russian cities. Our rationale was to create an exchange of best practices and raw material information from different regions to benefit isolated regions far from the center. And secondly, we hoped to create an environment where trust could develop between delegates while they were traveling and learning as a unit. Both goals soon were validated. We saw that delegates came to respect one another while training together in the U.S.; we learned that they were keeping in touch with each other upon going back to their different regions in Russia; and some even began having annual reunions to commemorate their trips to the U.S. Business partnerships began erupting and information between Russian regions became a common feature after the delegations returned home.

The goodwill and genuine connections made as PEP's delegations traveled throughout the '90s will ripple on from one generation to the next across Russia. PEP vignettes will be featured in Part III.

One of our stated intentions for PEP from the outset was to create an up-to-date program template adapted from the Marshall Plan, which could be used by other organizations in other countries in the future. This we have done. PEP is archived in entirety in about 100 legal boxes at Stanford University's Hoover Institute. Anywhere in the world that business and economic development is needed, this template can be modified for local conditions. The following elements were critical to PEP's success. We offer them as a model for future users.

- All program aspects of PEP were computerized with all information preserved on servers.
- Each delegation was industry-specific.
- Delegations of 11 Russians (plus two interpreter-facilitators) trained together.
- Fifteen-person vans were used for transportation. Volunteer drivers were used.
- Each delegation was comprised of Russians from at least seven different Russian regions.
- Training was researched and plans were written for a total of 80 industry sub-sectors.
- Training modules for each sub-sector were designed by U.S. industry professionals.
- CCI designed workbooks for delegates to document daily meetings and learnings.
- Delegates stayed in American homes—usually two delegates to a family.
- Russian-born professional interpreters and facilitators were used.
- Interpreters trained in specific industry sectors where they gained sector expertise.
- U.S. Embassy and American Consulates played a vital role vetting Russian applicants.
- Russian Partner offices publicized training throughout their regions. They interviewed, screened, and accepted candidates for the PEP pool. CCI San Francisco made the selections.
- U.S. staff marketers contacted civic clubs to explain PEP and signed contracts with clubs.
- U.S. staff officers alerted Russian offices to submit relevant candidates to the PEP pool.
- U.S. staff officers studied the candidate pool and made the choice about which Russians would travel on the different delegations.
- U.S. staff officers contacted Russian offices to prepare Russian entrepreneurs for travel.
- CCI U.S. staff coordinators watched closely over each delegation while in the U.S.
- Russian staff provided pre-travel training, survival English classes, visa support and post travel evaluations and long-term resources for the alumni.
- All Russian participants paid a percentage of the training (from 16 percent in the beginning, up to 100 percent by 2007).
- Delegates wired their training fees directly to CCI's U.S. office.
- U.S. Department of State provided CCI's operating expenses and part of the trainings in the earlier years.
- U.S. civic clubs provided approximately 40 percent of total costs through in-kind contributions.
- Civic clubs arranged pro bono accommodations, meals, transport, and business training.
- Civic clubs chose a local coordinator to oversee all aspects of Russians' trainings.
- Civic members interviewed CEOs and managers and helped develop training schedules.

PEP staff celebrating the acceptance letter saying that PEP would be funded by the U.S. Department of State!

Upper Right: PEP Delegates meeting their new trainers: Whole Foods delegation, New Philadelphia and Boardman, Ohio.

Right: Natasha Lipkina, original PEP Director, and Natalie Bosworth, Natasha's Deputy Director, with PEP schedule behind them.

PEP delegates in building materials delegation being exposed to standards in the wood industry.

Crop Farmers Delegation: Colusa, California.

Large Construction Delegation: Jasper, Georgia.

Supermarket Management Delegation: Rexburg and Rigby, Idaho.

Construction Delegation:
Atlanta and Jasper, Georgia

Retail Clothing Delegation:
Dallas, Texas

Taking the information back
home with video-cams. Large
Construction:
Saratoga, San Jose, California.

Legal Services Delegation:
Baltimore and Annapolis, Maryland.

"In 1990 we lost our positions at the Institute. My father and I conferred how we
could survive. He said, 'If Russia survives, paint will be needed. Nothing has been
painted here for decades.' We went to the library to study how to make paint and
what ingredients are needed. We located old Soviet equipment, tore it down, and
rebuilt our machinery to suit our needs." At left is a jury-rigged paint pulverizer
that ground particles in the beginning years. At right is their paint warehouse
ten years later when father and son were selling paint from St. Petersburg to
Vladivostok.

- Civic club members introduced delegates to the communities and arranged public relations.
- Business management training was mandated for every working day—no slacking off.
- Each work day ended with a brainstorm to identify what was applicable for use in Russia.
- End of delegation evaluations assessed lessons learned from delegates and coordinators.
- Upon return home Russians were evaluated by CCI Russian Office Directors.
- Program alumni shared information on return and helped prepare new PEP candidates.
- Long-term evaluations were carried out annually in Russian cities by U.S. CCI officers.
- CCI's eight Russian Partner offices and 60 regional satellite operations supported PEP throughout Russia by providing pre-travel and post-travel consultations and materials, plus developing business centers and business clubs, western business consultants and networking opportunities, creating conferences for alumni, doing public relations and providing a host of other related business opportunities.

PEP's "Closed Loop" System

PEP's success came from operating a closed-loop system, which started with advertising in Russia through all aspects of U.S. training and to post-internship evaluations in Russia. None of its operations were subcontracted out. All aspects were interactive. The loop allowed continuous monitoring from beginning to end. Problems with a delegate, home host, trainer, or interpreter quickly became evident within the loop and problem solving began immediately.

Annual computerized evaluations with participants were carried out in Russia one to two years after U.S. training. These evaluations provided a longer-term look at what the delegates learned in addition to providing surveys regarding politics, economics, values, and lifestyles.

Rotary for Russia

From the time the PEP program was under consideration, we knew we could depend on Rotary and other U.S. civic clubs (Kiwanis, Optimists and Lions) to sponsor delegations coming to their cities. Around 85 percent of the PEP delegations were sponsored by Rotary.

Rotary, however, was still a mystery to Russians. They considered this worldwide organization to be something like the Masonic Order about which they knew very little but were quite suspicious in the beginning. While interviewing PEP candidates in Russia, we told future delegates that American civic clubs, most likely a Rotary club, would sponsor them. Many were cynical, wanting to know, "What's in it for these Americans?" They firmly believed that people don't do something for nothing. We tried to explain civic clubs' motivation, but their conditioning was not ready to take in this new concept. So they came to America trying to figure out what was in it for their Rotarian hosts. At first they decided that CCI was paying Rotarians or that Rotarians wanted to get into lucrative business deals with them.

When they finally realized that civic clubs hosted them simply to build international goodwill, they were shocked. Learning that all the clubs have "service projects" providing service to those less fortunate, they were further amazed. For many it was Rotary's code of ethics, the Four-Way Test, that helped them see that Rotary (and other civic clubs) are a new way for business and professional people to live in the world.

THE FOUR-WAY TEST
Of the things we think, say or do:
Is it the Truth?
Is it Fair to all concerned?
Will it build Goodwill and Better Friendships?
Will it be Beneficial to all concerned?

Once back in their home cities, many PEP participants began to realize that Russia really needs civic club concepts in its new world of business development. Next they tried to figure out how such clubs could be formed in Russia. Searching out other local PEP alumni, they eventually united and some developed several Rotary "friendship" clubs. Following this, the new entities became "provisional clubs" and the last step was to become chartered by Rotary International. PEP alumni have chartered at least 25 Rotary clubs of which we are aware. Western Russia now has 45 chartered Rotary clubs, and Siberia and the Far East have 35 chartered clubs.

In the early 1990s, unbeknownst to CCI, Rotarians from Alaska, the Yukon, Washington state, and Texas traveled throughout Siberia and the Far East to introduce Rotary in those regions. Leaders Jack Randolph, Steve Yoshida, and Jim Aneff were more like circuit riders or missionaries as they carried Rotary principles from Magadan to Chita and throughout Siberia. Over a period of years they left 40 Rotary clubs in their wake.

CCI's role in spreading Rotary in Russia happened by chance rather than intention. When we began bringing Russian entrepreneurs to America, Rotarians in various states and cities gladly signed up to participate, arranged programs, secured home hosts, and entertained their new Russian friends. Because of the relations built with American Rotarians during their business training, Russian entrepreneurs began creating their own Rotary clubs when they returned home.

Kiwanis Clubs, Optimist Clubs, and Lions Clubs
We at CCI greatly appreciate the training and hosting roles played by Kiwanis, Optimists, and Lions Clubs that sponsored numbers of PEP delegations in American cities. Kiwanis sponsored 14 percent of our PEP delegations, with Optimists and Lions sponsoring the remaining groups. Their business training programs were of the same high quality as Rotary-sponsored delegations. Their members, while not as numerous, nonetheless provided exceptional education for their delegates and left joyful hosting memories in the hearts of their new Russian friends.

Photo of Olga Kriakova at the Lakewood Rocky River Rotary Club in Cleveland, Ohio. Standing is Carl Johnson, the "father" and tutor of the Volgograd Rotary Club. The latter was the first Rotary Club in Russia established by CCI Fellows.

Olga Kriakova sounding the Rotary Bell in her newly chartered Volgograd Club.

Evgenia Terekhova, director of CCI Vladivostok at the microphone at a Rotary function where PEP delegates were guests. At right is Grant Wilkins, former board member of Rotary International.

Alpine Kiwanis Club in Rockford, Illinois hosting a delegation of PEP Fellows. At the microphone is Zina Generalova, the first PEP facilitator /interpreter and the one who accompanied the most PEP delegations over PEP's lifespan.

Russia's Financial Crisis—1998–1999

The August 1998 Asian market crash brought Russia's unstable market economy down with a near fatal blow. Soon Russia was left needing to apply for and take huge loans from international lending institutions—as was the case earlier at the beginning of the decade.

The inept handling of Russia's economy and market throughout the 1990s is a story too big to document here. A CNN special website outlines Russia's fragile situation blow by blow. See website: www.pbs.org/wgbh/pages/frontline/shows/crash/etc/russia.html. The ruble was devalued once again, taking with it any remaining security for Russian people. The crash temporarily obliterated Russia's nascent small business sector. Company savings were wiped out, owners couldn't pay down loans, and ordinary Russians had no money with which to purchase products. CCI alumni e-mailed us that they had no idea how to recoup from this latest crisis.

Russia's 1990s ended in chaos and inability to cope with the latest circumstances— not unlike the beginning of the decade. The banking system was corrupt and bankrupt. Yeltsin was drinking and sick. And Russia's debt to the International Monetary Fund and the World Bank was in the billions of dollars.

Was there any hope for Russia to get back on her feet?

Part III

2000-2010

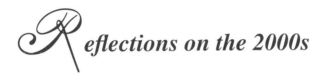

Reflections on the 2000s

It felt as if the scene was changing dramatically before our eyes. The heady days of private citizen exchanges had vanished. Big omnibus contractors were brought in to oversee most of the U.S. projects in Russia. U.S. government funding for organizations like ours was being cut, and few programs supported the needs of small businesses and average Russians. To keep our citizen-oriented work intact, CCI expanded rapidly—thanks to our numerous funders and Russian entrepreneurs who were increasingly paying more for their CCI business training.

I pause to share how difficult it has been to write Part III of this book. Sitting at my computer for hours on end, I debated with myself how to describe the many events that have complicated this decade.

These ten years could not be put into the simple categories that worked for the two previous decades—too much was happening. Furthermore, U.S.-Russia politics were becoming extremely complex. After much deliberation, I decided to cover the first decade of the 2000s in a year-by-year fashion, hoping to give the reader a sequential, bottom-up account of major economic and political happenings along with touching vignettes, the "feel" of this massive country undergoing rapid change, and the hope that we witnessed as Russian people began to pull out of their collective depression of the 1990s.

At the Turn of Russia's 2000s

Change in Russia's Leadership

Prior to the last minutes of the passing decade, a sick and incapable Yeltsin had held the presidential office. On December 31, 1999, Yeltsin stunned the world by announcing that he was leaving the presidency and was turning Russia over to a little-known, former KGB chief (his latest in a string of Prime Ministers), Vladimir Vladimirovich Putin. Reports were that the heavy-weight oligarch, Boris Berezovsky, told Yeltsin to vacate the presidency and appoint Putin, *"Because we can control him."* Putin became Russia's acting President until the next election, to be held on March 26, 2000. Moscow's Mayor Yuri Luzhkov and Soviet senior statesman Evgeny Primakov had planned to run for the presidency, as had several other liberal candidates. Russia watchers gasped at Yeltsin's choice to replace himself, and so did I.

A Whip-lashed Russian People Slowly Come Back

As the 2000s began, Russia's people were weary to the bone and nearly paralyzed from one crisis after another. Rejecting totalitarianism in the late 1980s, Russians had hopes that they might finally create a normal country in the 1990s. But soon that decade of criminality and lawlessness under President Yeltsin all but destroyed their dreams for a decent future. At the end of the '90s, we stood by helplessly as one more unexpected event, the 1998 financial crash, took its toll across Russia.

Right: V.V. Putin unexpectedly took over for President Boris Yeltsin at the end of 1999. Russia's entrepreneurs didn't trust Putin since he was an appointee of Yeltsin's.

Left: Interviewing CCI entrepreneurs via computer.

PEP 2000 evaluations for our alumni were grim. The financial crisis of 1998 was still hanging heavily over their struggling companies.

Olga Ponomareva, chief manager of a large private bakery, ponders her company's future.

PEP Fellows Dmitry Kalinchuk, Sergei Baranov, and Gleb Falaleev caught in a moment of reflection about how to proceed during turbulent times.

With Andrei Illarionov at the end of our first Kremlin meeting which focused on our belief that with some support, Russia's regional entrepreneurs could bring hope to the economy—which the Putin administration hadn't had time to think about.

In early 2000, we watched as some of our CCI alumni and other small businessmen across Russia's regions began to slowly hobble to their feet. Most of the country was still flat on its back. Entrepreneur types saw vacant store shelves where "foreign products" had sat prior to the 1998 crisis. As the crisis set in, foreigners pulled products back home and vacated the Russian market. Until now Russian entrepreneurs had not been able to compete with sleek foreign products, which Russian consumers preferred to purchase. But with shelf space empty, Russia's entrepreneurs began to get a toehold in local markets. They tried to duplicate foreign products and began to manufacture new Russian brands to fill the bare shelves. "Mattress money" that had been stowed away in private nooks, slowly found its way to the market. Russian shops began to reawaken and bartering increased.

An unanticipated factor began developing ... for the first time ordinary Russians began to accept their own grassroots entrepreneurs as "okay" people. During the 1990s, they assumed that all unknown Russians were not trustworthy, particularly those running small businesses. Now, these same Russian entrepreneurs were bringing food products and household goods to the shops at a time when no other products were available.

We also observed Russians' innate ability to endure—the strength to put one foot in front the other and trudge forward a centimeter at a time, regardless of the circumstances.

Putin's Ascension to Power

Vladimir Putin won the March 2000 election, and on May 7 he was inaugurated as President of the Russian Federation. The relatively small population of entrepreneurs throughout the country had voted mostly for opposition candidate Gregori Yavlinsky, but Yalinsky didn't have a chance against Putin. The latter's stock had recently soared at the polls due to his vigorous response to Chechnya's invasion of Dagestan (two states within the Russian Federation). Later we learned that quite a few CCI alumni in St. Petersburg voted for Putin because he had personally registered their small businesses during the turbulent 1990s—and they didn't have to pay bribes to him. This was an almost unique situation in the St. Petersburg Marienskii bureaucracy where he worked.

As a little known KGB officer stationed in Germany for five years, Putin had no history with anyone in the Kremlin who made a difference—and he had no constituency of his own across Russia. Word circulated throughout Russia that Putin would be steamrollered by the Kremlin's powerful clans comprised of the oligarchs, Soviet hold-overs, and intelligence operatives. In the beginning, Putin had little choice but to work with the power mongers left by Yeltsin. Would he eventually have strength enough to lead Russia independent of these dominant forces? Few, if any, thought so.

I knew from my one encounter with Putin that he was unusually bright for a bureaucrat, but I didn't believe he would have the courage to battle the Kremlin oligarchs, or the regional governors who ran fiefdoms throughout Russia. And I was quite sure if he tried that he would be assassinated.

Meanwhile, Putin, the outsider, quietly took office. At first it appeared he didn't wish to rock any boats. Almost immediately, American journalists registered alarm that Russia was in a precarious stage of governance and that the newly-elected president and former KGB chief spelled trouble for the West. From ground level working in Russia, we saw no evidence to support this interpretation.

PEP Became CCI's Largest Program During the 2000s

PEP brought vital private sector information and inspiration to Russian entrepreneurs, which encouraged them to believe in themselves and to experiment with new business ideas in their small companies. PEP also created trust between the Russian participants as they traveled to the U.S. and learned together in delegations. By year 2000 the program was running like a well-tuned Mercedes. Fortunately, we had attracted a cadre of professional Russian interpreters and facilitators who traveled with the delegations as the "voices" for the non-English speaking delegates and American specialists in training sessions. These trip facilitator/interpreters became big hits with both Russian participants and American home hosts and civic clubs. See page 260 for their names.

While PEP groups were coming and going across America, my eyes were increasingly riveted on the U.S.-Russia relationship which was degenerating by the month.

CCI's Driving Intention in Year 2000

We were determined to keep the doors open between America and Russia, to expand PEP's business training, and also to do *something* to interrupt the insidious chain of corruption that was endemic in Russia's public sector. Corruption impacted every entrepreneur's business we trained—it was estimated that 95 percent of the bribe taking came from local district bureaucrats. Russians themselves couldn't comprehend how to combat these corrupters. When asked what could be done to change corrupt practices, blank looks covered their faces. Apparently authorities and bureaucrats at all levels had perfected their clandestine methods of operating for so long, that average citizens couldn't fathom their inner workings; hence they couldn't conceive how to tackle the problem. For us standing outside the system, Russian bureaucratic mismanagement looked opaque and murky but not insurmountable. However, little did we understand how challenging corruption would become, both in local district offices and up and down the vertical chain.

Investigation of Russia's New Leadership—Vladimir Putin

My long-time friend, Elena Sadovnikova, returned to St. Petersburg for a visit. We sat down in the children's "museum" at the Fontanka art school. Readers may remember that Elena, Evgeny Velikhov and I put together the international children's art exchanges back in the late 1980s. These art trips saved the teachers from ignominy at the hands of Soviet bureaucrats and were also responsible for obtaining this coveted building, in which we sat, for a new city art school. Over the years Elena and I found that we had much in common. As a professional psychologist, I wanted to get her view on the new Russian leadership in the Kremlin.

Once we were seated, I lost no time asking, "Elena, what's your assessment of your new president?" "Volodya! (nickname for Vladimir)" she exclaimed. "I've known him since we were young!" She shifted into psychologist mode and began analyzing how she had come to understand Vladimir Putin over the decades.

"You know, he was always somewhat different probably because of his family situation, which was quite difficult. His father was at the "front" during WWII. He returned seriously injured. His mom was given up for dead during the Leningrad Siege but somehow survived. An older brother died during the Siege. Volodya was born after the war and grew up as the only son. The family was very, very poor. He was a serious boy—you may know that he liked martial arts. At school he took up for underdogs and had a patriotic streak in him. We were not surprised when he tried to go to the KGB before university. He was rejected and told to get his education first—possibly a law degree, which he did. At that time, we believed those who entered the KGB did so because they loved the Motherland and wanted to protect it. Today the KGB has a bad reputation, but it didn't then. At the time, that career seemed right for Volodya. He really hasn't changed much since then except for broadening his education and experience."

I mentioned to Elena that I worried whether Putin was strong enough to deal with the crooks left by Yeltsin in the Kremlin. She thought for a minute and said, "Well, you know ... if I had to predict what he might do with them ... if he follows his own natural inclinations, I would say the following: He will watch them for a while. He will quietly get their attention to let them know he is watching. He will throw up flares if they don't begin to change. If they continue, within a couple of years some of them will be in prison. This would be natural to his personality." She described Putin as a modest and good family man with inner strength. Interesting ... I would wait and watch.

Over the next few years, I sent Elena a couple of congratulatory e-mails when her predictions about Putin's actions began to show up in real time.

PEP Evaluations Across Russia's Regions—Mid-Year 2000

We crisscrossed Russia from north to south and east to west, interviewing PEP graduates in 18 cities, towns, and rural areas. Moving around by cars, buses, vans, and trains, we covered about 10,000 miles. A few PEP alumni were getting back on their feet; others were still faltering. Here and there they proudly showed us new production and business expansion much of which was inspired by their training in American companies. We wrote home excitedly, "Our PEP Fellows are the faces of the New Russia. They are in striking contrast to the oligarchs and the new wealthy Muscovites of the 1990s." Their evaluation quotes spiced up the reports we sent back to the U.S.:

"My confidence level increased ten-fold after my American internship. My position as vice president in my old firm was a good job, but after the U.S. trip, I found the courage to risk starting my own company!" – Evgeni Sosnitski, Rostov-on Don

"We are in process of restructuring our company with information I acquired in America. Your system of payment and employee incentive programs will be used next. We are basing our company on principles we learned in America." – Ludmila Andreeva, Voronezh

"No small contribution was made by the families with whom we lived. The experience and knowledge they shared with me was invaluable. I was like a sponge, soaking up everything they could tell me. I learned from them about the real America, not the American film series like "Santa Barbara" that we see on television." – Oleg Ushanev, St. Petersburg

Despite the positive feedback and accolades for the PEP program, our entrepreneurs went home from the U.S. to face a devastated economy and deeply corrupted public officials who considered large bribes their just reward for signing and stamping required official documents.

An Unexpected Visit to the Kremlin—late 2000

In 1998 CCI board member, Patricia Dowden, hosted a delegation of Russian bankers in Philadelphia. One of them, Oleg Plaksin, was recently appointed deputy to President Putin's new economic advisor, Andrei Illarionov. Plaksin was able to get us a meeting with Illarionov in the Kremlin. His office was next door to Putin's, perhaps an indication of the importance the new Russian president would place on Russia's economy.

Illarionov was relatively young and very interested in what we were learning about Russia's regional entrepreneurs. Even as an expert in his country's economics, he had no knowledge of, or experience with, Russia's grassroots economy in far away regions. By the meeting's end, he remarked, "Obviously, you know more about our Russian people than those of us here in the Kremlin." He also said rather soberly, "I never understood how difficult the role of the president would be until I came to this position. If President Putin moves slightly from one side of the narrow corridor to the other, he bruises either himself or someone else in power."

This was my first glimpse into the tenseness of the Kremlin clans Putin inherited from Yeltsin. With no constituency, no political party to support him, no power to take out the clans, Putin was all alone—and from what became clear, the Kremlin environment, for the most part, was a den of self-serving vipers.

> *Later I asked Oleg Plaksin whom President Putin goes to for counsel. He looked at me in complete shock at the question and answered, "He can't confide in anyone! If he did, it would be highly dangerous. They could betray him." I was stunned considering what it would be like to try to take hold of an out-of-control country like Russia, to try to figure out a workable strategy in isolation, and to not trust anyone around you—how could any human being survive or govern in such an environment?*

> *It became increasingly obvious to me why Putin began bringing St. Petersburg people to Moscow—they were dependable friends with whom he had gone to school and university, those whom he trusted during his early KGB years—in addition to those he worked closely with in St. Petersburg's municipal offices, like Dmitri Medvedev.*

> *World media called these new Putin appointees, the St. Petersburg "Chekists" (early Soviet secret police who ran gulags and other sinister responsibilities). These long-term friends of Putin's began to replace some of Yeltsin's Moscow-based oligarchs and others of their ilk within the Kremlin.*

U.S. Media Suspicions and CCI's Plan for Bold Action—December 2000

As year 2000 ended, U.S. mainstream media continued jaundiced reporting on much of what was happening inside Russia. I began collecting a folder of articles from major newspapers, which seemed to be leading their readers toward a "Cold War II" mentality. I could not understand how Western journalists were coming to their conclusions. We didn't see evidence for these concerns at ground level—if anything, Russia was beginning to settle down and was getting itself somewhat together following the painful '90s.

George Ingram, Former Deputy Assistant Administrator of USAID responsible for the former Soviet Union, and I discussed this worrisome media direction. He gave prescient advice. "You need to do something bold shortly after the beginning of 2001. President Bush and new Congress members will be warming their seats. Get their attention before they have time to formulate their ideas about the Russia policy—do something that will force them to update their thinking regarding Russia." He quickly calculated that the first week in March 2001 would be a good time to plan some sort of mega-event in Washington, D.C.

Within hours a daring idea emerged. We could bring a mass of CCI alumni from across Russia, perhaps one hundred of them, to Washington for Congressional and State Department meetings. This would be a group too large to ignore. They could tell Congress members what is actually happening throughout Russia—and they then could give recommendations about how to craft a workable U.S.-Russia policy that would serve both countries. Could young Russian entrepreneurs afford such a trip? We would find out. E-mails were quickly sent to CCI Russian offices. Messages flooded back immediately with names of alumni who were ready to pay the projected fees of $2,600 for travel and living expenses while in Washington.

Next we faxed Andrei Illarionov to inquire if we could bring the 100 entrepreneurs to the Kremlin after their meetings with U.S. Congress members. Our goal for the Kremlin meeting would be to deliver proposals to Russia's president to support small business development across Russia. An immediate "Yes" was faxed back from Illarionov.

Unfortunately, at this juncture we had nothing but a plan in our heads. We had not contacted a single Congress member and had never before carried out an event even remotely as sophisticated as this one. My assistant, Cathy Immanuel, and I pulled out the Congressional Roster and began making cold calls to Congressional offices. Most of them were intrigued at the possibility of speaking directly with Russian entrepreneurs. We spent the remainder of year 2000 planning for the mega-delegation of Russians to be in Washington, D.C., by March 2001. Meanwhile, PEP delegations were arriving and departing American cities one after another.

Thanks to CCI's talented program managers and staff who came to us after completing degrees in Russian studies, I had been able to pull away from the organization's day-to-day activities to create new programs and projects since the mid-1980s. These energetic young women and men sought non-governmental jobs that put them in direct contact with Russian people. They ran and refined complex programs at CCI, thus allowing me to dive into projects like the "100 Russians to Washington." See page 258 for their names.

$\mathcal{Y}$ear 2001

100 Russian Entrepreneurs to Washington, D.C.—March 5-9, 2001

The "100 Russians to D.C." project was an outstanding success. Every morning teams of Russians and CCI volunteers trekked to the metro to get to multiple Capitol Hill meetings. They weathered rain and miserable wind on day one and a snowy blizzard on day two.

Eager to discuss Russia's current situation, they weren't daunted by VIP Congress members. Meetings ranged from Senate and House Leaders, Richard Gephardt and Richard Lugar, to dozens of U.S. Congressional members, Congressional Committees, policy institutions, and the U.S. Departments of State, Commerce, Treasury, and Justice. In each venue they reiterated that Russian leadership was at last moving in the right direction and that their businesses were beginning to take off, thanks to training in American companies. Further they claimed that more than anything, Russia wants to be in close relations with the United States.

Leader Gephardt met with all 100 alumni and was visibly energized by this roomful of eager Russian faces.

Senator Lugar scheduled a 30-minute meeting with the entire group. After brief remarks Lugar told them, "I started out as a small business owner in Indiana. I know the struggles of creating a business. What I really want to know is how have you survived in Russia's tough and corrupt marketplace? What are your personal stories?" First one Russian got up and told his story, then others began standing up one after another, each

Congressman Richard Gephardt, Democratic Leader of the House of Representatives, in a sea of PEP alumni, some of whom he had met when he led the U.S. delegation to Russia to determine how U.S. taxpayers money was being spent.

After listening to 100 Russian entrepreneurs for two hours, then shaking hands with each of them, Senator Richard Lugar seemed excited by their spunk and their gratitude for his attentions to them.

Lugar being presented with books printed at Elena Budanova's private printing company in Ekaterinburg.

sharing details of their struggles and how they were overcoming them. Lugar beamed as he listened to these modern day Horatio Algers.

His aides whispered, "Sharon, it's time to break it up; the Senator has to get back to work!" I attempted to intervene in the story telling to give Senator Lugar an out. It didn't work. His aides then passed him a note saying it was time to leave. He responded by asking CCI alumni for more stories. An hour and a half later, Senator Lugar stood up with a magnificent smile on his face and asked to shake hands with all 100 of the Russians! His staff rolled their eyes. The air was electrified. Flashbulbs popped across the room. Finally, we left after two hours of fabulous interactions.

The five days of Congressional meetings were packed with discussions regarding key U.S.-Russia policy matters.

In the midst of it all, State Department representatives called and said there was an outside chance that the Russians could meet with Colin Powell, the new Secretary of State. It materialized on our final day in Washington.

Meeting with Colin Powell

Meeting with Secretary Colin Powell in the massive State Department conference room was the last and most prestigious meeting. Simultaneous translation was provided. The U.S. Seal of the Department of State and the American flag were prominent in the great hall. When all the Russians were seated, officials marched into the room with the Russian flag and placed it next to the American flag. Emotional and boisterous applause broke out across the entire hall.

Someone announced that the Secretary was approaching. An expectant silence fell on the crowd as Powell strode briskly into the room with a dramatic presidential presence. Mounting the podium to continuing applause, he began speaking extemporaneously.

He told the 100 how he once feared Russians and how he thought they were his enemy. Then he informed them about when he began to change his attitude. At that time he was in command of U.S. troops in Germany.

He reported that he kept a photo of the U.S.S.R.'s top general in his office to remind him why he was there. After the Berlin Wall came down, he met the Soviet general face-to-face. At an appropriate moment Secretary Powell confided to him that he had kept his photo displayed on his desk and for what reason. In shock, the general looked at Powell and said, "General Powell, I had a photo of you in my office for the very same reason." He related that they have since become good friends. Secretary Powell continued to share remarks with the group. Here is a short snippet:

> *"There is a sense of excitement about you and about the role Russia will play in the world unfolding in front of us .... What happens to Russia is important to your people, to our people, and to the entire world .... Your role is especially crucial because, in order to succeed in today's globalized world, Russia needs a vibrant small business sector .... Russia's future is for you to determine .... Knowing that there are 100 of you here today is cause for great optimism in my heart. The old days are gone; the cold war is gone. May those days never come back!"*

Standing under the two nations' flags, Secretary of State Colin Powell addressed 100 FEP alumni in the officious hall of the U.S. Department of State on March 9, 2001. This was Secretary Powell's first address to a foreign delegation following his appointment to the office of Secretary. He told them how he feared Russians, when he changed, and how much he respected their courageous efforts to build a business sector across Russia.

Secretary Powell on the spur of a moment asked if one of the delegates would explain how they started their business. Alexander (Sasha) Malashkin's hand shot up. Here he is telling his story of converting from a legal career to becoming a businessman.

As Secretary Powell finished his remarks and was rapidly striding out of the room, he broke ranks with his officers, dashed to the left, and waded through the applauding crowd to shake Sasha's hand. The entire room exploded with applause and excitement.

In closing, Powell asked if one of the entrepreneurs would share a personal story with him. Alexander (Sasha) Malashkin's hand shot up. His face beamed as he spoke. He told of graduating from law school at Volgograd University and having a wife and baby to support when the U.S.S.R. began imploding. In desperation he rented a truck, drove to Moscow, and purchased a load of cookies. He drove back to Volgograd and hired 15 babushkas to sit at central underground walkways and sell his cookies. In five days the cookies were all gone, but he had earned enough money to pay the grannies and to go back to Moscow for more cookies. He continued this activity. After eight months, he realized that he should work as a businessman, not as a lawyer.

Sasha reported to Secretary Powell that his wholesale food line now carries 1,600 products, that he employs 1,200 people full-time, and that he owns the largest wholesale food business in the Volga region. His story was later paraphrased by President Bush on prime time TV across America.

Out of time and amid thunderous applause, Powell quickly strode down from the podium toward the door. Unexpectedly, he made a speedy left turn and pushed his way through the applauding crowd of Russians to reach Sasha—and enthusiastically lurched forward to shake his hand. The large room went wild with surprise and applause!

Kremlin Meeting with Andrei Illarionov—March 13, 2001

Our group arrived back in Moscow on March 12. Buses brought us to the huge Rossiya Hotel at the south end of Red Square. Straight across the cobblestones from the hotel sat the ominous Kremlin wall with ancient towers. Centuries old churches with gold domes along with numerous administrative buildings were seen beyond the wall. This would be the first time that any of CCI's alumni would go within the massive structure, which in the past housed tyrannical leaders and governments. After a restless sleep, the group brainstormed early the next morning before proceeding to the Kremlin.

At 10:00 AM sharp, we began the trek across the centuries-old cobblestones leading to the Kremlin's well-known Spassky Gate that was constructed in 1491. It was here at the Spassky entrance that those deemed suitable to the insiders, were checked before being allowed to enter the Kremlin walls. In centuries past, even Tsars had to take off their headgear and bow upon entering this supposedly hallowed gate.

A dozen Kremlin guards were on hand to speedily register our large group. This day 100 ordinary Russian entrepreneurs were coming through the revered gate.

Entering the yellow buildings behind the Kremlin wall, we were taken through corridors and elevators to an upper floor. The meeting room we entered had blond birch paneling and was surprisingly inviting. At the head of the room, the only décor visible was a large red velvet seal with double-headed gold eagles. A podium stood to the right with a long table and several chairs that faced the audience. Our group of entrepreneurs carried hand-written notes to prompt their memories should they get a chance to speak. This day they would address themselves directly to the power of Russia and would tell the Putin government what it should be doing to support Russia's small businesses—a feat that no entrepreneur in the room could have ever imagined doing.

Andrei Illarionov and his deputies walked into the stately room. Instead of going to the podium, Andrei chose a low, hard-backed chair and sat down at the long table with notepad and pen in hand. He motioned me to make introductory remarks, following which one Russian after another stood, took the podium, and made thoughtful, astute

Jim Aneff, PEP's National Field Director, Tennison, and Madina Bikbulatova, Moscow Region Coordinator, followed by PEP delegates, on their way to their first Kremlin Meeting with Andrei Illarionov, then Minister of Economy for the Russian Federation.

An alumnus glanced up and snapped this photo as we passed by St. Basil's church.

Russia's regional entrepreneurs preparing to enter the auspicious Spaskii Gate at the Kremlin. For centuries a sanctifying icon has hung above the entrance. All those who entered had to do so with bared heads and supposedly penitent souls. Napoleon scoffed at this. It is said that a mighty wind rushed at Napoleon as he entered, took his head gear off—and he indeed entered the gate bareheaded.

recommendations that would hopefully get to President Putin. Illarionov and his deputies speedily took notes.

The delegates' topics ranged from Russia's endemic corruption and outrageously high tax rates to much needed legislation, loan guarantees, help with "public perception" of business, need for business education, and much more. Entrepreneur Piotr Prodiakov from Taganrog spoke from three pages of handwritten bullet points. As he left the podium, Illarionov reached toward Piotr's notes asking if he could have them. Piotr resisted, saying they weren't in proper form … to which Illarionov remarked, "But I can use them as is, please …."

It was an arresting moment with the Russian Federation's Minister of Economy clearly wanting input from a grassroots entrepreneur from Taganrog, a small city to south of Moscow in the Rostov-on-Don region.

The hour and a half sped by. I slipped Plaksin a note, telling him how important it would be for the group to hear from Illarionov and noting that our time was up. He whispered back, "Don't worry, Andrei will take the time to hear them all … this is important for him." Only toward the end did Illarionov take the floor. He congratulated the 100 on their survival through Russia's difficult transition and confirmed the importance of their visit to Washington policy makers, his belief in them, the extreme importance of private sector development across Russia, and his interest in staying in touch with them. Lastly, he spoke about new economic steps that the Putin administration planned for 2001 and 2002.

Illarionov requested that each entrepreneur write down his or her recommendations and get them to him through CCI. He assured them he would brief President Putin upon his return to Moscow. He explained that they didn't have answers in the Kremlin, that the answers for Russia were yet to be decided by people like themselves—that they would have to fight to build and to defend the principles behind democratic institutions across Russia. He assured them that he and Putin would support their fight. To our shock, the Kremlin meeting lasted three and a half hours. Our 100 Russian alumni left the formerly inscrutable premises knowing that their government had taken them seriously. They coordinated a way to get their input to Illarionov. Two weeks later Putin's televised remarks to the nation covered some of the exact points that were made during the entrepreneurs' meeting and that were sent to Andrei Illarionov.

Pondering the Meaning of It All

The Russians cleared out of the massive Rossiya hotel and headed toward their cities across 11 time zones. I sat alone in a corner café staring out of floor-to-ceiling windows at the Kremlin towers until the sun went down. It was a magnificent scene— snow, ancient walls, pink and blue sky, dusk setting in. For me it was a time for looking back, for brooding.

It had been 17 years since I'd first stayed in this old Soviet hotel and looked across a similar snowy expanse to the Kremlin walls. My mind recalled those days—concerns about bugged rooms, informers, ransacked luggage, body searches, trying to find ordinary Russian citizens with whom to speak, and secretly sneaking into multi-locked citizens' apartments for long evenings of heated discussions around samovars. These two Russia's seemed centuries apart—but as history goes, the transition between the two has been but a blink on the face of time. So much … so very much … has happened during this short interim.

PEP Evaluations–Mid-Year—July 2001

At the half-way point of our mid-year evaluation trip across Russia, we had visited 17 cities and towns. Traveling around by auto, bus, and rail gave us a chance to gauge rural fields, crops, livestock, villages, cities, highways, numerous eighteen-wheelers on roads, and new automobiles in out-of-the-way places. There was evidence of new life budding across Russia: modern clothing and middle-class housing developments surrounding the Russian cities. These positive signs were interspersed with the remains of a decaying Soviet world of crumbling buildings, vacant collective farms, and rusting industrial equipment strewn across the countryside. The signs of new growth reminded me of green shoots coming up from burned forests.

Russians were putting one foot in front of the other and slowly recovering. To me, what was playing out in Russia at this moment was the most fascinating evolution of any country on the planet.

At the beginning of the 1990s, this largest nation on earth turned upside down and threw off a severely dysfunctional system, which had controlled all aspects of their lives. During the rocky process, they tried to graft outside ideas from the West onto their Russian mentality and souls, and unfortunately, it didn't work well for them. Suffering one indignation after another including the inability to feed themselves, and the crumbling of their prestigious educational, medical, scientific, and military institutions, Russians were finally beginning to show signs of revival.

As for PEP evaluations, we interviewed our Russian alumni every day from morning to evening including weekends. We could have asked the computerized questions in our sleep—except that the answers from the entrepreneurs sitting in front of us were so fascinating that their heartwarming input kept us wide-awake.

The following is a quick summary of PEP entrepreneurs' most frequent responses in 2001:

- Russia: The country is beginning to stabilize; it is coming out of the "deep depression" of the 1990s; businesses are stronger; and Russians have more money to spend this year. (This input flew in the face of a just-released May 2001 issue of the *Atlantic Monthly* magazine that published a lead story and a front cover showing a gray-uniformed Russian soldier. The magazine cover headline read, *"Russia is Finished."*)
- Putin: All entrepreneurs we spoke with were impressed with his leadership; they said he supports business, has reduced taxes, and is honest with the country about the manifold challenges facing Russia.
- Chechnya: Roughly 95 percent support Putin's Chechen policy, but they still believe the situation in Chechnya will be impossible to bring under control.
- Criminalized mafia: Mafia is no longer a problem for Russia's small and medium-sized businesses.
- Corruption: From city to city Russians report that local public bureaucrats are now the "unofficial mafia" and the main deterrent to Russia's new market economy. Although bureaucrats don't physically harm entrepreneurs like the earlier criminalized mafia did, they demand bribes or stall giving official stamps and permissions until entrepreneurs' business opportunities go under—unless they pay up.

CCI's New Program to "Out" Corrupters—Next Steps: Transition to Transparency

We knew that Russia's entrepreneurs could be key to breaking through Russia's entrenched cycle of corruption at least at the level of small businesses. This alone made it incumbent on us to start an anti-corruption program since we had the largest database of small-business entrepreneurs in the country.

President Bill White of the Mott Foundation was contacted. Thankfully, again he was ready to invest in this latest experiment. We designed a program to help Russian entrepreneurs unite, go up against local public corrupters, educate on the costs of public corruption, and eventually to become a force against corruption across the regions. If we could get CCI alumni to join hands to oust public officials, the new program could ignite other groups of entrepreneurs to do the same throughout Russia.

Background for Russia's Pervasive Challenge with Corruption

What we call corruption today has existed since the first forms of communal living evolved many centuries ago in Russia and in other European states. Tributes (goods or money) to officials were part of the feudal systems. As European countries gradually began to adopt more broad-minded commercial practices, Russia's autocracy and expectation of tributes continued to be deeply embedded across the country. Russia's landmass alone along with the lack of transportation in the 19th century provided little socialization with other countries. For the most part, the mentality of Russian people developed far from the experimentations going on across Europe, Great Britain, the Nordic countries, and America. Although Russia freed the serfs in 1861, autocratic Tsarist rule continued many aspects of feudalism up to 1917. Russian subjects weren't allowed to take part in refining or reforming their society. They had to defer to all in official positions. This deference to power continued in the 20th century, when communist authorities became the latest of the top-down hierarchical overlords with which ordinary citizens had to comply or face life-threatening circumstances.

As communism broke up in the late 1980s, authorities' expectations of special treatment continued. Public officials made meager salaries and scraped to get by during this period. Envious of entrepreneurs who had begun to make money from private initiatives, they found ways to enrich themselves. Demanding bribes for signing official documents for these new businesses was just their starting place. Next, they created artificially contrived "inspections" and extra-legal "permissions" for which they extracted even more bribes. The amounts were capricious and grew exponentially. If entrepreneurs complained, they incurred the wrath of bureaucrats up and down the vertical chain who were sharing in the "take" with each other. At that time, there were no laws forbidding these activities, and if there had been, entrepreneurs could have never won against authorities.

The deeply ingrained system of bribe-taking was, and is, not only about money; it is also about Russia's age-old societal emphasis on having "connections" with people in positions of authority. This has been their way to get around laws and formalities; hence, if possible, Russians make connections with authorities wherever they find themselves. A law-abiding society has been difficult to develop across Russia due to the proclivity to bribe for favors and the use of connections rather than laws to solve problems.

Alyona Nikolaeva—Russia's Anti-Corruption Princess

In early 2001, a lovely and gutsy Russian entrepreneur by the name of Alyona Nikolaeva barged her way into President Putin's office and demanded that he begin an anti-corruption campaign. She told him about her family's struggle against corrupters after starting their small bread business in Moscow. They baked bread and sold it on Moscow streets. With their profits, they purchased and remodeled a defunct old bakery. Then they started a second business remodeling apartments. Meanwhile, they were being bled dry, first by mafia and then by bureaucrats who routinely increased illegal inspections and unscrupulous fees for bogus services.

Apparently Putin was taken by Alyona's outrage and swiftly created a non-governmental organization loosely affiliated with his office. She was appointed as director. In this position, Alyona had a bully pulpit to take on corrupters. When we met, she quickly recognized that CCI's alumni could be her closest Russian allies. We began working together. As Aloyna moved forward, Putin quietly invited 30 regional entrepreneurs to a meeting at the Kremlin to discuss these issues; among those invited were two CCI Fellows, Alexander Lubyanoi and Vladimir Leontovich. Lubyanoi had recently organized the Association of Volgograd Entrepreneurs. The 30 participants were queried regarding how rapidly they could arrange anti-corruption conferences in their cities; Lubyanoi and Leontovich from Volgograd said three weeks for their home city.

With political cover from President Putin, Alyona and a host of young colleagues plotted a series of regional anti-corruption conferences, the first of which was in Volgograd where CCI alumni had a strong following.

Everything sped up after Putin made the decision to focus on corruption, regional small businesses, and the establishment of a middle class across Russia. As for corruption, I hoped he would have some magic formula because bureaucrats were getting rich off of bribes and would be loathe to give up their streams of income.

Volgograd Conference on Corruption—August 4, 2001

I flew to Volgograd to attend this first-of-a-kind conference stimulated by Alyona. There was little advance notice. We had hoped to organize a conference similar to this one the following February in St. Petersburg; Volgograd had stolen our thunder.

The conference was held in Volgograd's largest auditorium with about 75 of our CCI alumni present in addition to all of the city's entrepreneurs they could collect. Volgograd's Mayor, Vice Mayor, and Volgograd's chief bureaucrats were required to be there since the event was ordered from higher up in the political chain.

The event was amazing to behold! Our CCI alumni boldly discussed, in front of Volgograd media and city officials, topics that were absolutely taboo a year before. They declared they would create a "hot line" to expose local bureaucrats. Mayor Chekhov, sitting in the audience, drew heavy criticism from them for protecting Volgograd's bureaucrats. He yelled back from the audience, "You haven't been angels yourselves!" It was hard to believe we were privy to this accusatory shouting match, which was unheard of behavior in Russia.

Putin's young representatives were impressive. They spoke with authority about his mandate. They urged swift action and startup of grassroots associations all across Russia, of which to our knowledge, Volgograd's was the first Association of Entrepreneurs to exist in Russia.

Sergei Polyakov, owner of a construction company, speaking at the podium of the first ever "Business vs Power" conference. This event was hosted by Volgograd's Association for Entrepreneurs. Alexander Lubyanoi, leader of the association, is sitting between the two flags. This was a bellwether event—one that demonstrated that entrepreneurs could go up against local and regional officials, if there was direct support from higher up in the official chain. This movement was initiated by Alyona Nikolaeva with support from Putin.

Alexander Lubyanoi, the quiet but strategic leader of Volgograd's entrepreneurs, encouraging an audience of CCI alumni from across Russia (at the St. Petersburg Corruption Conference) to join Volgograd by creating their own associations locally.

Above: Alyona Nikolaeva, co-owner of bakeries and construction companies with her husband, became a firebrand and ignited a movement to "speak truth to power." Entrepreneurs caught her vision and began to stand up against local bureaucrats. Next she created a nationwide anti-corruption conference in Moscow at which Putin conferred with small groups of entrepreneurs to collect data regarding corruption at local levels. Following this, Alyona put together the first ever nation-wide organization, OPORA, to assist small businessmen and women to carry out actions locally to clean up Russia's business environment.

That afternoon as the conference was in full force, Alexander Lubyanoi, the conference chair, took a telephone call and quickly left the podium table. Later we learned that his private dental clinic had been "torched." We knew the torchers would never be prosecuted, even if identified, since without doubt they represented some part of Volgograd's official bureaucracy. Later Lubyanoi shrugged his shoulders and paid to get his new clinic reconstructed.

Next Alyona Nikolaeva's team created a new national Association of Entrepreneurs called OPORA, which they intended to push forward as the central clearinghouse for ridding Russia of corruption.

Looking back on those heady days and the hopes that we all had for dramatically reducing corruption, I realize that we all were unaware of two inhibiting factors at that time: 1) most Russian entrepreneurs were unable to trust other Russians sufficiently to join or build associations together, and 2) quite a few Russian entrepreneurs were forced to develop quid pro quo cash relationships with officials to insure that their business documents were serviced.

They could not afford to go against public officials. Business competition was so stiff, and business realities in Russia were so difficult, it was quite understandable that these entrepreneurs would have to find ways to expedite relations with bureaucrats to survive. Several entrepreneurs admitted, "If I don't offer bribes in return for my official papers, my competition will, and I'll lose the deals to them." We understood and began encouraging them to include these costs into their cash flow projections.

Russia Reduces Business Taxes—Autumn 2001

To the surprise of us all, Russia's outrageously high taxes from the Yeltsin era were reduced to a flat rate of 13 percent, the lowest in Europe; corporate taxes were reduced to 24 percent. Small businesses got a big break—they could choose a tax rate of either 6 percent on gross revenues or 15 percent tax on profits. Across the country, CCI alumni attributed these tax breaks to Putin's strong interest in their well being.

Other legislation was also in process. A land reform bill caught my eye since I had begun to look for property in St. Petersburg. In 2000 my father left me a modest inheritance that was too small to buy property in San Francisco but enough to purchase an unrenovated flat in St. Petersburg before prices began to soar.

The End of a Tragic Day—September 11, 2001

A month later Pat Dowden and I were in Washington, D.C., to discuss Russia issues with Thomas Cochran, the National Security Council's Russia expert, as well as Congress members and State Department officials. We were in a taxi riding up Independence Avenue on the way to the Rayburn Building. The cab radio issued a dramatic announcement that two airliners had crashed into the Twin Towers in New York City.

At that very moment we were within distant sight of the area around the White House. The radio further announced that smoke was reported behind the White House and at the Pentagon. Immediately I glanced toward the location of the White House and saw only a small low, white cloud, but no smoke—then turned to look back over my right shoulder toward the Pentagon and saw a huge plume of ugly, gray-black smoke filling the sky.

The moment was surreal. Traffic was moving as usual; people were on their way to work; the day was magnificent. I was listening to the radio, but my mind was not registering the impact of what I heard and saw, and apparently neither the taxi driver nor Pat were registering the gravity of the news. It was bizarre.

Within seconds cars were in gridlock. We hurriedly got out of the taxi near the Rayburn Building across from the Capitol. Within seconds it seemed, people were rushing out of the Congressional buildings and rapidly sprinting toward us. It fully hit us. What was happening at the Pentagon had to be related to the Twin Towers in New York—and other targets in this immediate vicinity could be hit next.

My cell phone wouldn't work. Quickly I questioned others on the sidewalk if their phones were working. None were. There were no policemen to direct the traffic, which had come to a standstill. It was like being locked in a bullpen with no way to move and no way to contact the outside world. By this time, sirens were blaring near and far. We sprinted to a metro and got outside the district before everything shut down.

Something inside me that morning became an observer ... a sad, very sad observer. In the middle of possible next targets, it was strange to me that I experienced little or no fear or panic ... but just a realization deep inside that we Americans collectively, the wealthy big brothers of the planet, had been attacked. Why?

Could it be that we have become richer, more complacent, and walled off while others have become poorer, more desperate, and shut out—and that we have been politically self-focused and self-promoting at a time when the world has become smaller, more dangerous, and armed to the teeth? Whatever the case, splinter groups from some unknown destinations had turned on us with something as simple as our own airplanes.

The thought quickly grasped my mind—that the world desperately needs citizen diplomacy to the Middle East and other troubled spots around the globe—it needs bottom-up programs, track-two diplomacy like CCI's early projects in the U.S.S.R. A more humane American presence is sorely needed in those places to help balance U.S. military might. Perhaps American citizens' efforts could open minds and hearts once again—since clearly our 21st century weapons cannot protect us if our own planes are used as missiles to attack our great cities.

The U.S. Department of Commerce's Business Mission to Russia—October 16, 2001

Despite the shocking events of 9/11, a month later the Commerce Department forged ahead with plans for its trade mission to Russia. At the invitation of the Department of Commerce, I traveled to Moscow in mid-October to address the first U.S. Business Mission to Russia in seven years.

President Bush's new Secretary of Commerce, Donald Evans, arrived with representatives of 18 major U.S. corporations. He and President Putin have both placed high priority on jump starting numerous new business connections between the U.S. and Russia. Both presidents have also urged large businesses to build joint ventures with small and medium-sized enterprises (SMEs) wherever possible. The challenge has been that none of these giants had connections with this sector; hence the focus on CCI. I had 20 minutes to convince these VIPs of the scope and excitement of Russia's SME sector, during which they were apprised of ways Russian businesses could provide quality products and services for their corporations. Two CCI-trained Russian entrepreneurs with me described their rapidly growing five-year-old companies and how such Russian businesses could serve their larger business' interests. The event went well. American CEOs seemed genuinely interested in the Russian market, and we at CCI gained a new level of support in the U.S. Department of Commerce.

Bush-Putin Summit—November 2001

Presidents Bush and Putin met for the first time and seemed to develop a fairly cordial relationship. Relative to Putin, Bush made a comment that would become famous, *"I looked the man in the eye. I found him to be very straight forward and trustworthy, and we had a very good dialogue. I was able to get a sense of his soul. He's a man deeply committed to his country and the best interests of his country, and I appreciate very much the frank dialogue, and that's the beginning of a very constructive relationship."* President Putin remarked that each of their countries bore a special responsibility for maintaining world peace and security. However, he did comment that any unilateral action would make that process more complicated—a signal that difficult discussions regarding NATO and the U.S. missile defense system still remain to be worked out. Bush invited Putin to his ranch in Crawford, Texas, for their next meeting.

A First! OPORA Anti-Corruption Conference—December 4-5, 2001

The first countrywide OPORA Anti-Corruption Conference for Russia's grassroots entrepreneurs was held in Moscow December 4 and 5. Some 1,100 regional entrepreneurs traveled thousands of kilometers across Russia's regions to voice their concerns. Although initiated by Putin, the conference was driven by Alyona Nikolaeva and Russia's entrepreneurs. Over 300 of CCI's Fellows from 40 Russian cities came at their own expense. The CCI bloc was the largest and the most vocal at the conference. It was pure joy to sit in the back of the auditorium and watch these young CCI-trained men and women rise to their feet and speak. Several of them were singled out to present from the podium; a small number attended a group with Putin's advisors; and two were invited to a mini-brainstorm with President Putin and six other entrepreneurs.

After the conference broke up that evening, Alyona and her organizers appeared at my hotel room. Heady with the success, they reported that President Putin commented that CCI Fellows were "the most experienced and strategically thinking" of all entrepreneurs to whom they had access—and that their contributions during the conference were of major importance. Aloyna had one last request—that CCI Fellows be immediately canvassed to get information on two critical topics:

- Identify the corrupt "pseudo" administrative agencies that surround their local and regional officials.
- Identify, by industry sector, the absurd regulations by which their local public officials extract bribes.

It was December 5th and the information was needed in the Kremlin before December 19th when Putin's meeting with the State Council of Russia would take place. An SOS e-mail was sent to CCI's Russian Partner offices. In turn they sent SOS e-mail requests to their regional Fellows. Immediately, data began pouring in, which was forwarded to the Kremlin prior to Putin's December 19th meeting.

We all had doubted that Russia would ever get corruption under control. Now it appears that it might eventually have a chance to succeed—but it will undoubtedly take years to root it out of Russian mentality.

A CCI Program for Orphans—December 2001

During the holiday season, a call came from a CCI contributor on the east coast. Nika Thayer, a Russian-born American, raised in the U.S. and living in Connecticut, had $10,000 that she wanted to put toward helping disadvantaged young girls in Russia. Since there were a lot of disadvantaged girls in Russian orphanages, I suggested that we start there. Nika agreed. Next she said she would like to do something to help the girls develop work skills so they could make productive lives for themselves. I mentioned computer skills since the country was rapidly becoming computerized, and these skills would be greatly needed in the future. Nika liked this idea, and our conversation ended with an agreement that CCI would try to set up an experimental computer laboratory in a St. Petersburg orphanage. I e-mailed Volodya Shestakov to begin searching for an orphanage with a reputable director.

A disturbing announcement was made public in the last week of December of 2001. President Bush notified Russia and the world that he was unilaterally pulling America out of the Anti-Ballistic Missile (ABM) Treaty signed with the U.S.S.R. in 1972. This treaty had kept the world relatively safe for the past 30 years.

Year 2002

Allegations Against Russia Increase—as PEP Delegations Expand

Year 2002 began with heavy criticisms leveled at Russia by U.S. media including human rights violations in the Chechen war, Russia's control over its media, and Russia's officials' refusal to allow the U.S. to build permanent military bases in Central Asia. Russia was mute on these issues.

At the same time, CCI's San Francisco office was gearing up for the largest number of PEP delegations ever in 2002. Each season brought requests from Russian participants for new industry sector training. Russia's private market was maturing quickly, and new types of private businesses were suddenly in demand. Each new sub-sector requested required CCI to develop training modules and guidelines regarding how to operate successfully within these sectors. Business professionals were contracted to help with these tasks.

We were able to track Russia's private sector development by clocking entrepreneurs' requests for new types of training. For instance, during the mid-1990s, there were no requests for trainings in insurance, real estate, or small private banks—the society just hadn't progressed to the place where these sub-sector trainings were needed. Then all of a sudden in 2002, a rash of new requests for these industry sectors came in from numerous Russian regions. It seemed there was some contagion in the air wherein specific business needs were developing simultaneously throughout wide-spread areas of Russia.

PEP Evaluations—April 2002

Russia's evolution moved so rapidly during the early 2000s that each year brought dramatic shifts in mentality and in businesses. By March of 2002, I was eager to get started on the year's evaluation road trip to monitor the changes.

Once again in Russia's regions, we scanned population centers and countrysides by rail, noting fascinating changes occurring across this vast territory.

Something intangible was in process—it felt as though Russians had begun to feel that they had a new lease on life even though their circumstances were still quite limited. In the early months of the 2000s, just being able to purchase a new dress or coat or modern shoes seemed to build self-image. The next mark of progress seemed to be to go to a private dentist and get one's smile beautified. There was a corresponding renewed interest in Russian culture—particularly pre-revolutionary culture. Cities and towns began to look as though local people cared about their appearances; flowers were planted, grass was cut, sidewalks and streets cleaned. Russian faces and body language began to show a looseness and confidence not previously witnessed.

I wondered if any other country in the world was experiencing this much economic and sociological change? Russia 2002 felt really different. On the other hand, it was clear that there were millions of aging Russians who would never be able to adapt to the new reality; they lacked the mentality and skills to change. In addition, most of that generation would be gone by the time this difficult transition had given way to a new direction.

Volgograd's Risk-Taking Entrepreneurs

Evaluations in 2002 took me back to Volgograd where there were large numbers of new CCI alumni to evaluate. They were ready to share what they learned in American companies and to show how the information was being used in their local businesses. We visited their enterprises and saw evidences of considerable growth following their training in American companies.

Meanwhile, the Volgograd Association of Entrepreneurs, a growing hub of CCI Fellows, had become a formidable force in the city. A year earlier, 300 of them stalled a new city-wide tax proposed for small business owners. When they threatened to close all of their businesses, officials backed down. In April of 2002, the bureaucrats again attempted to impose a new tax, and the association struck once again, this time with 1,500 entrepreneurs in the streets with placards in air. They burned a female figure in effigy, who, they said represented their "hope" that Volgograd businesses would ever get a fair deal from the city's bureaucrats. All of their businesses remained closed that April morning.

The same day entrepreneurs in five other Volga region cities also struck, closing down their businesses in solidarity with Volgograd. This collective region-wide action gained attention. Local and regional officials decided they didn't need to raise taxes after all.

Since local media always sided with officials, the news of such demonstrations was seldom reported even inside their cities, let alone outside to other cities. Hence, this important news never traveled to Moscow some 550 miles away. Moscow journalists were later shocked to hear that two such events had taken place in Volgograd.

It appears that Russians have lived fairly circumscribed lives up to the very recent past. For the most part, they have remained in the cities where they were born and often lived in the same apartment for most of their lives; generally they had attended one public school, matriculated through their school years with one group of classmates, and generally graduated from their local university without changing cities. Their lives centered around their families and small circles of close friends.

National television and radio carried what authorities wanted them to know about people in far away places. Computers were not used for information gathering. I was surprised to observe that in the early 2000s, Russia's entrepreneurs assumed that their city was showing some economic progress but believed that other Russian cities were not. I found myself carrying "good news" about such things as the Volgograd Association of Entrepreneurs and other breakthroughs from one city to another since there were few ways for such information to travel. Entrepreneurs in some Russian cities were quite cynical when told that Volgograd entrepreneurs "struck" and that 1,500 of them closed their businesses on one day. Even in Moscow, this news was received with suspicion.

Traveling Out In the Volga Region

We decided to go to Uryupinsk to interview a cluster of PEP alumni whose small outpost was beyond Russia's extensive rail system. We caught a train to Alexiekov, a nearby farming community, with the understanding that a PEP Fellow's driver would meet us there and bring us to Uryupinsk. Our night train made short stops at towns along the track to deliver mail and packages; we had exactly two minutes at 4:30 AM to toss our luggage out to the pavement and de-board before the train pulled off again.

The night before, Volodya Shestakov and I began eating dinner in the train's old dining car. Sitting across from us were three young men discussing their business trips to Moscow. Thinking they might be interested in PEP, we excused ourselves for interrupting them and asked what kind of businesses they owned. They were in retail trade, computer business, and fast foods. The oldest was 37, the youngest 25. They were curious about us also, where we were going … and why. Soon they moved to our booth, after which three hours of fascinating interactions ensued. Topics ranged from business to corruption, then to culture and life values. These guys were clearly the new breed of Russia's entrepreneurs, quick thinking and expressive. They perched on the edge of their seats as though ready to take off in a hurry. Their lively eyes had the look of constant problem solving as they moved from one topic to another with hardly a pause.

Finally, one of them brought up lifestyles and values—whether Russia was losing its culture, whether it could be regained, and whether life with only economic values as a priority was worth living. The oldest, who looked like he could be a manager in a small American firm, said that he was happier under socialism "because my top value is my family. We got to spend more time with our children under socialism. We took vacations with them. Now my only thought is how I can earn enough money to support my boys, and I don't have time for family vacations."

Then out of the blue he asked, "Do 100 percent of Americans think Stalin was evil?" I answered truthfully, "I don't know, but probably so. What do you think about Stalin?" Brooding a bit he offered, "Well, I see him in historical context now. A lot of bad things, yes … but also Russia wouldn't exist today if it weren't for Stalin. We were a primitive country in 1920. Stalin pushed the country without mercy to develop it. If not for this, the Nazis would have easily defeated Russia in WWII. So I don't see Stalin as black anymore." The younger more talkative fellow, Igor, agreed.

Then the eldest began speaking wistfully about the life of ease and comfort that Americans have, saying that the U.S. should be able to "coast" from now on, now that America has reached such a high level of economic development. Pushed to explain, he confidently remarked that "America is a nation of managers. It will be easy in the future for the U.S. to maintain global superiority by hiring technological brains from other countries and by just managing those brains to get what is needed for U.S. citizens."

I countered his notion explaining how complex it is to run a successful democracy— and how complicated it is to keep a balance between citizens' demands and running the whole country wisely. He looked somewhat puzzled and said, "Does this mean that democracy isn't a perfect system?" I admitted it is not, and explained that any system, democracy included, must be constantly worked on and changed or it won't survive.

The model in his mind must have been based on the Soviet system where ideally managers told compliant workers what to do and the workers dutifully implemented their bosses' decisions. Russians, particularly those who have never been out of the country, seem to be searching for information that explains how things work outside their own borders.

On our departing, Yuri, the oldest, took my hand and shook it gingerly, saying how important it was for them to meet an American and talk over these ideas. Then he said he hoped I still would like Russia after going into this primitive region where life is so backward compared to my country.

I told him I'd been in this general region previously, that it wasn't new to me, and that I found it to be a good place with good people in it. Feeling his disbelief, I offered, "The countryside out this train window looks very much like my region in Kentucky when I was a little girl. My granny lived in terrain like this. She had a two-room wooden house and planted her garden every summer. She canned produce for the winter—it was her means of staying independent. She didn't have indoor water or plumbing. When I visited her, I went to the well to fetch water with her. People in rural Kentucky were good people." Yuri looked at me as if I'd just dropped in from Mars … and uttered, "I never thought any American ever lived like that!" Igor rapidly spit out his comment, "We only know about four-bedroom homes with three toilets for every American family." Our new Russian friends seemed incredulous. With that, we exchanged e-mail addresses, shook hands, and parted.

On to Alexiekov

We made it to Alexiekov, a tiny little farming community far off the beaten path in central Russia, where we expected to be met by a driver. We made the obligatory leap off the train at daybreak, but there was nobody there to pick us up. Looking around the dilapidated train station, we observed marked contrasts. Even so early in the morning, stocky little babushkas in scarves stood next to smartly dressed young women in spike heels and slacks. Old men in worn clothing ambled around the station among a few young men in business attire. All were waiting for a ride to somewhere. This was Russia in transition. What must it be like to exist in these two worlds, which mingle side by side and often collide on where Russia needs to go in the future? Fortunately, Russia's older generation is docile by nature while younger Russians are impatient to get to the next rung of the business ladder.

By 5:30 AM our driver still hadn't arrived. A worn looking old man asked if we needed a ride somewhere. We told him Uryupinsk, with the hope that we could find our PEP Fellows upon arrival. He agreed. Passing many kilometers of wheat, barley, and oat fields, we finally came to our intended town. The driver left us at the dusty little Uryupinsk Hotel. Not a car was in sight. One little hotel guard lady sat behind a wooden cage and sleepily peered out at us through a glass window. We sat down in the barely lit lobby until the town awakened. An hour later, a well-dressed young man bolted through the door. Looking exasperated, he hurriedly announced that he was our driver.

His car broke down on the road to Alexiekov. He called a friend to bring him a spare part. He spotted our driver and us on the road to Uryupinsk, with our luggage piled up in the back of the old car. His friend helped, fixed the problem, and then they waited and flagged down the driver returning from Alexikov to ask where he had let us off.

Here our driver stood in the dusty little hotel—out of breath, and deeply apologetic. Quickly our luggage was hustled out to a handsome new Russian car, and we were on our way through Uryupinsk's quiet, tree-lined streets to a new "private motel."

After washing up a bit, we met the group of Uryupinsk alumni and learned that they were running quite successful businesses in this out of the way place. Last year they organized their own association of 19 entrepreneurs (based on the Volgograd model) primarily to support each other as they struggled with bureaucratic interference. Much like American civic clubs, they made the decision to put emphasis on bettering their local community for all of the town's people. Membership in their association required no smoking and no drinking—this alone must have reduced the club's ranks.

Recently, the group hired a young journalist and started their own private newspaper with the mission to build respect for local entrepreneurs and to expose the illegal actions of local bureaucrats.

Their largest "service project" this year was to bring back the town's holy icon, the Mother of Kazan—which endeared them to the local population. They created a parade to celebrate and show the town the lovely icon, which was then presented to the local Russian Orthodox Church. This season the association also outfitted their local youths' soccer team with new togs.

So aspects of civil society are being built even in little out-of-the-way corners like Uryupinsk. Incidentally, local entrepreneurs here are as culturally refined and educated as those in Russia's two capital cities. This fact continues to show itself across Russia, which always gives me pause to wonder how the Soviet Union accomplished this feat.

Months later, our CCI San_Francisco office received an e-mail reporting that "Uryupinsk newspapers announced today that local entrepreneurs have taken over the city." One of the CCI entrepreneurs we met while there was elected Mayor of the city, and two others were elected to the City Council!

CCI's RISE Program in Afghanistan—May 2002

In another part of the world, a CCI program was jumping borders. Our friends at the Foundation for Global Community (FGC) in Palo Alto had kept an eye on Afghanistan's deepening economic and social crisis as America's attention turned toward Iraq and away from Afghanistan. FGC members were searching for strategies to assist Afghans to retool their society and get back on their feet following the U.S. war with the Taliban in 2001.

Nancy Glaser, a CCI board member who developed St. Petersburg's RISE (Russian Initiative for Self Employment) Training Center, and I attended one of FGC's early meetings. We offered the possibility of our RISE training center and micro-loan program in St. Petersburg as a model—it seemed perfect for Kabul's needs. FGC leaders found the idea interesting.

Soon Nancy accompanied a scout trip to Afghanistan where the first plans for a training center similar to the RISE center were put together. We contacted President Bill White of the Charles Stewart Mott Foundation to ask if the Foundation would support several Bay Area Afghans to accompany the group to Kabul. Once more President Bill White was ready to invest in an international endeavor to provide training for grassroots citizens—this time in Afghanistan.

In Kabul, Nancy and the group assessed the situation. The needs were obvious. Reliable Afghan contacts were made, and the possibility of growing a training center for men and women became the goal. Bay Area Afghan, Nasir Durani volunteered to move to Kabul for the next year to get the training center organized and running. Smaller amounts of money began to come in, but it was not nearly enough to do the job needed. Thousands of Afghans needed to be trained in tasks and responsibilities they had never previously handled.

Ambassador William Taylor, the current U.S. Ambassador to Afghanistan was one and the same as Bill Taylor, State Department's Director for Russia during the 1990s, who was so very helpful to our PEP work. We sent Bill a proposal with hopes he could help with the Afghan Center. Wheels turn slowly, but eventually a U.S. grant was received.

Zoom Forward to … January 26, 2011

A meeting with Nasir Durani today caught me up to date with the Training Center in Kabul. Since his first visit there eight years ago, Nasir has lived in Afghanistan nine months out of each year. The original Kabul Center now has 31 affiliated Afghan Centers in outposts across Afghanistan. The centers primarily train women in work skills, health care issues, literacy, and a program that teaches them their rights as citizens. Rona Kabiri, a young Afghan woman who came up through one of the outlying centers, is graduating from the Monterey Institute for International Studies (MIIS) in Pacific Grove, California, in May 2011. She will return to her region in Afghanistan to work for women's rights and economic and political reforms. These centers are evidences that one small idea and a handful of American citizens can initiate projects that grow in time to amazingly large programs.

Out to the Ural Mountain Regions—June 9, 2002

The rail to the Ural mountain region between Moscow and Ekaterinburg is near 1,000 miles. The Urals are the north/south dividing range between European and Asian

Russia. All along the route, the train window framed many images demonstrating the patience and revival of Russian people.

A case in point: as we approached the small town of Glazov, one of thousands of small outposts across this nation, several small villages first came into sight. Closer to the little town, aging unpainted wooden houses appeared, which were bordered by neat gardens. Then came fields of rusting metal from large industrial machinery, silos, train tracks, tankers, and broken-down storage buildings. Next were graying multi-story residential block buildings ala Soviet era—with dusty roads, cars, and people scurrying back and forth. Finally, the local train station came into sight. This lovely little pre-revolutionary Glazov train station had a freshly-painted exterior with blossoming flowers and perfectly swept walkways surrounding it.

With a 20-minute stop at Glazov, we hustled out of the train to purchase cabbage and mushroom pies, boiled potatoes and eggs, tomatoes, onions, and whatever else we could feast on for lunch. The town's "grannies" were hawking their wares and trying to interest us in whatever else they had in their baskets.

Russians waiting for trains looked like those in regional cities and towns. About half of them were wearing fashionable clothing and stylish shoes. Their postures indicated that they had a purpose, were on the move, on time or trying to be. As our train moved out of town, we saw a sizeable suburb of new red brick private homes on the horizon— evidences of local initiative and recent middle class development. These five elements— aging villages, Soviet industrial relics, Soviet block houses, a touch of Tsarist elegance, and new wealth, are seen every day all across Russia.

Today's Russians are greatly concerned about the dying off of their villages. Village life has a special heart-tug for Russians regardless of how far they go or how rich they get. They photograph village life, paint village scenes, and the wealthy collect canvases of serene Russian village life. Their great museums down to small private galleries exhibit numerous celebrated village painters (if you have a chance, visit the famous Tretyakov State Gallery in Moscow).

When I tell Russians that I remember when villages died out in America, they consider it a great tragedy—like a death in a family. Yet it is happening now all along this seemingly endless train track to Siberia and many train tracks throughout Russia. Many Russian villages today appear to be vacant heaps of unpainted, leaning structures with little to no life in them. At least for now, Russians still have their small country plots (dachas) that ring their cities. This is where they can get back to nature and put their hands in the soil—which seems to replenish something deep in their Russian souls.

Ekaterinburg, Capital of the Ural Region—June 11, 2002

We arrived in Ekaterinburg on the early morning train and carried out a full day of evaluations. At 6:00 PM several CCI alumni excitedly burst into the room with flowers. We piled into cars and headed toward the outskirts of town. Passing wooden village houses and patches of trees, we made a sharp left turn and were soon on a nicely paved street with two and three-story red brick houses on either side. In mid-country USA, these houses would cost about $300,000. In San Francisco they would cost at least $2 million. Here in Russia, construction has been inexpensive by our standards—but in any case, we were in another world simply by turning down a country lane.

We pulled up to a splendid home with a fine iron grill fence. Carefully manicured gardens filled the front yard. PEP Fellow Ludmila Mafeeva, owner of Ekaterinburg Auditing and Consulting firm, opened the door. We walked through the living area to her large enclosed sun porch, which looked out onto a backyard filled with green vegetable tops and fruit trees. Neat rows of growing edibles extended all the way out to Ludmila's new Russian bathhouse, or banya.

PEP alumni arrived bearing food. I questioned, "Is this Russian potluck?" "NO," I was told. "Russian women would never think of it! This is American potluck, an idea we picked up while in the U.S." I'd never seen such an informal meal in Russia. We crowded around the big table. More alumni arrived and makeshift tables appeared. Late-arriving CCI fellows drew applause. Plates were filled for them as they made their rounds of handshakes and hugs. I was struck by their obvious delight to be meeting with each other.

Toasts began. CCI was toasted over and over until it became embarrassing. American hosts and volunteers' names, unknown to others around the tables, were offered up with great respect.

Lastly, Ludmila stood up with profound dignity and said she wanted to toast to "tears." She sadly explained, "On September 11th we were all struck dumb ... we were in complete shock with you ... we wept, we grieved, we could think of nothing else, we felt your pain as our own pain ...." Heads nodded around the table as men and women alike silently agreed. It was so very touching.

Observing the companionship and genuine affection in the room made me wonder. Why are these Russian business people so close with one another when Russians traditionally don't build wide networks with those unknown to them? Had these Ekaterinburg people gone to school or university together prior to their PEP trainings? I asked. No, none of them had known each other before they completed their trainings in numerous different PEP delegations.

Then I recalled that Lena Novomeiskaya, CCI's director of the Ekaterinburg office, frequently brought them together throughout the years for business seminars where apparently they began to get to know each other. Now they are joined at the hip, members of the same Rotary Club, purchasers of each other's products, and most importantly trusted colleagues.

If not for PEP and Lena, these Russians still would not know each other—and none of this richness of spirit and life would be taking place. One entrepreneur told me privately that his "new PEP friends" are closer to him than his life-long friends since these new friends share the struggles of creating businesses, and they help each other with challenges when problems arise—and that his older school friends don't understand him today and aren't interested in his new life.

Evaluations: Chelyabinsk in the Ural Mountains—June 15, 2002

Chelyabinsk is near the epicenter of a huge nuclear accident that occurred at a local Soviet nuclear weapons site in 1957. The Soviets never admitted that the accident happened. It is rumored that the CIA knew about it almost immediately but kept it secret. Better known today is the local Techa River, which is said to be one of the most highly radiation-contaminated areas on the planet. Nuclear wastes were indiscriminately dumped into the Techa river for years, thereby creating a chain of health consequences downstream.

Despite this catastrophic environmental situation, Chelyabinsk people love their territory. There are over a thousand sizeable lakes here. Deep sea diving is a local sport. The weather is extreme—from unbearable heat in the summer to minus forty-five degrees Celcius in the winter.

My long-time friend, Vivian Castleberry, traveled with me out into the Ural regions. She was last in Russia in 1987. A journalist by profession, Vivian registered every detail. Having just returned from visiting European capitals for a month, she concluded that Russian women and men look more European than American, noting that Russians and Europeans "dress up," whereas Americans increasingly "dress down." Many local women here in Chelyabinsk still wear high heels for everyday street wear, as is common in other Russian cities.

A quick sampling of a few of the PEP alumni we evaluated this year:

Alexander Kalinin, age 38, was part of a wholesale foods delegation hosted by a Rotary club in Baltimore. In 1991 he was a young nuclear missile cyberneticist who became jobless when the U.S.S.R. imploded. Alexander began purchasing food products in other regions, which he shipped into Chelyabinsk's markets. Today his wholesale business employs 200 workers, while he increasingly spends his spare time developing social and educational programs for troubled youth.

Mikhail Markov, age 36, a poultry equipment manufacturer trained in a meat processing delegation in Nebraska where his delegation was hosted by Rotary. *"I can't say what was most important about my trip to the U.S. It was something bigger than can be described. I am very happy that I could see everything about how a business should work with my own eyes. I asked more questions than anybody in my delegation."*

Svetlana Yermakova, early 40s, a dentist in a Dental Clinics Delegation to Colorado and Wyoming reported, *"My dream is a new dental building like I saw in Colorado. My internship was fantastic. Americans took great interest in sharing their experience with us. The dental hygienist concept was new information to all of us. Immediately on return to Chelyabinsk, I started hygienist training and service for our patients."*

Vladimir Kovolev, 46, trained in a private architect delegation. He explained, *"I build large buildings, cottages, trade centers, and reconstruct churches. My trip was SUPER! I saw the construction process directly. Beyond the professional program, staying with families was the best part of the trip. We learned about America through human relations. The trip wouldn't have touched our souls if we had lived in hotels. People who accommodated us were absolutely wonderful, and I fell in love with them!"*

Natalya Pashnina, 40, a restaurant owner in a Casual Dining delegation went to Wichita Falls, Texas. When we arrived for her interview, we walked into the most unusual restaurant we had ever seen. It was exquisite and all done in neutral tones. Indirect lightning, slip-covered chairs, and floor-length tablecloths lent a formal ambience. Natalya and art students created the decor using the cheapest of materials: paint, gypsum, scrap metal, and the least inexpensive fabric in Russia—cloth for military coverings. Natalya confidently reported that Wichita Falls, Texas, is the most wonderful place in the world, *"I noted family relations between wives and husbands, how they related to their* *children and their friends. It touched me that they held hands and blessed the food at the table. I understood that in my pursuit of business, I'd left some important things out of my life. I came home with renewed determination to make my family life wonderful again. My husband is a much happier man now,"* she reported.

A Summary of 2002 Evaluations Across Russia

• Bribes: Russia's economy as still greatly impacted by local bureaucrats who demand under-the-table cash, but some entrepreneurs admitted that there had been a slight change for the better. One said, *"We feel the wind blowing from the top. Each time Putin speaks out against corruption, our bureaucrats get more nervous."*

• Changes in business environment: "Barter" is becoming a thing of the past, "cash transactions" are no longer the rule. Most businesses now use bank transfers. This mostly has happened within the past year. Few businessmen and women take out bank loans—they use revenues to build their companies. Cell phones ring incessantly during interviews.

• Putin as president: Different generations see different elements in Putin. Entrepreneurs see him as themselves—dynamic, assertive, healthy, sports-minded, a sharp thinker, someone working on their behalf. Academics perceive him as well educated, multi-lingual, one of whom they can be proud. Older people see him as a "strong leader," a good Tsar, unlike Boris Yeltsin. Young people see Putin as a modern leader bringing Russia into a western mode, for which they are hungry.

• What PEP gave them: 1) A chance to observe how the world's most successful economy operates, 2) business ideas to adapt and implement in their own companies, 3) a chance to study management techniques in real-life situations, 4) an opportunity to observe civic clubs (new for Russia), and 5) a chance to live with American families, which, all agree, was the most memorable part of their U.S. experiences.

• Unexpected boosters: American CEOs "shared their business secrets" with them. The Russians received lots of encouragement and acknowledgement while in the U.S.— which they don't usually get in their home cities. The PEP experience gave them a "leg up" in business compared to their Russian competitors who hadn't experienced out-of-country training.

A Look at St. Petersburg—Summer 2002

After the U.S.S.R. broke up, St. Petersburg was the slowest of Russia's cities to show change. Its thousands of run-down historic merchants' homes in the city's center had housed the poorest-of-the-poor 'communal dwellers' for the past 80 years. During the Communist era and since, these aging people had no money for repairs; hence, the city had appeared worn out and shabby for decades.

As real estate laws became dependable, well off Russians and foreigners began purchasing these downtown properties from their elderly owners. The new owners began upgrading their investments; and the Russian Federation launched new renovation projects of historic buildings. This year, St. Petersburg began to take on a new face across the city. Scaffolding moved from one block to another; centuries-old buildings were resurfaced and painted in pastel colors, cobblestone streets reappeared, and the historic parks of the Tsars began blossoming after being overrun by weeds for the past several decades.

Orphanage Project Update–Angels for Angels Program—September 15, 2002

Volodya Shestakov searched St. Petersburg and found an orphanage and a director of which he approved; it was Children's Home #32. Aza Vasilevich, the director and "mother" of some 45 orphans, was delighted to experiment with installing a computer laboratory in her orphanage, even though it was not legal. I arrived to meet Aza and inspect the space. The Children's Home was old, but was spruced up with lots of photos of the children in holiday costumes, on nature trips, and hugging Aza and each other. It had all the earmarks of a well-run family environment. Our funder, Nika Thayer, approved the orphanage. She made a second request, that computerized English lessons be taught to the orphans, since she believed their futures would be considerably enhanced with a second language. We purchased five computers, software, and printers and started the first computer laboratory in Aza's St. Petersburg orphanage.

A CCI oversight trainer was hired; the first computer lab began as an experiment. Nika soon made sufficient funds available to start another lab in a second orphanage. Orphans from ages 10 to 17 years old were taking computer lessons after school and slowly becoming proficient in the new technology.

Over the next several years Nika Thayer, our sole Angel benefactor, provided enough funds to bring five children's homes into the program. These orphans began creating computer-generated newsletters and competing in contests with other sister orphanages; then a bit later, they were competing with orphanages in Moscow whose directors had also managed to get computers in some of their homes. Nika was delighted that her money was finally accomplishing what she desired.

CCI's Anti-Corruption Conference in St. Petersburg—September 30, 2002

Our CCI corruption conference was by "invitation only." This insured a safe environment in which our alumns could speak freely about corruption without fear of informers or officials. Registrants came from 74 cities across Russia. All were CCI Fellows. Major topics included: 1) documenting the status of, and solutions for, all types of bribe taking; 2) creating a strategy for uniting entrepreneurs across Russia, and 3) developing a plan for moving forward rapidly. The Volgograd Entrepreneurs Association led the most important sessions, since they had the longest experience in confronting corrupt officials. Entrepreneurs with little experience mobbed them for more information during intermissions.

Alyona Nikolaeva, the entrepreneur who spearheaded OPORA last year, electrified the audience. She has become a firebrand since Putin agreed to give presidential cover for her controversial work. In the past year, she has spoken across Russia, encouraging entrepreneurs not to be afraid and to stand up against bureaucrats.

Pavel Kuznetsov, Director of the Working Center for Economic Reform and, a young reformer from Moscow, gave a fiery presentation providing assurance that the Russian government was indeed pushing reform to support Russia's small business sector.

Bernie Sucher and Robert Courtney, two successful American entrepreneurs working in Moscow, gave talks on leadership and uniting business people across Russia. After revealing their battle scars from running their businesses in Russia, they were well received by CCI Fellows. Several representatives from the American Consulate and USAID officers also attended.

"Open microphones" permitted participants to ask questions and make comments after the sessions. Thirty round tables were followed by full session reports. Flip charts, video, and computers captured information. By the end of November, results were to be delivered to President Putin's advisors.

I purchased property in St. Petersburg this year. It may take years to get it renovated since only the external meter-thick brick walls are useable. To my dismay, I learned yesterday that my realtor paid a $300 bribe to get a phone installed!

$\mathcal{Y}$ear 2003

The New Year Begins

On January 1, our first e-mail for the year read, *"Happy New Year from Dallas, Texas! We have just discussed dates for our next PEP delegation of Russian women lawyers. We want them to come on April 10 through May 4. Our Annual "Women Helping Women" Awards Dinner is scheduled for April 30, 2003. We want our new Russian friends to attend. Thanks!"*—Carol Donavan, PEP delegation coordinator.

Running PEP had become a 365-day-a-year operation. My laptop picked up e-mails wherever I traveled. CCI's Russian-speaking staffers carried cell phones 24/7 to manage flight schedules and emergencies. An ever-growing number of American volunteers were meeting planes regardless of the day or hour they landed. They organized and supervised training in local companies, interacted with Russians in all sorts of conditions including medical emergencies, and put them back on planes three weeks later loaded down with cutting-edge information, warm feelings, and gifts for their Russian families.

U.S.-Russia Relations Floundering—February 2003

Since taking office in 2000, President Putin had made partnership with the U.S. a top priority for Russia—and in doing so, he frequently bucked Russia's hard-nosed foreign policy and military establishment who were still embedded in Cold War suspicions of America.

In 2001 Putin okayed the United States' use of Russian military bases in Central Asia much to his military establishment's dismay. Next, he glossed over Washington's decision to pull out of the ABM treaty at the end of 2001, then accepted NATO's expansion into the Baltic nations that rankled much of the population, and has been giving strong support to the U.S. government's campaign against terrorism.

The U.S. administration's request for Russia to send troops to Iraq this year has been a huge problem for Putin. It ignores the fact that Russia has had a long-standing trade relationship with Iraq, and has billions of dollars invested there. The Russian people have always looked at Iraq as a friendly and cooperative trade partner. Further, worn thin by the continuing Chechen war within their own borders, Russian citizens across 11 time zones would have mutinied at the notion of sending their sons to a war in Iraq—or for that matter, sending Russian troops to any war to please another nation.

The Rumble of War with Iraq

The buildup to the Iraq invasion felt to me like déjà vu of the U.S.-U.S.S.R. missile buildup that catapulted our little group into action in the early 1980s. The following e-mail spilled out onto my computer.

A Letter to CCI Constituents: Another War Looming?—February 13, 2003

Dear Friends, We've been through a similar threat of war before—and an even more dangerous one. In the 1980s we faced a massive missile buildup, enemy-making by government officials and U.S. media, and dire intelligence reports. Ten years later, history showed us the truth—the CIA stood accused of grossly misreading the 1980s intelligence regarding the U.S.S.R.'s capabilities and readiness for war. Their excuse? "Intelligence communities must look at 'worse case' scenarios."

None of us could have dreamed that circumstances with the U.S.S.R. would be reversed in 20 years. Iraq's circumstances may also be reversed in the next dozen years. Yes, Osama Bin Laden and his network need to be taken out, but bombing Iraq won't touch them. **We must find a totally new strategy.** *Unlike enemies of the past, those in the world who want to destroy us today can't be identified. They mingle in any crowd and sit on airplanes next to us. There is no war-book preparation—no precedent for what we face today.*

We are in a modern day "David and Goliath" situation. People with slingshots and rocks are taking aim at us—we, who have the ultimate in 21st century military technology. These seemingly insignificant individuals are hitting us where it hurts the most. How can we deal with this totally new phenomenon? This is the real question. It is not whether we should go to war in Iraq.

If we do start a war in Iraq, we will be less safe and less trusted by other nations. We will have more enemies around the world, and we may run headlong into a devastating economic crisis, which could take down our beloved country as we know it today.

And finally, as we Americans watch our TVs and see our fire power light up the skies over Baghdad ... will we think about the stark tragedy and havoc being wreaked below— the babies, small children, teenagers, young mothers and the elderly—the horrific burns, broken bones, the abject terror of a whole human population?

What would I do if I were President Bush? I would sink to my knees and pray to understand how to use America's resources and people power to spread goodwill and advantage—rather than using heinous weapons against innocent populations just to take out one leader. I would invoke an "unexpected miracle," something like the unexpected turn of events in the U.S.S.R. just 20 years ago. Sound naive?

Our leaders invoke the name of God pretty easily these days. Let's include prayers and goodwill to our national strategy. Let us consider using a huge amount of grassroots economic development as the carrot in Iraq—and to make it clear that Palestine becomes a recognized state and that Israel gets its borders totally protected. This is all completely doable; it just takes political will and a different consciousness. Then I'd ask Peace Corps and Rotary International to turn their attentions toward the Middle East for five years. Let us pray for this kind of solution—not another war, which could result in a horrible quagmire.

Deeply worried about the outcome of the war in the making, but with no means to influence the Iraq situation further; I left for Russia to continue our less controversial work there.

The Khodorkovsky Scandal Brewing—March 2003

Investigations of Yukos Oil Company by the Putin government are underway. Mikhail Khodorkovsky, Yukos' owner and Russia's richest young oligarch, began to seriously challenge Putin's deal with him and his fellow oligarchs (those who illegally made off with the U.S.S.R.'s huge money-making enterprises in the 1990s). Putin's openly stated deal with the oligarchs in 2001 was more than fair in my estimation—it was that they could keep their ill-gotten, enormously wealthy Soviet enterprises, but they had to pay taxes on all of their revenues in the future and stay out of Russia's politics. Khodorkovsky has refused on both counts.

Our conversations with Russia's entrepreneurs have made it abundantly clear that they have no sympathy for Khodorkovsky—and hold a completely different point of view of this oligarch than the one being pushed by western media.

Meanwhile, CCI's grassroots work continues in the midst of this minefield of national and international intrigue. Interviewing Russia's entrepreneurs and capturing their stories of courage and success keeps us emotionally gratified and believing that we are doing something to make a small difference in the U.S.-Russia relationship.

The 300th Anniversary of St. Petersburg
St. Petersburg Host Heads of States from 40 Countries—May 27-31, 2003

As the Khodorkovsky showdown heats up, St. Petersburg's 300th Anniversary, has provided an excuse for the new Russia to host 'heads of states' from all across the world.

The grand celebration in St. Petersburg this year is about "City Day" or their 300th Anniversary, but also it is an attempt to try to heal remaining rifts between Russia, Europe, and the U.S. that have become more complicated with the Iraq war that began just two months ago.

Throughout Russia, the anniversaries or birthdays' of cities are of utmost importance to local residents. This is part of Russia's national culture. Regardless of the size of the city or town, they celebrate their ancient artifacts, battles, cultural institutions, industries, universities, schools, and leading citizens. Parades, floats, and fireworks are normal fare even in very small towns.

Heroic efforts were made to complete the renovation of palaces, parks, bridges and historic residential houses in time for the anniversary. Few of us expected it could have been accomplished. But it happened like clockwork; scaffolding on historic buildings disappeared overnight. Decorative lighting outlined grand architecture and bridges in the evenings.

When President Putin greeted the world's leaders gathered here, St. Petersburg was ablaze with gold leaf, pastel paint, pilasters, and angels—all enhanced by warm weather, leafed out trees, and lilacs in bloom. While political elites held official meetings, the city was full of gawking tourists being stunned by one splendid piece of architecture after another. I walked around among them hardly believing what my eyes were taking in now that the scaffolding had all been removed. The grim, dilapidated museum city of the past had given way to one of the most spectacular metropolises in the modern world.

Mid-Year PEP Evaluations—June 12, 2003

My assistant, Heidi Hartman, flew to Russia to assist with 2003 PEP evaluations. Her following e-mail note to friends in the U.S. revealed what she is seeing of today's Russia with her "fresh eyes."

I hardly had a moment to breathe between evaluations. At the day's end we were rushed off to a reception for one of Ekaterinburg's entrepreneurs. It was a great opportunity to meet the people behind the amazing stories we have heard about in our San Francisco office. I've never been one to obsess over Hollywood types, but I imagine meeting these PEP entrepreneurs offers me about the same excitement that others get from meeting movie stars.

After the reception, we were rushed into another PEP Fellow's car for a 2.5 hour road trip. We left Ekaterinburg with a huge golden sun behind us. Up ahead we began to see the wild forests of birch trees stretched along the roadside .... occasionally a small village would appear .... then more forests. Sharon, CCI's President and my traveling partner, is discussing political and economic issues with our driver. My eyes are distracted by a peaceful babushka riding her beat-up bicycle along the side of the road.

It is now nearly 11:30 PM, and the sun has just begun to go down. I see old factories belching smoke out of their aging pipes and realize that in my mind, I have turned back in time. It is reminiscent of the Soviet era. The Soviet factories stand fairly close to nearby rundown apartment complexes. Drying clothes hang from the windows. We turn a corner ... there are huge above-ground metal pipes everywhere. We drive through this deserted side of town. We see typical aging Soviet apartment buildings. The driver says we are lost. Sharon and I are exhausted. It is midnight. We agree that anywhere with a bed will be great. Some twenty minutes later, after asking three by-passers on the road, and then "off-roading" over barriers and through some trees, the driver finally found our hotel.

It is not really a hotel at all, but rather an old school building under repair. Once inside we are led to our rooms. It is a mini-oasis among the troubled areas through which we have just passed. We have hot water, a microwave, and a living room! Amazing. The hotel ladies downstairs are taking great care of us bringing us fresh fruit, cheese, juice, bread—everything they have. I never realized how nice it is to come home to such an inviting place, especially after the long hard days we have been putting in. I'm not sure how Sharon does it. It exhausts me! After evaluations here we will be put on a night train going out to Izhevsk, which is near Lake Baikal in Siberia. – Heidi

I am struck, more on this trip than any trip before, by the immensity of the task that Russians have before them—and by the countless liabilities they've inherited from the Soviet system and Soviet mentality. Perhaps it's the travel over thousands of miles in the Urals and Siberia, witnessing the same industrial relics scattered across the countryside—abandoned livestock farms, the litter of poles and wires, and the hectares of once-upon-a-time trains with rusting red stars on engine cars. All of this I continue to observe from the train windows, wherever the tracks take us.

Deeper into Russia—June 22, 2003

Our travels took us to remote Russian cities that American tourists seldom visit. These included: Perm, Ekaterinburg, and Chelyabinsk in the Urals, and Omsk, Tomsk, Tyumen, Novosibirsk, Novokuznetsk, Krasnoyarsk and Irkutsk in Siberia.

Novokuznetsk: A Soviet-era train dropped us off in this formerly "closed" Soviet city. I remember this city well from 1984 when Tucson citizen diplomats, after traveling with CUUI to other parts of the U.S.S.R., tried to establish a Sister City relationship with Novokuznetsk. The city couldn't receive outside visitors, so our Tucson colleagues were somehow able to get in touch with Novokuznetsk's mayor and asked if their delegation could meet with his city council in a nearby 'open' city. They agreed. A small official group from Tucson traveled all the way to South Central Siberia to an unknown destination to meet their Soviet counterparts. Eventually, Tucson and Novokutnetsk solidified their sister-city relationship by letters, which, in those days, took six weeks or more to be delivered to either side.

Today Novokuznetsk is, of course, an open city. Unfortunately, it is rumored to be the fourth most industrially polluted area in Russia due to metal smelting. Debarking the train we expected to find one of the most degraded environments in the country. Instead, we found ourselves in an amazingly green city with new, multi-story red brick residential buildings with turrets, domes, and roofline cutaways reminiscent of old Russia's ancient fortresses. On occasion they sat next to crumbling Soviet-style high-rise apartment buildings.

Among PEP evaluations and interviews, our agenda included, a press conference that was held in a huge bank building that completely blew our minds. Polished granite and marble was present everywhere we looked. Gleaming floors bounced back mini-lighting from ceilings, giving the appearance of stars above and stars below. It was dizzying to walk down the corridors.

Unexpectedly, at the press conference, three recently returned PEP Fellows made presentations to Novokuznetsk journalists and future PEP candidates, about their U.S.

training. This was the first time I'd heard "Russians talk with Russians" about the advantages of PEP training. Their stories almost moved me to tears as they told each other about their American "parents" (home hosts), trainers, and new friends in the U.S. One alumnus, who trained in Fort Worth, Texas, with a Newspaper and Publishing delegation, reported that his experience in America, without doubt, was a life-changing event for him. Upon return home, he published a series of three full-page articles in his newspaper regarding what he observed and learned in the U.S.

Our Novokuznetsz hotel was typical of so much in this country as it converts from Soviet days to the new Russian world. The hotel was a hybrid structure: to the front it was an old, run-down multi-story Soviet apartment building with a new asphalt drive that wound around its periphery. At the back of the building was the distinctive entrance of "Hotel Hope." Three floors had been converted into a small hotel with modern conveniences including soft, elegant Italian furniture. After so many nights of sleeping on trains, we found this hotel to be sheer luxury. The workers were customer friendly, and upon realizing we hadn't had dinner, hotel ladies brought us fresh hot blini with tvorog (cottage cheese) and three kinds of homemade jams.

Tomsk: Among other alumni in this city, I interviewed Mikhail Koffman, an educator-turned hotel owner, who was renovating the old Soviet Tomsk Hotel. It sits in the town square across from Tomsk's newly spruced up pre-Revolution train station. Mikhail was re-surfacing the hotel's entire exterior, changing all windows, building a business center, enlarging sleeping rooms, and adding modern baths in the eight-story hotel—all with a three-year loan from the bank. He was in a race against time to attract sufficient guests to repay his loan. Working seven days a week, he hopes to do the impossible. Michael trained in Salt Lake City, Utah, where he gathered hundreds of ideas for his hotel. He was a walking torrent of words. He told about falling in love with the Salt Lake City people, their Rotary Club, and the PEP program. He is driven by his vision to duplicate Salt Lake City hotel services here in the heart of Siberia.

Krasnoyarsk: This city revealed the same mix of excitement that was found in other Siberian cities. Gratitude for their American training prevails in each place. It was remarkable that here too, as with other Russian cities, there were few if any differences between Siberian PEP Fellows and their counterparts in western Russia's two capitol cities. Their educational, intellectual, cultural, and energy levels were the same. This must be attributed to the standardized Soviet educational system that was laid down across the Soviet Union many decades ago. Children in every Soviet city, even rural areas, learned from the same textbooks, took the same tests, and were held to the same high standards. Barring intellectual disabilities, Russia is a nation of exceptionally well-educated and cultured people.

Omsk: Like other Siberian cities, Omsk appeared to be a strange amalgam of former centuries intermixed with the 21st century. For instance, in one city block in Omsk, we noted centuries-old, tilting, wooden Russian houses; one lone peeling Soviet high-rise apartment building; and a shining new, multi-story structure of granite and glass. Untrimmed weeds and bushes around the old Soviet building phased into perfectly manicured flower beds and carefully laid patio stones around the new high-rise. The visual image was jarring.

If we foreigners gawk at the magnitude of this transition, what must the average Russian citizen be thinking? Russians are known for their deep and almost "mother-like" identification with their own cities. These new architectural structures scattered around must be pleasing to their souls, even if they can't all live or work in them.

The Ural and Siberian cities were a combination of traditional regional warmth and bustling economic activity. PEP Fellows across the regions work long, intense days. It is necessary in such a difficult environment. Siberian business life is a constant struggle to outsmart officials and to out-compete fellow entrepreneurs. In the midst of it all, the influence that three weeks in American companies made in their psyches and businesses has been enormous.

CCI's Twentieth Anniversary—September 16, 2003

For most years we hadn't had time to celebrate, but CCI's twentieth anniversary seemed deserving of recognition. Twenty years ago on this day, the original CCI founders, and a film crew of four apprehensively boarded a jet headed for the U.S.S.R.

The twentieth celebration was a magical event of "Telling the CCI Story." We packed a huge banquet hall in the historic Presidio with participants who had helped implement our various programs throughout the years. Original 1983 "Citizen Diplomacy" trippers, past and present CCI Board Members, past and present representatives from all of our major programs, CCI Russian facilitators and interpreters, Rotarians and Kiwanians, past and present staff, funders, and other dear Russian participants wandered around looking for, and finding, old-time friends and colleagues.

CCI's Board Chair, Arlie Schardt, opened the ceremony. He called us to remember the critical period in which our organization was born. The 1983 travelers were invited to the podium. They spoke about the deep impact the trip had made on their lives, then, numerous participants across the room stood and relived their early remembrances. The event for me was a Camelot experience—a magical evening caught in a moment of timelessness where faces were glowing, and the world felt lovely and in tune with some far greater purpose than we understood.

A New Way to Address Russia's Corruption—September 2003

Following the celebrative weekend, we were back in CCI's office and onto our next big undertaking—corruption reduction across Russia. There was never a resting place—always something big and seemingly important was beginning to take form. Thankfully, these big ideas came in a sequential way. Generally, a large problem would begin to loom on our horizon. Energy would gather around it, and then we would begin creating a solution. Once the solution was devised, it dominated our attentions and all energies were focused toward achieving the result. Fortunately, we never had to deal with two separate mega-ideas at the same time.

So far, what we were doing vis à vis corruption had not created significant impact on the situation—so we decided on a bold new strategy, something never tried by anyone before. We would give Russian entrepreneurs training in how other nations of the world had systematically reduced corruption. Unable to take them to numerous countries, we decided to take them to a city that had Embassies from countries around the world. We would execute the new program in familiar territory, Washington, D.C.

We consulted Transparency International (TI), the leading corruption agency in the world, and selected the top 15 nations that had reduced corruption step-by-step within their borders. They were the following: (1) Finland, (2) Iceland, (3) Singapore, (4) Denmark, (5) New Zealand, (6) Sweden, (7) the Netherlands, (8) Australia, (9) Norway, (10) Switzerland, (11) Canada, (12) Luxembourg, (13) U.K., (14) Austria, and (15) Hong Kong. Admittedly, these are smaller countries, and Russia is the largest country in the world. But we felt that some of the solutions could be used by both small and large nations.

We made "cold calls" to Embassy officers. They questioned who we were to make this bizarre, first-ever request? We explained our history, that this was a stand-alone project, that Russians would pay costs for their trips and training, and that it was in all countries' interests to help Russia solve its corruption problem, since trade with Russia in the future was sure to become more likely. They began to soften and listen. The remainder of 2003 was spent organizing the details on the Washington side, then setting up systems to invite Russians, interpreters, translators, U.S. volunteers and staff. The last goal was to schedule a briefing in the Kremlin when the Russians returned to Moscow.

Looking back, I don't know how we ordinary people had the nerve to begin such projects. But here we were in the middle of another one.

An Extremely Difficult Year for U.S.-Russia Relations—2003

Russia's refusal to send troops to the Iraq war set the tone for U.S.-Russia relations for the foreseeable future. Once the decision was made, a barrage of damning articles regarding Russia's internal Chechen war, Putin's "consolidation of power," "the erosion of Russia's democracy," and human right's issues, appeared repeatedly in American media—with no regard for Russia's history or the progress made over the past two decades.

Russian entrepreneurs we interviewed saw the issues leading to these accusations through quite different lenses. To them the Chechen war was a fight against Islamic terrorists within Russia's own borders. They could see no other way to handle the fearful situation. As for consolidation of power, they saw Putin's efforts as necessary, given the lack of democratic infrastructures and the inexperience of Russia's people with self-governance. To them it wasn't a matter of rolling back democracy, since there had been no real experience with democracy under Yeltsin—and none for a thousand years in Russian history. Elections and "free media" were not free in the 1990s; they were for sale to the highest bidder.

Russian entrepreneurs were smart enough to know that a façade of democracy could not be thrown over their out-of-control nation—in their estimation, nothing but a strong hand would work. As far as force goes, it was all that Russians had ever known. It appeared to them the only way to deal with Chechens-turned-terrorists and criminals in the streets.

The Year-Long Media Frenzy with Khodorkovsky Continued to the End of 2003

Mikhail Khodorkovsky and the prospects for Yukos Oil Company created sensational headlines in U.S. media throughout 2003. It was the perfect storm for stereotyping and enemy-making. Russian citizens who got their news from the Internet were indignant with the international coverage. In their opinion, Khodorkovsky hadn't worked for his riches—he had stolen them from the Russian people—and he wouldn't even pay taxes on the enormous revenues he was making. They had no tolerance for him or other flagrantly wealthy Russians who drove Jaguars and the like through Moscow streets while millions across the country were hungry and barely surviving.

Khodorkovsky was jailed amid sensational stories in the U.S. media. My perspective on Khodorkovsky was that he is the most handsome, the most clever, and the most dangerous of all of Russia's oligarchs, aside from Boris Berezovsky who had already exiled himself to London to avoid trial for numerous alleged crimes. As for Khodorkovsky, he openly declared he would "buy" Russia's Duma (he had already begun doing so—and Duma officials were cash hungry), make laws to protect the oligarchs' new fortunes, create a parliamentarian government, and make the office of Russia's presidency irrelevant. How would an American president deal with a competitor who could buy the U.S. Congress and make the U.S. presidency irrelevant?

Lastly, Khodorkovsky was in final negotiations to sell a large portion of his ill-gained multi-billion-dollar asset, Yukos Oil Company, to Exxon-Mobil when he was arrested.

He had talked openly about his plans, so his own words insured that he would be imprisoned on one charge or another. As it happened, he was eventually tried in a clumsy trial and sent to prison for nine years for tax evasion. A parallel of sorts exists in U.S. history: Al Capone in Chicago was sent to prison for tax evasion and died behind bars, while numerous other charges lay in the wake of his life.

Year 2003 ended with shrill condemnation of Russia and Putin in American media. Those of us who understood these events differently had no access to the public forum. We spoke to Congress members, giving them our assessments, with the hope of keeping the doors open to the new, and admittedly uneven, Russian Federation.

During the 1990s, I was proud that the Clinton administration directed funds toward constructive programs for Russians. I treasured my relations with U.S. State Department officials and am grateful to have been part of their efforts to train Russian people in private sector skills after their seven decades under communism—which left them totally ill prepared for the tasks ahead of them.

During the 2000s, I watched as the reservoir of goodwill from the Gorbachev/ Reagan years evaporated. Power politics began to take hold of America's Russia policy. Mainstream media fell in line with the politics. I looked on with increasing apprehension as the U.K. and other European newspapers went along and printed biased information on Russia. I continued to wonder, who could profit from creating another Cold War.

*Y*ear 2004

2004 Started with Mixed News
Orphans Program Gets New Grant!

Nike Thayer surprised us with an unexpected gift to develop more computer labs in Russian orphanages. We gratefully began ratcheting up our work for 2004.

Another positive note came from Andrei Illarionov in the Kremlin who confirmed a meeting with 100 PEP alumni following the Washington, D.C. Anti-Corruption Symposium in March.

On a less optimistic front, the U.S. Embassy in Moscow announced large funding cuts for Russia, which undoubtedly will affect CCI.

Anti-Corruption Symposium in Washington—March 18-26, 2004

After months of preparation, one hundred PEP Fellows arrived in Washington, D.C. to learn how other nations of the world have reduced corruption in their countries.

John Pepper, chairman of the board of Procter & Gamble, keynoted a day-long seminar for our Russian entrepreneurs preceding their Anti-Corruption Symposium. Norway's Embassy flew in Madame Eva Joly, their country's pre-eminent anti-corruption lawyer. She gave a rousing presentation to CCI Fellows about "risk taking" and how to run corruption investigations for which she is well known across Europe.

The next day, 15 subgroups of Russians went to Embassies throughout Washington for full day trainings. We hoped our alumni would get a 360-degree view on how to

The famous Madame Eva Joly from Norway discussing corruption questions with Natalie Yakimenko at CCI's Corruption Symposium in Washington, DC.

Giving report-out from Embassy meetings.

Hands up for questions from delegates during evening report-out sessions after attending 15 different Embassy trainings.

Debating which points to put in the report for President Putin to be delivered during their meeting with Illarionov a week later.

Heidi Hartman, Manager of CCI Special Projects, listening and facilitating in a Moscow hotel room as the delegates hotly debated what should go into the final document to the president.

rein in corruption. The embassy meetings were followed by evening "report out" sessions during which all entrepreneurs could hear the essence of what the other subgroups had learned from their sessions. Teams of "scribes" captured input on flip charts that later was culled over to put into a document intended for President Putin.

By the end of the week, it was clear to us all that dealing with corruption successfully was quite similar from country to country. Radical differences in economic, ethnic, and cultural backgrounds seemed to make little difference. The critical elements are:

- active support from the country's political leaders
- introduction of strict legislative reforms
- institution of strong oversight mechanisms
- creation of public education programs for adults and children
- active judicial oversight and prosecution
- reduction of discretionary roles of officials
- introduction of swift and heavy penalties

Some 55 anti-corruption training sessions were held with embassies and international agencies such as the Organization for Economic Cooperation and Development (OECD), World Bank, International Monetary Fund (IMF), and Transparency International, U.S. Departments of State, Justice, Commerce, and Treasury, American Bar Association, FBI, policy institutions, watchdog organizations such as Center for Public Integrity and International Center for Journalism, judicial specialists, and investigative journalists.

Loaded with fresh insights, CCI entrepreneurs spent their free time drafting a document for their upcoming Kremlin meeting.

Anti-Corruption Techniques Transported to Moscow—March 27, 2004

During the flight and after landing in Moscow, delegates obsessed over the statement being prepared for President Putin. Staying up half of the night in hotel halls, corner cafes, and their bedrooms, they tried to craft a set of precise solutions that would get Putin's attention. Heidi Hartman, CCI's special projects manager, became the middle person between heated factions as entrepreneurs debated each concept to be entered into the evolving document.

Prime Time Russian TV with Vladimir Pozner—March 28, 2004

Sunday morning we all boarded buses for Ostankino, Russia's central television center in Moscow. Upon arrival we were led into a complex of buildings, and then onto a fashionable television set. In the center, a large birch roundtable and chairs were waiting for our four designated PEP Fellows. Circles of raised theater seats around the area accommodated the remainder of us. The set was ablaze with whirling lights. Pale blue and silver dominated the scene's décor.

Vladimir Pozner, Russia's iconic television journalist, entered the room followed by a train of makeup people. I hadn't seen him since the early '90s. Memories flooded back to a completely different world in the '80s—a time when Pozner was candid with us when nobody else was. I sat there wondering how this man had kept faith with the Russian public throughout these long and tortuous years. Still today he remains a top TV anchor and is seen weekly throughout Russia and the states of the former U.S.S.R.

Taped in the morning in Moscow, the program would be seen at 6:00 PM across each of the eleven time zones in Russia's far out regions and nearby states.

On the set with Vladimir Pozner: the prime time program was seen over 11 time zones as CCI alumni spoke about the taboo topic of corruption that impedes Russia's small business sectors across the country. An estimated 90% of corruption in Russia occurs at the local district level.

100 entrepreneurs were seated in circular bleachers around the central interview table. They gave input by handheld devices.

Sergei Frolov, Dmitri Kalinchuk, Igor Zyablitsev, and Mikhail Yartsev being interviewed by journalists at Moscow's International Press Center following the D.C. and Kremlin events.

Pozner answering questions on stage at the program's end. Madina Bikbulatova on left. Beside her are two alumni who later were elected to city Duma in Uryupinsk.

Pozner opened the show by quoting President Putin regarding the need to eradicate corruption throughout the country, and then began interrogating the four Fellows seated at the table. Those of us in the audience were simultaneously polled using hand-held electronic devices. Our responses showed up immediately on a background screen. The screen also displayed statistics showing that Russia's small business development lagged far behind other nations due to the country's endemic corruption.

Pozner asked the four alumni for their personal experiences with corrupt officials. Sergei Frolov described his shocking story about using Russian law to imprison the Tula region's top Fire Inspector for four years. The others spoke about destruction of their businesses by bureaucrats, and one accused Russia's entrepreneurs for offering bribes to officials to expedite services—a topic seldom spoken of by Russia's businessmen. Time whizzed by as TV audiences across Russia heard for the first time on nationwide television how corruption actually impacts their entire society. The hour program came to an end all too soon.

By the following day, friends of alumni from across Russia were calling and advising delegates not to come home, warning that everyone had seen their faces on the Sunday program. Others called congratulating them for their courage in speaking out so boldly. At least for the moment, the Fellows felt empowered by bringing media attention to this gravely inhibiting issue; most brushed off concerns of safety for themselves and their businesses.

Two-Hour Kremlin Meeting—March 29, 2004

The much-anticipated meeting at the Kremlin took place the next day. Andrei Illarionov, Russia's Minister of Economy, had previously met with another large delegation of CCI entrepreneurs in 2001. He quickly began interrogating this latest group and taking notes. One delegate after another came to the podium with critical content absorbed from ambassadors and other VIPs with whom they spoke.

After two hours of intense input from our alumni, Illarionov took the podium and thanked them for taking their time and money to collect this data in America and responded with his own personal outrage at the current situation across Russia.

During this amazing meeting, it struck me that these Russian regional entrepreneurs were interacting with one of the highest authorities in all of Russia today. They were making suggestions, listening, advising and debating the issues with Illarionov as equals. I wondered in how many countries around the world this could this be happening in 2004.

Illarionov clearly was fascinated by their reports. He urged them to build websites, become public figures, and to create associations when they returned to their regions. He assured them that he would definitely discuss their specific points with President Putin. During the final minutes, Dmitri Kalinchuk, a St. Petersburg entrepreneur, presented Illarionov with a formal copy of "35 Recommendations to the President" in a leather portfolio; it was inscribed *To President Vladimir Putin, from Russia's Regional Entrepreneurs.* Andrei Illarionov was visibly "in sync" with his informants.

We knew for sure that the 35 recommendations made it to Putin when two weeks later, the points began showing up in his addresses to the nation.

Meeting The New York Times Correspondent—April 1, 2004

Bernard (Bernie) Sucher, Moscow-based American financial expert, gave the incoming *The New York Times* Russia reporter, Erin Arvedlund, my e-mail address. We met. She told me her New York boss was interested in corruption in Russia, and she needed to find a very unusual corruption story. Sergei Frolov's case was the most dramatic one we had come across. We arranged to meet with Erin in Tula, south of Moscow, where she could capture the particulars of Frolov's fascinating case herself. She was intrigued by the idea of interviewing a Russian entrepreneur who had stood up to corrupt institutional power and won using Russian law in local courts.

We met in Tula and went to Sergei's new three-story "supermarket" for the interview. Erin appeared captivated by Sergei's story and unique court battle and left shortly thereafter for Moscow to write the article. She told me to start looking for it in *The New York Times*. I stayed in Tula to conduct additional PEP evaluations. After a week the story still hadn't come out. I e-mailed Erin, and she related that she was having trouble getting the article accepted in the New York office—but said to keep looking. I did and still no story. I e-mailed again. Finally, when I caught up with her, she reported that the article wouldn't be printed—that the New York office wanted more stories about cases like oligarch Michael Khodorkovsky.

> At that time by my estimation, the Times had already printed some 50 front-page stories regarding Khodorkovsky—all omitting key facts and rehearsing only one side of his complicated story.

> I was crestfallen! It seemed so important to get Frolov's story out to the American public, to demonstrate that there are clean Russian entrepreneurs who are radically different from Russia's oligarchs—and at least one of them was able to pursue justice against the bureaucrats and won using Russia's, albeit unstable, court system.

In frustration, I decided to write up Frolov's story for CCI's constituency—with the hope that a newspaper might ask for his contact information. It follows here:

Russian Entrepreneur Puts Regional Fire Inspector in Prison on Corruption Charges

> Sergei Frolov is a rags-to-riches young Russian whose story would excite any red-blooded American entrepreneur. Some of you met him in Texas in 2002 when he trained on a PEP supermarkets delegation hosted by Huntsville, Houston, and College Station Rotary Clubs.

> I first interviewed Sergei in his original store in late 2002. It was an old Soviet building that showed decades of hard wear. We walked up four sets of stairs looking in on each floor and found only merchandise for Russia's working class.

> On the top floor we came to an elegant door—the only one in the whole building. Entering it we were in Frolov's rather small office. Sergei had renovated the room in 19th century Russian motif. Powder blue walls with white moldings created an elegance that masked the drabness of the rest of the old Soviet structure. Inside this room, Sergei looked like an Austrian banker behind his

Sergei Frolov, son of a coal miner, began his business life selling tennis shoes on the sidewalks of Tula. He recently built the largest supermarket in the city. Sergei has the distinction of taking Tula's regional Fire Marshall to court for demanding a bribe and won his case using Russian law. The official received and served a four-year prison term.

Frolov ran for and won a seat in the regional Duma were he attempts to push civil society issues from the bottom.

Sergei was obviously excited about his groups' input as he presented their ideas at the Corruption Symposium in Washington, D.C.

Nonna Barkhatova, right, started battling 'power' years ago. She has a fierce sense of protection for Novosibirsk's entrepreneurs who support her Small Business Center and its work across the region. Following the Symposium in D.C., she organized meetings with local officials, wrote articles in newspapers, and confronted individual officials directly about their roles in corruption.

Shown with Nonna is Piotr Prodyakov from Taganrog who owns a wholesale food distribution business. Piotr is one of many PEP entrepreneurs who are committed to reduce the hold of corrupt bureaucrats on Russia's small business sector.

mahogany desk. The room's only decor was his framed CCI diploma, a small bronze Texas boot on his bookcase, and a framed photo of Russia's President. I was totally impressed with this young entrepreneur's demeanor and the contents of his store.

A year later in 2003, I set up my second interview with Sergei and other PEP alumni in this conservative, bureaucracy-stifled city. We caught a taxi to Sergei's newest "supermarket" near downtown. I was shocked when our car drove up to the brand new building! It was a huge, sky blue, mirrored-glass and gleaming metal structure with "FROLOV Trade Center" boldly placed in the center of the tall building. To my memory this was the first business we had seen in Russia that was personalized by an entrepreneur's family name. It has been an unspoken rule among Russian entrepreneurs not to flaunt their personal names as part of a company title.

Inside, the supermarket was a visual treat; shades of light blue were noted everywhere. It sported a smart information center just inside the front doors, a chic women's makeup shop straight ahead, followed with half stairs up and down that led to various levels of shopping. This was the building that almost didn't happen due to outrageous bribes. The Tula fire inspector alone wanted $50,000 just for permission to renovate the building; he later reduced it to $20,000.

Angered by this predator's demands for a bribe, Sergei made a first-ever consultation with the FSB (successor to the KGB) to learn if they would give him "cover" if he created a legal case and tried to take the Fire Inspector to court. This was an unheard of strategy for a Russian entrepreneur. The FSB replied, "This is precisely what the President wants us to do. Mark your bills, pay the bribe, and then take him to court. If you can't win in court, we will get him on marked bills." Sergei hired Kostya Ivanov, a brilliant and angry young lawyer whose private legal business had been destroyed earlier by Tula officials. The two began building the case. Sergei related that, "Swarms of municipal and regional authorities came down on my business, trying to find legal flaws on which to hang me. They threatened to drive me out of town, but my course was set. I would try to beat them with Russian law." One consequence occurred when hooded thugs broke into his home and roughed up his pregnant wife. This necessitated bodyguards for the family from thereon.

My third visit to Sergei's store in 2004 was with Erin Arvedlund, The New York Times reporter. Sergei's trial was over; his three-story, ultra-modern super market was selling everything from live plants and clothing to bathtubs and fur coats. As we strolled through different areas, Sergei explained his life to Erin, starting with his background.

This "dollar millionaire" is different from Moscow's infamous oligarchs. He was the son of a miner and a collective farm worker; Sergei was their seventh *child. He got a bit of education in engineering, dropped out to do a stint in the army, and then went back to the university. As the U.S.S.R. collapsed in the '90s, his parents became destitute, so he again dropped his education, this time to support them. He traveled to Turkey to get tennis shoes to sell on Tula's sidewalks. Later he shuttled clothing into Tula's kiosks, and next he set up a small retail store. Local mafia was ever-present, and Russia's nascent business environment had no laws on which to depend. Sergei created a one-stop-shop for products that any struggling Russian family might need. It succeeded and he continued to expand. He hired young people and trained them himself. Today his department managers look no more than 25 years old, and they give excellent customer service. Sergei recently ran for the Tula Region's Duma (Congress) and was elected.*

Following a long interview with Erin in his new pent-house office, she seemed to think his was a terrific story and took off to Moscow to write it. Volodya and I had tea in Sergei's cafeteria before departing. I became aware of a couple of well-dressed young men in business suits who were seen earlier strolling the aisles in the supermarket. Here they were again, this time having lunch across the room. Then I noted that they were quietly keeping an eye on who was coming in the door. Later as the two left the building, one hopped into the driver's seat of a parked SUV, the other followed Sergei from behind. The three of them drove away. I was reminded of the price that Sergei still pays for going against the grain of Tula's culture of official corruption.

Unfortunately, Arvedlund's article never made it into *The New York Times*.

Meeting with The Economist's Journalist—April 7, 2004

Once again Bernie Sucher connected me with a young journalist, this time from *The Economist*. His assignment was to write a major 12-page special on Russia for their May issue. We sat down for a two-hour interview in a Moscow restaurant. After he asked numerous questions, which seemed to insure getting negative responses, I stopped the interview and remarked that he was asking the wrong questions. I began to enumerate what I thought we should be asking about Russia these days. He looked puzzled, as though my list of questions was different from anything he had thought of before. His fingers raced over his little fold-out keyboard as I explained what was going on inside and outside of Moscow, along with what needed to be reported on and why.

Following my outburst, he came up with some really intelligent questions. After answering them, I launched into my pet vexation—the misinformation put out by his colleagues in key western newspapers. My passion about the subject seemed to overwhelm and confuse him. Finally, he informed me he had been in Russia for only 18 months and was now packing to go to the Middle East. He gathered up his portable keyboard, stuck it in his pocket, and raced off to another appointment. As he left, he said something like, "Well, I appreciate what you've had to say. It helps me look at things a little differently."

I mentally beat myself up for pushing this young guy farther than he wanted to go, and assumed he was just being polite to this white-haired, out-spoken grandmother. Later I got the following note from him:

"17 Apr 2004 18:47:55 +0400. 'Dear Sharon, the article won't be out until May 21. Let me know if you have trouble getting it, and I'll make sure you receive a copy. Thanks again. It was, by the way, inspiring to talk to you. It gave me a positive twist on Russia.' – Gideon Lichfield"

Before leaving for the Middle East on April 28, 2004, Gideon sent a lengthy e-mail to JRL, the daily e-list of articles on Russia that all Russia insiders scan, a quote from which follows: *"Looking at my fellow Russia-watchers, I'm reminded of a pack of male baboons in fights for territory. There are a lot of us, and we are all talking at once. To be heard we have to distinguish our voices. And to do that, we have to stake out a position and defend it aggressively as baboons do. Ironically, it is made worse by the fact that ... we, unlike most of the world, read (only) what is published in English. This is like taking all the baboons out of the jungle and putting them together in one small room to fight it out."*

I would add that when journalists are listening only to each other, rather than traveling the country as investigative reporters, they all end up missing the most critical stories that need to be reported on—and they post similar U.S.-centric sensationalized "opinions" that end up as "news" in our mainstream media. This is part of what is amiss with our Russia coverage today.

As for *The Economist's* 12-page special on Russia, it came out in May of 2004 and was balanced and in depth reporting on Russia. I questioned if *The Economist's* editors had overlooked his piece—or if Gideon risked writing a balanced piece since he was ready to leave Russia on a new assignment, and his editors let it go by.

U.S. State Department Withdraws Funds for CCI's PEP Grant—May 12, 2004

The U.S. State Department informed us early in 2004 that in all likelihood they would need to prematurely withdraw PEP's 2004/2005 funding due to needs in the Middle East. Despite everything we did and all the people in Washington with whom we spoke, nothing changed their decision. However, we had banked formerly allocated State Department funds, which could not be taken from us. State Department lawyers allowed those funds to gradually be spent down over the following two years.

Novosibirsk, the Capital of Siberia—June 23, 2004

Among other Russian cities, our mid-year 2004 evaluation trip took us to Novosibirsk. This center-of-the-country metropolis of 1.5 million citizens looked and felt like a real capital city with solidly built granite buildings, wide boulevards, lots of greenery, and everywhere evidence of private sector development. But it was a tough place. Recently the city's vice mayor was assassinated for some shady corruption deal. He was not the first, nor was he expected to be the last.

By 2004 a powerful voice had emerged in Novosibirsk to unify Siberia's grass roots entrepreneurs. Nonna Barkhotova, an entrepreneur herself, stepped onto the scene several years earlier as an organizer of local business owners. Previously, she studied small business development in England. After meeting and convincing George Soros to fund her numerous ideas, she built a Small Business Development Center (SBDC) in Novosibirsk. Later Nonna found ingenious ways to finance her vision for developing Siberia's small business sector. She began western-like monthly business luncheons with speakers, and a string of classy conferences. She scheduled monthly seminars taught by U.S. and British business consultants throughout the year. Most of her entrepreneurs participated in PEP management training in American companies.

Upon return from the Anti-Corruption Symposium held in Washington, D.C., in March, Nonna and her PEP alumni immediately went to work. They held three press conferences on corruption issues, got leading Siberian newspapers to write articles about what they had learned at the Symposium, and invited city officials to round table discussions regarding reducing corruption using the strategies that other countries have used. I sat in on one such meeting with amazement. Official bureaucrats around the table seemed cowed by this mission-driven lady's fearless passion to tackle the city's entrenched corruption.

Irkutsk: Meeting Vladimir Donskoy, Russia's Most Honored Rotarian—June 2004

Arriving in Irkutsk to conduct PEP evaluations, we were picked up at the train station by Vladimir Donskoy, the father of Rotary in Russia. He took us to our lodging in a large complex of white buildings. We soon realized we were not in a hotel! Dozens of people with white patches over one eye were walking through the halls. A plaque on the wall finally ended the mystery. We were in one of the private-public medical institutions of Dr. Svyatoslav Fedorov, Russia's world-famous eye surgeon. Later we learned that the hospital's director was a Rotarian; so we had the privilege of lodging there at the rate ordinary Russian patients pay.

Donskoy was first introduced to Rotary at the end of the 1980s. Absorbing Rotary principles like a sponge, he became fixated on spreading the concepts throughout Russia. Over the years Vladimir translated the bulk of major Rotary materials into the Russian language. Thirty-seven Rotary Clubs from the Ural Mountains to the Far East were nurtured and chartered by Vladimir during the 1990s.

Irkutsk and the Decembrists

In addition to present-day private sector influences, Irkutsk's unusual history has contributed to its openness and cultural life. In the early 1800s, Irkutsk was the gateway to one of the termination points for the famous "Decembrists," the young enlightened nobility of Russian aristocracy who were exiled to Siberia in chains for their reformist ideas. Such was the fate of aristocrats who believed that serfs should be freed, and more democratic forms of governance should be installed across Russia. This fascinating history can be found online by Googling "Russia's Decembrists."

Within a couple of years of their husbands' exiles, some of the Decembrists' wives left their families and their children in St. Petersburg. They journeyed to far away Siberia—traveling across thousands of miles of unbroken territory to get to their husbands. These sophisticated, cultured women lived in prisons with their men, even birthing babies there. Years later, the couples and their small children were allowed to leave the prisons and to settle in Irkutsk and other remote Siberian cities.

The Decembrists brought culture to the then backward regions of Siberia. They built sturdy homes within compounds, and soon began giving musical performances to local people. Some of the displaced aristocrats and their wives were quite artistic; all were instrumental in developing the classical arts locally. As a result, Irkutsk early on became a mini-hub of education and culture. One of their homes built in the 1800s is now a museum that is furnished with elegant 19th century furniture. Walls display framed sketches by the Decembrists, which depict their lives in prison cells far from the country's cultural center in St. Petersburg.

Smitten by this place, I asked my Irkutsk friends to leave me there alone for a couple of hours. There were no other persons at the compound except for a caretaker. The whole area seemed to have a familiarity, a strange air about it. After slowly walking over the grounds and pondering how life must have been for those women and their men, I sat down on a deteriorating shed porch and found myself brooding over what this nation and its people have endured since these young noblemen made their first attempts to breathe democratic principles into Russian life—and the price they all paid for being so far ahead of their time.

What is Irkutsk like today? To me it seemed to be a city of 600,000 inhabitants caught somewhere between the Decembrists, the Soviet era, and the 21st century.

Finally Getting to See Lake Baikal

Finishing evaluations with Irkutsk's PEP alumni and interviewing new PEP candidates, we departed next for Siberia's Baikal, the largest fresh water lake in the world. CCI completed a major mapping and rehabilitation project for the Baikal watershed during the '90s. This would be my first look at the region.

Lake Baikal is considered a "spiritual home" to Russian people; they claim it has some mystique about it that can't be described. And it seems so when there. As mentioned in the 1990s section, this huge body of water and basin was sacrificed to industrial development during the Soviet years. Our task under a USAID grant was to provide the model plan for rehabilitating the region. Aspects of the plan are still being implemented by different groups participating in the on-going work.

While visiting Baikal during this trip, we went native and stayed in a Buryiat village with Hank Birnbaum, a transplanted American doing forestry work in the Baikal Basin. Hank's home looked like early American pioneers' places. We picnicked at the edge of the great lake with a Buryiat couple that wanted nothing more than for their humble place on earth to be spared development and tourism and for themselves to be left alone in their austere environment. What a privilege it was to sit there and contemplate what is of value and what isn't. Soon we were off again with memories of those few days wafting in our craniums.

International Relations Still in Turmoil—August 1, 2004

Summer 2004 was rocky for Russia. The fate of Yukos Oil Company and Mikhail Khodorkovsky still dominated international news. The company most likely will splinter taking down Russia's most highly publicized business in the West. Putin, in typical Russian style, hasn't bothered to answer his accusers; he simply moved forward, apparently doing what, in his mind, needed to be done next.

Concurrently, he began the drumbeat for drastic reforms in several spheres: banking, military, the bloated administrative apparatus, and the social sphere. These reforms are sure to cause problems. Some go straight to the heart of Russia's privileged class—and oddly enough, even the opposite end of the population, Russia's pensioners.

Soviet "holdover benefits" (free transport and many other services for veterans and the elderly) are at stake—this has produced street demonstrations among the elderly across Russia. These are considered to be "rights" by the electorate. It was reported this year that over 50 percent of Russia's population still receives some form of monetary payments from the new Russian government. These payments were put in place during the communist era—they constitute a serious drawback to the new country and the development of a real private sector.

Will these reforms backfire or work with the population? As far as Russia's masses go, some of Putin's initiatives in the past have appeared to backfire, but eventually they paid off. Russian people are living better, and Russia's economy is growing. Even in remote regions, people are beginning to feel that they have a future, which is their litmus test. Russians in the streets understand that difficult decisions have to be made in order to go forward. Amazingly the polls continue to show 70 percent approval ratings for Putin.

The West, with its totally different history and democratic standards, doesn't understand the multitude of challenges that must be dealt with if Russia is to work toward becoming a stable country.

Putin's tasks over the next four years are enormous. Somehow he must push reforms forward, deal with the political fall-out caused by them, and reduce the gaping chasm between Russia's "haves" and "have nots." More than 40 million Russians (30 percent of the population) still live below the poverty line—while Russia's multi-billionaires travel the world, spending their enormous and ill-gotten wealth from Russia's natural resource base. This egregious dichotomy has yet to be resolved.

I believe by 2015, we will look back and see that this rocky period in Russia's evolution had to take place—and that the challenges being worked through today, will be seen to have been steps in the right direction.

To those who are critical of Putin, my question is, "If not Putin, who?" Who else could take on these immense transitional tasks and hope to come out with a Russia on her feet? I see no one in Russia today who could come close to winning an election, let alone tackle these intrinsic challenges. And the next question is, "Is there any precedent in the history of the world that shows how a formerly autocratic, out-of-control, mammoth nation can use only top-of-the-line democratic methodologies to achieve a 180-degree redirection within a 20-year period?" If so, let's get the model to Russia for duplication. If not, let's give Russia some slack and the time to carry out this first-ever agonizing experiment.

I wonder if Putin and his few trusted colleagues have looked squarely at the chessboard on which they are forced to play and have opted to take calculated risks where they see few choices. Is their gamble that, with tough moves over the next few years, the country may get across to the other side of the board where Russia can then ease controls and increase the democratizing process? I personally suspect this is their underlying strategy. However, it defies conventional Western thinking.

Our Locked in Beliefs May Surprise Us in a Few Years

Between 1985 and 1995, totally unexpected scenarios occurred in the U.S.S.R. and Russia—all of which have defied the West's best predictions. These should give us pause to question our predictions of today.

For instance, in 1980 who would have predicted that:

- a communist leader would ascend to power and start glasnost and perestroika in 1985,
- Soviets would be free to travel abroad as they wished before 1990,
- the Berlin Wall would fall before 1990,
- there would be a mass exodus of Jews by 1990,
- the U.S.S.R. would collapse under its own weight by 1991, and that
- the Putsch (attempted coup) in August of 1991 would self-destruct in less than a week?

The West's locked in beliefs in 1980 about what was possible regarding the U.S.S.R. didn't materialize. So what is a circumspect stance for Western bystanders, in face of what is transpiring across Russia today? It seems wise to make room for unexpected changes and to recall how many decades it took the U.S. to achieve a balanced and fair democracy. We need to back off and be patient with today's Russia—which is in rapid transition.

Russia Grieves Once More: Beslan School Tragedy—September 1, 2004

The news of the Beslan School tragedy first reached my ears during a 7:00 AM Rotary Club meeting in Westminster, Colorado, where I was the speaker for the morning. The young Rotarian giving the invocation asked special blessings for the children hostages in Beslan, Russia. I was on pins and needles waiting for the invocation to be over. The news was unimaginable: 1,100 school children and teachers were taken hostage by Chechen terrorists on the first day of their academic school year. (Over the next three days, 338 of them would be killed in explosions and fire.) I sent an immediate e-mail of condolences to our friends across Russia. My pre-planned trip deposited me in St. Petersburg the next Saturday. I wrote the following e-mail the first day after I arrived.

The grief here in St. Petersburg is palpable. There are small and large memorials on the sidewalks. Yesterday I took a six-block walk from my home. In that short space, there were two small, obviously citizen-initiated altars that I passed—one in front of a local TV store and another in the front of a small business. Russian people, a thousand miles away from this disaster, had simply put out small tables, draped them with simple fabric, added newspaper photos of Beslan children, lighted candles, and put flowers on the homemade altars. Passersby added more flowers. Blossoms were spilling over to the sidewalk by the time I came along. From Russian teenagers to grandparents, people were standing in front of these little alters in silence, some dabbing away tears. No words, no organizers ... just ordinary people grieving.

If this is taking place within a six-block range of my home, what is going on in other cities across this nation? My morning e-mail revealed that some of our Russian friends are traveling hundreds of miles to be with their families to mourn this tragedy together. Others mention that potential terrorists live throughout their cities.

In the U.S. we had one horrific terrorist attack on New York and Washington, D.C.—it shook every American to the core. Here in Russia there have been dozens of serious terrorist attacks on metros, apartment buildings, theaters, airplanes, and trains. No one feels safe taking public transport, going to sleep in their flats, attending performances, traveling by air or rail—and now sending their children to public schools.

As an onlooker of this day, I recall with deep empathy that Russians obviously know well how to grieve; they have had lots of experience at it. Their 20th century was full of unrelenting grief and mourning: millions of family members were whisked away at night to gulags before being exterminated—families couldn't mourn openly for fear of incurring the same fate; then over 26,000,000 of their own died in WWII, not to mention deaths in other sieges, wars, earthquakes, Chernobyl … and now from terrorists within their own country. What Russians can't fathom about Beslan is that the terrorists targeted innocent children; this is a first-ever for their country. In face of such tragedy, Russians don't appear to think about "getting even." They just internalize the losses and mourn. Paranoia exists in this country with good reason.

Post-Beslan Response from Western Pundits

American mainstream media used the Beslan events to disparage Putin, Russia's police and military, and the entire operation. Surely Russians were doing the best they could under the circumstances. I pause to remember how Russia and President Putin responded to our events of 9/11. Russia was the first country to send deeply-felt condolences to President Bush and the American people, they created altars on their streets and in front of the American Embassy—they mourned with us without analyzing causes and circumstances or assessing blame.

Year 2004 ended as it started—with accusations and hyperbole in American media surrounding anything happening throughout Russia. For me, a citizen diplomat, it remains intolerable to see the diplomacy of the '80s and '90s going down the drain of history.

End-of-Year Note to Constituents—December 31, 2004

Dear Volunteers, thanks to you, this has been a transforming year for many Russian entrepreneurs across Russia's time zones. You took these young business owners into your companies, communities, civic clubs, and homes. You trained them and exposed them to a radically different way of organizing business and community life. You shared them with your friends and colleagues. This created goodwill between the two countries during a year in which it was sorely needed.

CCI heads into a crucial turning point in 2005. The State Department funds we had saved for a rainy day are being used up more quickly than we anticipated. We are slashing expenses, shrinking space, and reducing staff and salaries. Russian participants are paying ever-higher fees for training.

If Russia was more stable and relations between our two countries were proceeding normally, it would be another matter—we would declare victory and let PEP fade into history. But 2004 has been an extremely tense year between these two nations, and PEP is one of the few remaining open doors for these countries, so we must continue.

Thank you so very much for your many contributions to our common goal for a safer world. We wish you a wonderful New Year!"

$\mathcal{Y}$ear 2005

Stereotypes at a Holiday Luncheon—January 2, 2005

I sat at a post-holiday dinner with a large group of family members and some new acquaintances in Bend, Oregon. At my end of the table, the discussion turned to my work in Russia. Responses were stereotypical. "Is Putin turning into a Joe Stalin?" "So Russia is going backwards again." I listened and finally commented that western media seriously misrepresents Russia's reality today.

The day before, a long "special" about alcoholism in Russia's villages was on the front page of this small town's newspaper. A family member reported seeing it in the Portland paper a few days earlier.

I was reminded of how fast such articles travel these days. First *The New York Times* or the *Wall Street Journal* prints the piece, then state capital newspapers pick it up, and finally third and fourth-tier small town newspapers around America print it. The same story, most likely written by a young reporter who never got out of Moscow, has circulated throughout the U.S. leaving its residue of suspicion and sordidness throughout the whole of our population.

As for Russia, of course, there is alcoholism in their villages. These are the rural people who haven't been able to figure out how to survive without cradle to grave socialism. There is alcoholism in Russian cities for that matter; but to circulate this oppressive piece as a holiday story across America, is a strange twist of journalism, particularly when constructive change going on in Russia never gets mentioned.

Later I left Bend in a possible snowstorm and got near Mt. Shasta before being turned back by state troopers. Checking into a local motel, a chatty owner inquired what I did for a living. When I mentioned working in Russia, his face turned grim and he retorted, "Russia's going backward again; Putin has his KGB pin back on!"

Pertinent questions come up for me: Do we in America need to have an enemy? Do we need to put other countries down in order to feel good about ourselves? David Fogelsong, A Rutgers historian, chronicles America's 130-year history with Russia in a recent book, *The American Mission and the "Evil Empire" with a subtitle: the Crusade for a "Free Russia" since 1881*. Why has Russia become our "shadow" in psychological terms?

What will happen if America, the U.K., and Europe blackball Russia? As with any country, Russia must have allies and trading partners to survive. If denied relations with the West, Russia will be forced into less desirable options with countries such as China, Iran, and North Korea—which will be far from our national security interests.

Rotary District Conference #5160 in Ashland, Oregon—April 2, 2005

District Governor Susan Wait requested that I keynote her large District's celebration in Ashland. Leaving Russia the day before, I arrived to find Rotarians already displaying their accomplishments of the passing year. Scores of booths showed evidences of humanitarian projects around the world that this District alone had accomplished during the past ten months. Over 500 Rotarians were gathered to celebrate these happenings.

I have become increasingly aware of how well suited Rotary's principles, philosophy, and activities are for Russia as it continues to grow a private sector to replace the top down communist mentality. My keynote remarks lauded the district clubs for their exemplary participation in CCI's PEP program and explained why Rotary is so important for Russia today:

- Rotary provides a safe space for strangers to meet and to begin to build trust with each other.
- Rotary provides leadership mentoring for local men and women.
- New presidents and officers are voted in annually, thus no one stays in power for long terms. This prevents hierarchical leadership from forming.
- Rotary promotes individual responsibility and volunteerism.
- Rotary is based on ethical principles to guide personal and organizational decision-making.
- Rotary's Four-Way Test is a trusted code of ethics for all aspects of life.
- Rotarians respect diversity and honor all ethnic groups and nationalities.
- Rotary requires group service to disadvantaged populations, locally and internationally.
- Rotary is an international body of 1.2 million professional people throughout approximately 200 countries. They welcome fellow Rotarians when visiting their cities. This is an enormous benefit for Russians who travel abroad today after having been cut off from international contacts for much of their history.

A First! Three PEP Delegations Simultaneously—April 2005

PEP enthusiast Allen Kerr of Columbus, Georgia, sent us a request to host three PEP delegations simultaneously in April of 2005. At the time Allen was 80 years young, but he exhibited the energy and enthusiasm of a 30-year-old. Three PEP delegations had not been attempted before, but we knew he could round up the business trainers, volunteers, and home hosts from his large base of Georgian Rotarians—and he did! I flew down to Columbus to witness these triplet delegations on ground. It was exciting, and it appeared that most of Columbus' citizens were involved. They trained separately in different industry sectors but came together for large functions. It went amazingly well. Allen sent the following note shortly after putting the three delegations on the plane headed back to Moscow.

> *"In my wildest flight of fantasy I don't believe I could have asked for a better or more satisfying PEP experience than the one we just completed here in Columbus. When the three PEP delegations departed Columbus this past Sunday morning, a big crowd of enthusiastic well-wishers gathered to see them off!"*

I immediately left Georgia for Russia to do PEP's 2005 evaluations. During 2004, CCI brought the largest volume of PEP entrepreneurs ever to American cities, thereby providing a "bumper crop" of new alumni to interview.

Tales Among the PEP Mid-Year Evaluations
PEP Encounter on a Russian Train—June 15, 2005

We had just completed evaluations in Volodga in Northwest Russia. The dining car from Vologda to St. Petersburg had no vacant tables. I asked a young Russian awaiting his meal if Volodya and I might share a table with him. He agreed, registering no particular interest or opposition. After a few minutes, I decided to try to involve this young man in citizen-to-citizen chat. Apologizing for my poor Russian, I introduced Volodya and myself and asked his name. He said it was Alexander Perfiliev. "Are you going home to St. Petersburg?" I asked. He replied that he wasn't, and that he was from Vologda and would be visiting St. Petersburg and two other Russian cities.

I inquired what kind of business he was in. He said that he owned an insurance business and then modestly revealed that his company had new partners in Kazan and Voronezh. Excusing his poor English skills, Alexander said he wanted to practice his new language. He broke into halting English and explained with a big smile that he trained in Springfield, Illinois, last year where he had an opportunity to learn "U.S. big experience" in the insurance industry.

"Do you remember what program you were in?" "No." he responded, "Maybe I can remember; let me think … something like Center for Initiatives by Citizens?" Volodya broke out in an uncharacteristically loud chuckle. Our new table mate instantly looked confused. Volodya quickly explained who we were and what we were doing on the train.

Alexander was completely undone. He broke out in smiles, laughter, arm movements, hands over eyes, several "No's! "Couldn't be! Impossible! My friends from internship won't believe me if I tell I've met you!" I kept quiet enjoying the scene and waiting for Alexander to settle down so I could do a short PEP evaluation. Somehow or another, we had missed contacting him for evaluations while in Vologda. I began asking questions and Volodya sprinted off to get my computer.

A cascade of exclamations rolled out from Alexander—his gratitude to CCI, his overwhelming thanks for his CCI facilitator and interpreter, respect for American people, his love for Larry Miller (the local insurance executive who arranged insurance training sites for Alexander's delegation), admiration for Rotary concepts, a new depth of understanding of the philosophy of insurance, and on and on and on. I began taking notes on a paper napkin while Volodya fetched my computer.

With Volodya interpreting, Alexander dispensed with English and continued excitedly in his native Russian language. "American people are very friendly, so wonderful, and so helpful. We learned absolutely new techniques we could never get in Russia. Previously, we all had traveled to Moscow to get lectures, but these classes were taught by Russian trainers—one needs to see, hear and "feel" these things in their own context. It was so important to go to the U.S. and to be in the middle of big experience to understand how insurance works in real time. Now I have new partnership with Kazan delegate from my delegation (Kazan is 2000 kilometers from Vologda) and also partnership with a delegate from Voronezh. All of us delegates are now in close touch—we telephone and advise each other."

He continued, "Russia's insurance experience has been wild. Earlier there were 5,000 insurance companies in Russia, nobody understanding what they were doing. Now it is more stable—about 1,500 insurance companies survived across Russia. Being in Springfield was like a gulp of fresh air for us. Our fears were dispelled, our hopes confirmed, and we could see that insurance is a legitimate business. We saw paperless insurance companies for the first time. We had heard of them, but didn't believe it was so. Then we saw them in Springfield, and now we begin to implement "paperless concept" into our Russian companies! We learned that all documents for insurance in U.S. are standardized. This allows the building of large insurance networks. In Russia each company has different documents, which hampers the development of networks that are very needed for success. We also began to understand the use of agents in America and how they can work with several insurance companies. This is very important for us in Russia. We don't have any of this experience. Nobody here is qualified. Someone must go outside the country, get the experience, and bring it back in to others. I must get more of this experience. Can you help me get back to U.S. for a month of study when my English is better?"

Leaving Alexander and Volodya to continue their talks, I wandered off down the rather bumpy corridor to my berth for the night.

Arrested in St. Petersburg—September 18, 2005

After moving around western Russia, we came back to St. Petersburg for the next round of evaluations. I went to bed early to get a good night's sleep before another long day of interviews. A rap came at my door at about 11:00 PM. By this time of night, I'm the only inhabitant in this three-story building, except for the old guard who sleeps downstairs.

I became wary when the rapper didn't answer my query from behind my locked door. "Who's there?" I asked again. No answer. And again I inquired. Finally a voice that sounded recognizable said, "Sharon?" Thinking it probably was the old guard, I opened the door onto the black hallway. By light from my apartment, I saw two dark figures in uniforms. They flipped open ID holders showing their photos for identification. I stood staring at these guys, wondering why on earth they were at my door in the middle of the night!

After examining my passport, they instructed me to get dressed and come with them to the militia station. Having heard stories of Russian thugs in police uniforms, I had no intention of going anywhere with them. Further, they spoke no English, and my Russian wasn't good enough for me to be certain I wasn't walking into a trap. Our noisy verbal exchange brought the house guard up the stairs. He quickly called Volodya and the director of the art school in which my small apartment was located. By 1:00 AM a sizable group of Russian friends had arrived. They advised me to stay behind my door and go to bed. I locked myself in and went to sleep.

At 7:30 AM Volodya knocked on the door reporting that the militia had "guarded" me since I locked my door. They and my friends had stayed up the entire night sitting in hard backed children's chairs down on the first floor! The militia men were now insisting that we go to the station. First, I wanted to get in touch with the U.S. Consulate. By 8:30 AM the Consulate representative returned my call. After listening to my story he informed me that I was not in compliance with a new Russian law, so I must go to the station. Dressed in professional attire, I took off for another "first" experience in Russia.

What law had I broken? For 14 years when in Petersburg, I had lived at 34 Fontanka Embankment on one of the city's many canals. My apartment is located in a non-profit art school. The building wasn't designated as a residential building, but during the '90s there were no laws, so it had made no difference where foreigners lived. After the Moscow apartment bombings by terrorists and the Beslan attack last year, Putin began to put more laws in place to try to deter terrorists from roaming freely in Russian cities. The law for foreigners living in unregistered properties had become a newspaper topic. But for some reason, I just didn't think it would apply to me. Obviously, my luck had run out. Different scenarios flipped through my mind as we sped through Petersburg streets en route to the Chekhov Militia Station.

Entering the aging building, a ruckus was underway. The bulldog sergeant in charge was barking orders at everyone in sight. We passed three small iron-grilled, pad-locked cells (one occupied). Volodya was allowed in my cell as my interpreter. He was already fading from being up all night. Our tiny room was open on two sides with bars, and was empty except for a small pocked table and three half-broken chairs. The entire CCI entourage of Russian friends planted themselves firmly at the station as though they belonged there. Occasionally they popped their heads around the corner, making excuses to come in and out of the holding area around the sergeant's desk where we were visible—they were letting it be known that they were "watching." Their cell phones were ringing incessantly; they had alerted myriads of PEP Fellows in other cities who were calling back and forth with recommendations and cautions.

Rumors were rampant. "Factions in Russia are trying to embarrass President Putin during his trip to the U.S." "Someone upstairs in the FSB is trying to intimidate Sharon because of CCI's Anti-Corruption program." "You will surely be deported from Russia by tomorrow." "Kommersant (Russia's business newspaper) is ready to cover the story, which will automatically jump to U.S. media in New York." Dismissing all of these rumors, I forbade any newspaper involvement. My instinct was to be honest and open, maintain goodwill, and take my chances. Deportation was the worst I could think of— but instinctively, it just didn't make sense that this would happen.

Morning came and went, each hour dragging into the next. Bullpen voices lessened in volume by noontime. CCI "watchers" sent in a sack of grapes and apples that we gratefully devoured. We returned to waiting. A rumor circulated that a court hearing might possibly happen before 6:00 PM. All hopes were quashed by 5:30 PM since time was running out. Were we to sit in these same broken chairs and lay our heads on this pocked table all night? What kinds of criminals would be jailed during the night shift? Volodya caught bits of conversations about new corpses being brought in and not enough workers to guard them until forensic specialists arrived. There were also complaints between workers about low wages and long working hours. Around 6:00 PM a rumor circulated that two plainclothes FSB men had just come into the station. As we awaited the outcome, we overheard that two other Americans were being deported from St. Petersburg this evening—one for some sort of crime, the other for mental illness.

Meeting the FSB at the Jail

Half an hour after the plainclothesmen arrived, we were requested to come to the second floor of the station. The hall and stairwell looked foreboding and very Soviet. At the end of the corridor, we entered the office of the chief of the militia station. A framed photo of President Putin hung on the wall behind his desk. In front of us stood two men looking for the world like young American guys—one in modish blue dress shirt and khaki slacks, the other in a handsome red ski vest. After shaking hands I commented that it was good to meet people from their agency. They looked rather curious. I explained that their colleagues in other cities have come to CCI offices across Russia to get information about our work; and that I prefer to speak directly to them, thus avoiding second-hand information. The casual attitude seemed to break the ice. From then on, we dealt openly about my non-compliance with the latest Russian law.

The lead FSB fellow in the red vest, Ilya, first asked if I had any "claims" against the militia or them. It seemed strange! I thought it just the reverse; the militia had claims against me. I admitted to decent care and attention to my rights as a foreigner. Ilya offered that the Russian side didn't want any public attention around my case but emphasized that I had broken three Russian Federation laws: 1) living in a school, not a residential building; 2) no proper registration (which I thought I had); and 3) refusing to heed the request to come to militia station last night. As for the latter, I told that they should surely understand. "I'm a lone woman, in a dark hall at midnight, and two men appear who I've never seen before, and I'd had no contact with my Consulate. Furthermore, no criminal law had been broken." I explained that to be awakened in the middle of night felt to me like "Russia during the gulag days!" With this, both young men instantly looked startled—as though they had never considered how this experience might feel to a foreign woman. I ended with, "No woman in her right mind would go out alone at midnight with unknown men dressed up in uniforms!"

With a look of shock and frustration, they both agreed—but said that nonetheless, Russian law had been broken, and there had to be some sort of penalty. I offered that perhaps CCI's work in behalf of Russia would be taken into consideration. Opening my computer in the chief's office, I began a slide presentation about CCI's programs across Russia. They were astonished. After about ten minutes, the head fellow said soberly, "By all means, we see these years of work for our country—we hope nothing has happened today that you will hold against us or against Russia."

Edvard then inquired with abject puzzlement, "We understand that you own property here in Petersburg. Something we don't understand is why have you not registered yourself at your own property?" I explained that my property was under renovation and not livable. He replied that it made no difference; I could still be registered at my property and stay any place I wished in Petersburg.

A short time earlier, a Russian attorney declared to me that it was impossible to register one's residence before renovation of property was completed. This is one of a thousand examples where Russian citizens, even their specialists, cannot keep up with their own laws. Russian laws have been written, revised, and updated so frequently over the past 10 years that even legal experts can't stay current with the changes.

Finally, Ilya offered their FSB phone number and e-mail address saying that if questions arise in the future about Russian laws, to call and that they would save me from a lot of problems. He explained my case would go to court Monday, September 19, 2004. The fine would be 1,000 rubles (about $35), which could be paid within 30 days at any one of the local Cberbanks around town.

This saga is the latest of hundreds of normal-to-bizarre human encounters experienced over the years. These kinds of events have been used to experiment with a conviction that an attitude of openness and goodwill will produce the best outcome possible; and conversely, an attitude of superiority, anger, or blame will result in the least favorable outcome. Once again, the experiment was yielding good results.

A Citizen Diplomat's Day in Court—September 19, 2005

The court day started out dark, windy, and rainy. We were instructed to show up at the Chekhov Militia Station at 11:00 AM. A chunky young man in full uniform was waiting outside to escort me to court. Some blocks away, we entered a weathered old 19th century building, passed through a metal detector and walked up marble steps to the second floor. The building appeared to have been renovated recently, but the architecture looked as if it had been built to be a courthouse from the beginning.

Several cases were ahead of mine. We sat on very hard wooden benches for a couple of hours. Occasionally, a pleasantly full-bodied young woman in an attractive olive pantsuit and high heels came out from a set of double doors to make an inquiry. She lent considerable contrast to the 150-year-old surroundings. My volunteer lawyer friends were doing what lawyers everywhere do. They wanted to "win" by constructing a series of fabrications to tell the judge about my situation. But this was not in keeping with my experiment. After much persuasion, they agreed to play it straight. At last we were invited down the long carpeted hall and through tall stately court doors. The courtroom was furnished with three high-back, black chairs over which hung the red and gold Russian Federation coat of arms. Below was Russia's red, white, and blue flag.

To my utter surprise, in the middle black chair sat the young woman who was previously in the olive pantsuit. Now she wore a black judge's robe. Looking professional and in charge, she began the proceedings. She questioned my PEP lawyer carefully and then asked me several questions. With facts in hand, she excused herself to deliberate, leaving us to continue sitting on the hard benches. Quite a long time later, she returned to her chair, asked more questions, and then retired to deliberate again, all with the seriousness of high court. Again, we sat for what seemed like an interminable period of time.

At last she came out with official papers in hand—a computer-generated document she apparently had inputted herself since there was no clerk around. She read the entire circumstances of my case, what had been submitted as evidence, and her final deliberations.

She announced quite seriously that the verdict was the following: there was insufficient evidence to convict me of any charge, and the case was to be dropped with no further investigation. Her official reasoning was that the registration paper in my passport (arranged by our CCI director) from a "local service" that I thought to be legitimate, was not. Unknown to me and our CCI director, Olga Chubarova, who purchased the registration, it turned out to be a fictitious agency at an address that didn't exist! Court dismissed.

I walked up to the young woman, now out of her black robe, and asked for a photo with her. She seemed delighted. She asked about the art school in which I had lived for years and offered winsomely that she was searching for an art school for her seven-year-old daughter and inquired if she could come by Fontanka for an enrollment interview. We gave her instructions to the school.

It felt like a series of concentric circles had somehow come together in a completely unexpected manner; I left the courtroom exhilarated with the outcome.

For follow-up, I invited the FSB fellows over to my unsanctioned Fontanka apartment the next day for lunch to see the rest of CCI's Powerpoint. They came and seemed truly surprised to meet people who do this kind of work in their country.

Outrage over Russia's New NGO Legislation—October 2005

Meanwhile internationally, another U.S.-Russia row was exploding. Putin was leading the drive to create new laws to regulate Russia's scrappy nonprofit sector, particularly the foreign NGOs (non-governmental organizations), which had been educating Russian people on "opposition politics," democracy issues, and other activities that had begun to make Russians suspicious of them. The thorny subject turned into another platform for the Western press to disparage Russia for "clamping down on democracy"—this latest accusation would dominate hundreds of front-page articles over the next year or two.

Throughout 2005, delegations of Russian entrepreneurs were coming every month for training in American companies. During their visits, they were treated like family members in American homes. Despite the media barrage of suspicion and cynicism, when real people from the two countries came together, a certain magic was predictable. Not to say that all was perfect. On occasion a challenging personality got through our selection screens on both sides; but on the whole, the gratitude and goodwill created in our little PEP world kept us buoyed up when political circumstances were seemingly more out of control than ever.

As 2005 came to an end amid frustration, I wrote an article about the U.S.-Russia NGO flap that was raging and hoped it would be picked up by Reuters and other news sources. It was destined to get some attention in 2006.

Year 2006

Fort Worth Star-Telegram
Publisher J. R. Labbe
By Sharon Tennison
Printed: January 1, 2006

Reining in Russia's NGOs

Alarmist headlines abound in American newspapers as President Vladimir Putin prepares to sign a new bill to govern Russia's non-profit or non-governmental organizations (NGOs), as well as foreign NGO's operating on the territory of the Russian Federation.

As Russian authorities are accustomed to doing, they have offered few explanations regarding the need for this legislation. Russia's new non-profit organizations are vehemently opposed to any tampering with their usual way of governing themselves. Heated debates are occurring on Russian TV with Putin's harshest critics participating.

Is the NGO bill healthy or harmful for Russia? It could cut either way; it won't become obvious until implementation begins. Meanwhile, there are good and bad NGOs in Russia—both domestic and foreign. Regrettably, some of the latter have supported activities that are illegal in America today.

In 1938 the United States found it necessary to restrict foreigners whose intentions were to sway public opinion and policy in America. The Foreign Agents Registration Act

(FARA) was Congress' response to the large number of German propaganda agents who were active in pre-World War II America. Our FARA legislation was updated as recently as 1995.

Like the United States, Russia is undeniably interested in limiting foreign influence in its domestic politics. Although their fears are discounted by the West, Putin and many Russians harbor deep concern that foreign and domestic NGOs may be fomenting a "color revolution" in Russia, as they suspect happened recently in the new states of Ukraine and Georgia.

The Kremlin is further challenged by Russia's wealthy exiled oligarchs who have funneled a great deal of money to Russia's NGOs in order to destabilize the Putin government. To date, laws like FARA don't exist in Russia.

In most countries, NGOs rely primarily on philanthropy from their own citizens; hence, their activities reflect the will of their own people. This is not so in Russia. Foreign and oligarch support in Russia has led to NGOs' pursuing objectives contrary to those of the average Russian citizen and to the stability of the fragile new government. This wouldn't go down well in any country.

To align NGO activities with citizens' interests, the Putin administration needs to legislate tax incentives to encourage Russian support for Russia's NGOs, thereby creating a base for in-country private donations, not foreign or oligarch funding.

Russia's not-for-profit sector is in serious need of regulation. It still hasn't developed the legal underpinnings to assure transparency of expenditures, operations or funder information—all of which are crucial for societal trust and civil society development.

Russia is inching toward a democratic society, but it isn't close yet. The country's long history and harsh conditioning cannot be radically transformed in two short decades. Pushing Russian society and the Putin government faster than they can go at this juncture will incur consequences that serve neither Russia nor the West. Lecturing Russia to move farther and faster than they can will only backfire on us—and them.

I was somewhat mollified that my article was printed in the Fort Worth *Star-Telegram*. Even for experts in the Russia field, it has been near to impossible to get an article in mainstream media if it takes a position different from current editorial policies.

Saving our Huge PEP Program

Year 2006 started with our revising PEP business training modules and materials to attract owners of larger Russian businesses who could afford to pay for U.S. training for their top managers. Jim Aneff, PEP's National Field Coordinator, developed a plan to entice a nationwide team of American volunteer recruiters to replace paid CCI staff whom we could no longer afford to keep on payroll. Meanwhile Rotarians and Kiwanians across America prepared for the PEP 2006 season with gusto.

A Russian Hero is Given U.N. Award for Averting
Nuclear War in 1983—January 16, 2006

Today the United Nations in New York City presented the "World Citizen Award" to a retired Russian colonel. Stanislav Petrov was honored as the "Man Who Averted Nuclear War" on September 26, 1983, (during the time our first travelers were in the

U.S.S.R.). He made a heroic decision on that day that prevented a nuclear war, which could have destroyed the United States, the U.S.S.R., and the entire planet.

Petrov was in charge at Russia's main nuclear command center when the alarm system's warnings went off, indicating a nuclear missile attack launched by the United States. With sirens wailing and his console flashing MISSILE ATTACK and START, Petrov was in shock. "START" was his instruction to launch 5,000 Soviet missiles to obliterate America cities.

The Soviet procedure manual demanded that he immediately notify his superiors of the attack. Petrov disobeyed. For almost five minutes, while holding the hotline phone in one hand and his intercom in the other, he barked orders to personnel to get back to their desks. Summoning up his firmest voice, he called his Kremlin liaison officers and reported that it was a false alarm.

Today he admits, "I wasn't 100 percent sure. Not even close to 100 percent." Unknown to Petrov, a new and unproven Soviet satellite system had picked up a flash in Montana near a Minuteman II silo. Five other flashes followed. It did appear that the Soviet Union was in imminent danger.

It was later determined that sunlight reflecting off of clouds in Montana had caused a faulty satellite computer assembly to report a missile launch flash.

Upon clarification of this event, Petrov was discharged from his duties for not following official orders—but meanwhile he had saved the world from nuclear annihilation. Petrov had never been acknowledged in the U.S.S.R., Russia, or the U.S. for his planet-saving decision in 1983. Today at the United Nations in New York in a small and unpretentious ceremony, Petrov was finally vindicated and honored. This elderly gentleman now lives a simple life outside of Moscow.

Council on Foreign Relations Task Force Report on Russia—March 26, 2006

The long-awaited official Council on Foreign Relations Report on Russia, overseen by former Senators John Edwards and Jack Kemp, was delivered to the public today. It is entitled "Russia's Wrong Direction—What the U.S. Can and Should Do."

As feared by those of us at CCI, the report turned out to be a disparaging 97-page document written to affirm the superiority of the United States and to blame Russia for its current deficiencies and direction. It concluded saying that "Russia's cooperation with the U.S. is central to achieving America's interests,"—as though Russia has no economic and strategic interests of its own. This tome landed like a bomb in the middle of U.S.-Russia relations. See the CFR Report: www.cfr.org/publication/9997.

PEP Evaluations and Vignettes—Mid-year 2006
Kazan, Tatarstan Autonomous Region—June 7, 2006

I traveled to Kazan, a lovely 1000-year-old Russian city east of Moscow, to conduct evaluations and to attend the PEP Fellows' tenth anniversary in this city. A collection of 160 Kazan PEP alumni known as "The Golden Heart Society" held a conference that featured how to become socially responsible business people.

We drove up to the Kazan Business Center, a lovely new structure of light stone and polished granite. An eager journalist on the sidewalk rushed up with a question, "How does a socially-responsible business operate in the U.S.?" While the question was still being answered, organizers ushered us inside. The large meeting room was elegant. Men and women in professional attire packed the seats.

I was seated at the presidium table with Tatarstan's Deputy Prime Minister, Mr. Ramonov. He spoke passionately about the necessity of government and business to join hands to help with the many dire human situations across Tatarstan. Among other questions he posed was, "How can we create a more socially-responsible business sector in Kazan?" I tried to sum up the history of America's socially responsible business experience, hoping it might offer a model for Ramonov and Kazan's entrepreneurs.

It felt so good to see these U.S.-trained entrepreneurs and their city leaders asking the right questions for their entire society and struggling to come up with good answers. I already knew of numbers of Kazan business owners who had taken on chunks of socially responsible activities outside of their business lives—so the climate was fertile for new initiatives.

Yaroslavl—June 11, 2006

Yaroslavl is another thousand-year-old city north of Moscow. The back road route to get there felt like moving through Russia's long history; dense forests, ancient churches, small wooden villages, deserted "one-industry" towns that were built and then vacated by Soviet power, and, in between, small towns with outlying communities of new red brick homes—more evidence of "middle class" development.

Seven PEP Fellows met us in an elegant Yaroslavl restaurant in the middle of downtown. High-end furniture, classical music, and exquisite food began a remarkable evening. We must have been treated to the most lavish eatery in the city. Discussion followed as one PEP story after another tumbled out revealing the impact that American training and home-stays had made on the lives of these alumni.

My trusty laptop captured their words. Slava Kuzmin held up his glass and said, "Although this PEP experience for my business was truly great, I want to say that the most important part for me was living in the home of Jack and Karen in Kansas City. It was in their home that I learned about the heart of America, and I started to understand your great and ordinary American people, and I began to feel that Americans are our friends. They were so open to us … so kind … and so warm. It was the most important thing about PEP for me." I had hoped to get into political and economic discussions, but Yaroslavl Fellows' priority was to revel once again in their stories about their U.S. training and new American friends in their host cities.

Yaroslavl's YMCA

Pat Dowden and I entered a gate that led into a scrubby yard of small industrial buildings. Earlier, she had been helpful in making connections between her Philadelphia YMCA and a middle-aged Russian who interned there.

A nondescript sign on one wall said YMKA. Inside the door we found a Russian version of America's YMCA. The founder, Nicolai Kurochkin, who interned at Philadelphia's YMCA, greeted us—this institution was his brainchild. Inside the premises, we found a community center comprised of a large room for group meetings, a non-alcohol bar, pool table, fitness center with equipment and mirrored walls, photography room, small rooms for family consultations and a sleep-over room for out-of-town guests. Finally, we came to a tiny YMCA office for personnel, most of whom were volunteers. They shared with us a computerized presentation showing their accomplishments and plans for future directions. Even though Yaroslavl is a third tier Russian city, Nicolai has become the

All-Russia coordinator for YMCA International. His center is operating pretty much like startup YMCAs around the world—again, more evidence of civil society development in Russia's outlying areas, which didn't exist a few years ago.

Rybinsk, Russia—June 13, 2006

A gray SUV arrived in Yaroslavl to transport us to Rybinsk where two PEP alumni businessmen manufacture "valves" for huge oil pipelines. Anatoly Chistiakov, the general director of Fobos, Inc. (PEP 2004, Alexandria, Minnesota) and Alexander Ivanov, Fobos' commercial director (PEP 2001, Midland, Montana; Pleasant and Saginaw, Michigan), have been partners since the company's inception in 1995.

Rybinsk, with a population of 250,000, is off the beaten path in Russia. In the 1800s, this town was the gateway to the Volga River route to St. Petersburg. The famed Ilya Repin painting, "The Volga Boatmen," was inspired here. At that time, the city was known for the hoards of local men who leashed leather straps around their bodies and pulled merchant boats up through the city's shallow waters.

After sinking into ignominy during the Soviet era, Rybinsk is now a fascinating contrast of recently restored 19th century buildings alongside other structures on the same block that are in total disrepair. So it is in many places, as Russia digs its way out of the 20th century with the help of bright young educated men like Anatoly and Alexander.

Alexander was the first to find PEP's training program on the Internet. He contacted CCI and signed up immediately. Anatoly followed as soon as the appropriate PEP delegation became available for him. Both men shared stories of what their out-of-country experiences had meant to them. They received us in their corporate offices. A few years ago, the two purchased the fourth and fifth floors of this weathered 19th century building in the center of historic Rybinsk. Slowly they renovated it to "Euro standards."

They also persuaded local officials to give them an aging Soviet structure on the outskirts of town for a production site. At the time, it had no water or heat. They bargained to get the structure free in return for renovating it, which was common practice in the '90s. Together they scavenged discarded Soviet equipment, broke it down for parts, and created usable equipment for their specific needs. Gradually new equipment was purchased, and the old building was made habitable year round. Anatoly and Alexander have never taken out a loan; they have used only "reinvested revenues" for capital improvements of Fobus.

A visit to this production site revealed a huge space with a large overhead banner in Russian that read, "We Strive for Perfection!" Workers dashed around stacks of pipes, cutting machines, welding operations, and huge pieces of steel equipment. Their chief product is an oil pipe valve, which joins huge field pipes and redirects oil flows. One of their valves was placed as a decorative focal point in the center of the large building. It was about the height of my shoulders; they mentioned that this valve was not the largest that they manufacture. Anatoly and Alexander's valves have earned the top stamp of approval from Russia's largest oil companies. Today their production is ready for major investors.

Rybinsk Rotary

Alexander organized Rybinsk's only Rotary club when he returned from his PEP training. Fortunately, we were there on Tuesday, their Rotary day. Following a typical Rotary luncheon and meeting, several Rotarians took us to their primary service project— CANDLE, a temporary home for Rybinsk's street kids. Some children are brought to this halfway house by the police; others were turned into the authorities by neighbors; some are identified by schools; and some children just show up at CANDLE's door when they have no place else to go.

All of the children were undersized. One room of two to five-year-olds was heartbreaking. One little fellow's breathing was so labored that he was severely incapacitated. He arrived the previous day and had just been diagnosed. Doctors said he couldn't live much longer without heart surgery. Rotarians were trying to get him transferred to Moscow, but money was still in short supply. We were touched by the tenderness the Rotarians felt for this little fellow and made small contributions to his welfare.

It was an impressive visit. Alexander's assistant, Sergei, drove us back to Yaroslavl. We learned from him that he and his wife are adopting a child from CANDLE ... not because they can't have their own but because their hearts have been so moved by the plight of these street kids. Sergei mentioned that other Rybinsk Rotarians have also begun adopting these children. Asked if this is new for Russians, he replied that it is. "Why now?" we asked. He puzzled a few moments and said with some uncertainty, "Well, maybe it's because we can afford to adopt for the first time .... and today we have more home space in which to raise children than we ever had before."

Later we learned that the little fellow at CANDLE survived open heart surgery in Moscow and now lives in the capital city.

Western Russia Becomes its own Rotary International District—June 18, 2006

This was a historic day for Rotary in Russia. The newly designated Rotary District #2220 includes all of Western Russia, north to south, and out to the Ural Mountains—90 percent of Russia's population lives in this huge geographical area. Russian Rotarians and fellow Rotarians from 20 countries traveled in Moscow to celebrate the event. Heretofore, this entire area had been put under the sponsorships of Finnish and Swedish Rotarians.

The events took place in a large convention center outside of Moscow. The center's floors were filled with energetic Rotarians. PEP alumni with familiar faces were darting back and forth. Americans were well represented in the crowd. As I walked into the center I accidentally bumped into Jim Aneff, CCI's National Coordinator. Walls and tables were decked out with photo boards of Rotary projects and student exchanges with other countries. The spectacle would have made Rotarians the world over proud to see the service work being accomplished by clubs of this new district.

Music began to swell through the space as we all made our way into a large hall with theater seating. The elevated stage's presidium table was covered with Rotary's traditional blue fabric. Rotary International President Carl-Wilhelm Stenhammer and the current Rotary Governors from Finland and Sweden sat at the presidium table. Thick red curtains were pulled back to reveal a huge screen with a Rotary slide show in motion. It showed scenes of Russia's new private sector development, Rotary projects, historic monuments, Russia's children at play, the faces of Russian citizens hard at work, and Russia's president. It demonstrated who and what Russia is today from the eyes of its own people. The country's national anthem filled the auditorium and brought us all to our feet. Western Russia's first District Governor Elect, Andrei Danilenko, was invited to the podium.

> *Andrei, the young 14-year-old boy we met in 1983, has been fascinating to watch over the years. As mentioned earlier, he was reared as a Soviet boy in Moscow by an American mother whose ancestors came from Russia. He visited the U.S. every couple of years, and since his early teens had met a constant stream of Americans of goodwill who visited his Moscow home. Brought up in an agnostic environment, he was influenced by Christianity after interpreting for Dr. Robert Schuller of the Crystal Cathedral Ministry who visited Russia frequently in the 1990s. Andrei has a deep understanding of both Russian and American mentalities; hence, he straddles both cultures with patience and grace. This unusual background has produced a young man who seems to feel a strong pull to weave together his Russian and American roots.*

> *Throughout the years, Andrei has been quite entrepreneurial. During his 20s, when Russia faced potential famine, he threw his energies into experimenting with vegetable growing to determine how plants could produce better and faster yields. When officials weren't interested in his ideas, he decided to create a small demonstration farm himself. Soon hundreds, then later thousands of hectares of idle land north of Moscow turned into his new private farmlands, which provided produce for Moscow's restaurants. He then expanded and went into dairy farming. At this writing, his businesses are flourishing due to the innovative technology he has introduced. In 2009 Andrei became Chair of the new Russian Dairy Farmers Association, and in 2010 he was appointed the Chair of the Committee of Russian Farmers to help chart agricultural policy for Russia's Ministry of Agriculture.*

> *Rotary may have been a magnet for Andrei since the organization brings together people of good intentions, encourages community-building projects, and is an international endeavor—values, which appear to be deeply embedded in this young businessman.*

At the celebration of District #2220's creation on June 18, 2006, Andrei Danilenko was formally inducted as Rotary International's first Western Russia Rotary District Governor in an officious ceremony befitting of the occasion. Rotary International past presidents and governors charged him with Rotary responsibilities and presented appropriate Rotary emblems and ribbons amid much fanfare. Andrei gave a rousing acceptance speech in Russian, which he translated into English, sentence-by-sentence, to assure that all in the hall understood as he spoke. Seeing this kid, who many of us watched growing up in the 1980s, take his place among the top Rotary International leaders of the world, was an unforgettable experience. Andrei, who never had a father

Andrei Danilenko, first Rotary International President for the new Western Russia District #2220, being presented congratulations by Rotary International President Carl-Wilhelm Stenhammar.

President Putin assisting with feedings at Andrei's farm.

Andrei responding to the audience's full approval of his new title and the Rotary responsibilities ahead of him.

Andrei's dairy farm visited by prestigious guests—at the time, President Putin and at his chief protégé, Dmitri Medvedev.

Vladimir Donskoy has become the living embodiment of Rotary across Russia. He was a Fulbright student in the 1980s during which time he became acquainted with Rotary principles. Since then he has tirelessly worked to disseminate Rotary principles in Russia and to create goodwill between Russia and the West.

He was the first Russian Governor of the large 5010 District in 2004-05— covering the area from Russia's Ural mountains all the way out to the Pacific ocean, Alaska and the Yukon of Canada.

(Above) Rotary club in Ekaterinburg, Russia, which was initiated by Lena Novomeiskaya, PEP Director and her delegates.

Rotary Club in Omsk, presentation from a PEP delegate just returning home from America.

Could you have guessed she would become the Rotary District Governor of District #2220 in Russia!

Nadezhda Safronova on her first trip to America where her delegation was hosted by Ivan Cornelius.

Nadezhda proudly showing her PEP diploma flanked by her Rotary home hosts, Ivan and JoAnn Cornelius. Nadezhda was introduced to Rotary at Ivan's Rotary Club of San Leandro, California. Later she became a member of Ekaterinburg's Rotary club, then became club president, and was later elected Governor of the Western Russia District 2220 for 2010/2011.

figure he can remember, now has hundreds, if not thousands of responsible Rotary men for models, all of whom love and respect him. After the ceremony was over, the halls and corridors felt magical.

Greensboro, North Carolina's Mike Sigmon ran into a Russian PEP Fellow who immediately cried out, "Mike! I'm a Rotarian now; thanks so much for sponsoring our club!" Mike recognized him as one of the Russian entrepreneurs he had hosted in his home years earlier.

A lovely young woman approached me saying, "I'm from the Ulyansk Rotary club, and I want to tell you that CCI and PEP are the salvation of our business people in Ulyansk. I am your CCI representative in my city, and I can say that PEP is changing the lives of our entrepreneurs. Our Rotary club is active in several spheres and our members are dedicated to Rotary and to American people." An endless stream of proud Russian Rotarians stopped by to make warm comments and to collect congratulations on finally becoming their own masters in Rotary International.

A 10-Story Monument to American People from Russia—September 11, 2006

One of the best kept secrets in America's 2000s is the ten-story, multi-million dollar pavilion and huge "Tear Drop" monument in Bayonne, New Jersey. A Russian artist Zurab Tsereteli, President Putin, and the Russian people gifted this monumental work to the American people in sympathy for our 9-11 disaster in the heart of New York City. The names of those who perished on 9-11 are etched in its granite base.

The 175-ton complex took months to create in the revered Russian foundry that cast the Bronze Horseman of Peter the Great in 1782. It was shipped from St. Petersburg to America in five parts where it was installed by Russian craftsmen during 2005-06. The structure is located at the peninsula of the Harbor and is lined up with our Statue of Liberty on the New York side of the water.

President Putin, the mayor of Bayonne, and a few local dignitaries quietly dedicated the gift in 2005 before installation was completed.

On September 11, 2006, it was dedicated in a small ceremony. Former President Clinton and a handful of representatives from the current administration were present. There was no national publicity. A short article appeared in *The New Yorker* magazine, which mentioned that the monument was in place.

Later in 2008 and 2009, the story somehow began to get blog exposure. When I heard about it, I was sure this was a fictitious story. A quick visit to Google revealed that indeed the story was factual. If you haven't known about this huge complex, Google "Russian 9/11 Memorial" to view this powerful and all but ignored gift to the American people.

A Look at an Oligarch's Empire—September 28, 2006

Over the years, I have harbored strong feelings against Russia's privatization period and its new "oligarch class," which spawned the era that brought such dire consequences to ordinary Russian citizens.

Stanislov Petrov, the Russian commander who refused to send nuclear warheads to America on September 26, 1983.

A monument that Russia presented to America in 2005/06. Few Americans knew of the gift, since mainstream media didn't cover the delivery or the months-long installation of the 10-story edifice.

"To the Struggle Against World Terrorism" was conceived by an artist in Russia. Zarub Tsereteli was walking the streets in Moscow, as the events around 9/11 unfolded. Struck by the outpouring of grief felt by the people of America and all people, an image of a tear monument formed in his mind.

Shortly after the attacks, Tsereteli visited ground zero and found the perfect place for his vision.

The memorial is made of steel sheathed in bronze.

Standing 100 feet high, its center contains a jagged hollow space. Inside the space hangs a 40-foot stainless steel teardrop, representing the sadness and grief over the loss of life—but also the hope for a future free from terror for all humankind.

Etched in granite on an 11-sided base are the names of the nearly 3,000 citizens killed in the 1993 World Trade Center bombings and terrorist attacks on Sept. 11, 2001.

During evaluations of CCI's EDP entrepreneurs in the 1990s, a young Russian sat down across the desk from me in Moscow. He appeared to be in his late '20s, was tall and serious. He lived and worked in Norilsk in the far North of Russia. It turned out he wasn't in small business at all. He was one of the chief accountants at Norilsk Nickel, a huge metallurgic company north of the Arctic Circle. I was shocked to learn that he had gotten through CCI's screens and had already been trained in American companies.

Having heard rumors about his 32-year-old boss, Vladimir Potanin, and how he had gotten controlling shares in the huge U.S.S.R. nickel company during the 1990s, I was somewhat testy with this young man. He admitted that his boss was indeed young, maybe too young, but he defended him saying he was smart and hands-on with the company— and that he provided perhaps the only hope that this monster Soviet company with tens of thousands of employees in the far North could survive. The young man apologized for manipulating himself into the CCI program but argued that the U.S. experience was extremely useful to him and the huge company. He explained that business principles are fairly scientific, and what works well in small companies also provides models for larger companies. His logic and demeanor won me over.

Years later when our PEP funding was dwindling in 2006, it occurred to me that perhaps Russia's "oligarch elite" might consider becoming patrons of our PEP program. Surely they would see the advantage of growing a healthy small business sector across Russia. From the periphery, I had always kept an eye on Potanin after meeting his young accountant in the 1990s. So I decided I'd try to get an appointment with him. Fortunately, a friend at the USAID network in Moscow knew Potanin and helped me to get an appointment at Interros, the giant holdings of the oligarch. Internet information told me that Potanin had not only resurrected Norilsk Nickel and other large corporations, but has also implemented a nation-wide leadership program to educate Russian youth throughout Siberia's far-flung regions and is also quite interested in Russia's classical arts.

On September 28, 2006, a Moscow driver delivered me to Interros. The huge complex is elegant but understated. I didn't get to meet Potanin, but spent considerable time with one of his Interros' directors. The erudite man had done his homework and surprised me with his knowledge of CCI's programs and mission. Our meeting was more of a discussion about PEP's work and Interros' non-commercial and cultural pursuits than my needs for PEP. However, it was of value to me.

I learned of Potanin's deep interest in preserving Russia's 900 years of art from icons forward to modern masterpieces. He recently took a large collection of Russian art to the Guggenheim Museum in New York, where he is a Trustee. He is also Chair of the Board of the world-famous Hermitage Museum in St. Petersburg to which he has contributed significantly by buying back Russia's lost art from the pillaging of the earlier decades of the 20th century. But I was most impressed with his efforts today to educate Russian children across many far away regions in Siberia.

It isn't clear to me how Potanin obtained his wealth during Russia's privatization period, but he seems to be doing good things with it by 2006. Norilsk Nickel and his other holdings have flourished. He may or may not decide to be a patron for PEP, but my micro-glance into the world of vast wealth resulting from the privatization period was an eye opener—and one more wrinkle in the multi-faceted Russia, which so few of us outsiders get a chance to comprehend.

A Broken Water Pipe and a Lawsuit—October 9, 2006

In 2003 I purchased property in a nearly destroyed St. Petersburg house, which was built in 1825. Like all other historic buildings after the 1917 Revolution, the house was carved up into tiny communal rooms where multiple families shared one kitchen and one bath during the 20th century. Six families had lived in the 150-meter piece I purchased. Finally, I managed to get the money together to start renovating it. When all of the partitions were removed, only the external meter-thick brick walls, a few internal meter-thick brick walls, and huge floor beams remained. These had sustained no damage over the years. Sub-floorings were replaced. Next a new heating system was installed.

Two weeks after the system was put in, one of my new heater pipes exploded; hot water temporarily gushed out and down into the flat below. It happened to be an art studio leased from the city of St. Petersburg to a long-time performing soprano at the Kirov/Mariensky Opera and Ballet Theater, which is a block south of the property.

I was eventually presented with a lawsuit, which included 100 percent damage to two grand Bechstein pianos, several full-length fur coats, scores of Italian dresses and as many pairs of shoes, all of the furniture, a library of antique books, antique paintings, and a tanning machine. Lawyers and legal advisors came and went during the build-up to the case. The initial day in court (to be covered a bit later) made me wonder whether a fair trial could ever take place since I was going up against an icon of St. Petersburg's cultural world.

Chelyabinsk Gets a Face Lift—October 16, 2006

Back in the Ural Mountains again for 2006 PEP evaluations, we were hosted by CCI Fellow Alexander Kalinin. He wanted to show us the city's latest accomplishment. Our car pulled into a downtown parking place. Alexander remarked that we needed to walk from here since no cars are allowed now on Kirov Street, Chelyabinsk's main boulevard.

A cold brisk wind blew as our feet hit the cobblestones. Soon we were in a colorful, enchanting pedestrian mall that went on for blocks in either direction. Elegant French lamp posts lit up the walkways; charming new shops and restaurants lined the cobblestone walkways; trees with miniature twinkling lights added delight to the mall; and bronze sculptures of life-size men and women seemed to come alive.

In front of the historic Chelyabinsk Administration building stood a bronze statue of a turn-of-century country peasant scratching his head as if trying to understand a large riffled book of laws. Half a block away in the middle of the mall stood another bronze turn-of-century figure—a tiny-waisted, bonneted elegant lady, dressed "to the nines," primped in front of an oversized bronze oval mirror that was riveted onto the walkway. Further down in front of a new 24-hour Bank-O-Mat, we spotted another bronze figure, this one a "down-on-his-luck" derelict that appeared to have just been thrown out of the bank. He was in sharp contrast to the present 21st century backdrop. Further down the mall, more bronze figures playfully perked up the chilly night. It was Sunday evening; the mall was full of women under 40, dressed in spike-heeled suede boots, dress jeans, and fancy jackets. A few couples with strollers and bundled up small children were noted. Volodya, my interpreter from St. Petersburg, exclaimed loudly, "I feel I'm abroad! I've never seen anything like this in Russia!" Following our evening promenade, Alexander, Volodya, and I sat down to discuss the next three days of PEP evaluations.

Chelyabinsk was economically devastated when the U.S.S.R. broke up. Like many Soviet cities, what they manufactured during the Soviet period, was no longer in demand in Russia's new world. They didn't have oil as did nearby regions, but Chelyabinsk did have precious metals deep under its subsoil. Eventually this industry was brought back, along with other new small manufacturing and services that local people developed. Today the city is a bustling economic success that is far from Russia's capital cities.

Alexander Odolskii, PEP Fellow in Chelyabinsk

Alexander was part of a PEP Casual Dining delegation in Murfreesboro, Tennessee, in 2003. His newest Family Entertainment Center was another treat in Chelyabinsk. Driving up to the complex, the Center looked like a fusion of two or three oversized coliseums. The restaurant in which we ate was in the subterranean parts of the Center. This 12,000 square meter (129,000 square feet) complex houses four movie theaters, eight restaurants, two bowling alleys, 75 billiard tables, and games and entertainments of all imaginable types. There is no entrance fee. "For pay" activities seemed endless. Three years ago we visited Odolskii's first entertainment center. It has been sufficiently successful that this new center named Megapolis was built last year. Alexander, the creative genius behind these businesses, looks about 40 years old and has three children, ages 2 to 10 years. He enjoys the businesses but complained that there is not enough time to spend with his growing family.

Of the several hundred people in the center that Monday evening, I appeared to be the only foreigner. Those we saw enjoying this mega-space were not wealthy. They were the 30's crowd, ordinary parents with babies in buggies, and teenagers. Megapolis appeared to be the city's indoor playground. In its huge interiors one could browse around and graze on ethnic cuisines ranging from Russian to Indian to Japanese. Games and sports could be played in a safe environment. There was no evidence of security except for metal detectors at the front door.

I questioned Alexander as to how he kept the crowds orderly and clean cut. He explained that he cooperates with the city's anti-drug specialists who play pool and enjoy other activities for free, in return for watching for unacceptable behaviors or substance abuse. As a result, life within the giant complex remains welcoming and peaceful.

So what does this entertainment center and the downtown mall visited the day before, have to say about the spending power of Chelyabinsk and Ural region citizens? A lot. Local people are employed, the middle class is growing, and ordinary Russian people are beginning to enjoy themselves.

The Politkovskaya Murder—October 22, 2006

This high-profile murder focused on one of the most egregious problems in Russia's post-Soviet era. With guns freely circulating during the 1990s for the first time in their history, life has been considered expendable to those with money and axes to grind.

Courageous investigative reporters have zeroed in on big business criminal groups and the fierce ethnic factions freely roaming the country. Anna Politkovskaya was one of these. Her grievous assassination prompted thousands of articles in Western press incriminating Putin, the Kremlin, the FSB, or some combination thereof—without a shred of evidence to support these accusations.

A quick glance on the Internet reveals that not only was the outspoken Politkovskaya haranguing the Russian government over the war in Chechnya, but also even more dangerous, she was reporting on and harassing Chechen leaders in high places. There is considerable suspicion by serious analysts that she was taken out by those around Ramzan Kadyrov, current president of Chechnya, or one of the Caucasus mobs which she excoriated. Kadyrov was appointed to the Chechnya presidency by Putin, after his father's assassination, not because he would necessarily make a good leader but because there was no one any better to "keep the lid on" in that highly volatile region, which has been so challenging for the rest of Russia. In any case, a methodical investigation was warranted and is still being carried out. As of this writing no one has been convicted—as with most murders of other high-profile journalists or business tycoons.

Chechnya is looked at by many as a radicalized state within Russia. Violence is an accepted way of life in the region, as are honor killings. One can make the case that the Chechens' resistance to being communized in the '30s, the tragedy of their mass deportation under Stalin, along with their feudalistic culture, has created a people given to heated passions and violent resistance to any who get in their way.

My strong suspicion is that most of these contract killers who commit such murders get out of the country speedily and are somewhere in the islands living high on the ill-gotten hit money. Meanwhile those who pay for the contracts are driving around Moscow or Grozny as usual—making it next to impossible to convict and bring anyone to trial for most of these murders.

Fast forward to June 2011. After a lengthy criminal investigation, Rustam Mahmoudov was arrested and charged for Politkovskaya's murder. Mahmoudov has a long history of kidnappings, racketeering, involvement with criminal groups and suspected murders.

October 7, 2011. Der Spiegel reports that Dmitri Pavlyuchenkov, a Moscow bureaucrat, head of a special unit of Moscow police, and compulsive gambler who made extra money to pay off debts by shady services to criminal groups, has been indicted as both co-conspirator and chief witness in Politkovskaya's murder. Involved is a circle of Chechens along with Pavlyuchenkov (who is incriminating Berezovsky). There is no connection between any of these people and President Putin.

Litvinenko, the Latest Flashpoint in U.S.-Russia Relations—November 6, 2006

The poisoning and death of Alexander Litvinenko, a former low-level KGB agent and former employee of exiled oligarch, Boris Berezovsky, created scandalous world press. Again Western media jumped to accuse President Putin of orchestrating this murder. A deathbed letter in English supposedly from Litvinenko accused Putin of his poisoning despite the fact that the dying man didn't have English skills. Obviously, someone who had interest in blaming this murder on Putin did the writing in addition to paying for the public relations campaign surrounding this highly publicized death. Two questions need to be asked: who profited most from Litvinenko's death and these accusations, and who would be most damaged by them?

Aside from Litvinenko himself, Putin was obviously the most damaged since, as would be expected, world mainstream media vilified the Russian leader for months. It was herd journalism at its worst. Not a shred of serious evidence for this murder has been linked to Putin or anyone connected with him. And again Putin did not bother to defend himself. Who gained? Those who had axes to grind with Litvinenko and at the same time got their agendas against Putin satisfied.

Media Storms Rage—December 10, 2006

As 2006 ends, mainstream media continue pitting the United States and the West against Russia. Putin finally responded with an old Arabic proverb, "The dogs bark and the caravan moves on."

Again I ask myself who or what is behind this? Is it just unregenerate humanity that needs to make enemies? Could it be that "once an enemy, always an enemy?" Could it be the media alone? If so, is it the journalists? I finally concluded that it is not; journalists are hired hands. They write what is expected by their papers in order to receive a paycheck. Is it the editors? No, they are hired hands too. Is it the publishers or owners? Who sits on the boards of these major media outlets? With whom are they connected?

Whatever the case, surely the geopolitical handwriting is on the wall and should be obvious: Russia is getting up off her knees in the 2000s. This vast country has a preponderance of the world's energy products under its subsoil, which will make it a powerful nation in this new century. Russia is an intelligent, educated, and cultured nation. Who in their right minds would be interested in pitting the U.S. and the West against Russia again? Lastly, history has proven that Russia is an "endurer" state; even when outnumbered and poorly trained, Russia has gone head-to-head with any power that came up against it in the past—including the massive Nazi regime in the 1940s. Are groups of powerful people forgetting this?

American citizens must find ways to change this course—we can't afford to stand by and watch another warring relationship rebuild between America and Russia in the 21st century.

An Idea to Offset the Impact of U.S. Media—December 15, 2006

At the end of 2006, we asked ourselves, "What can CCI do to force honest discourse in Washington about America's increasingly dangerous media, which pits the West against Russia?"

We could take another mega-delegation of 100 Russian alumni to Washington to give their points of view to Congressional members on the Politkovskaya and Litvinenko murders, accusations against Russia's leadership, and the state of Russia today. But these days we have no funds for such projects. It occurred that we could put this idea out to our CCI constituency with the understanding that if they considered it a worthy idea, collectively they could send in small checks to contribute toward the effort.

Throwing bread out on the waters, I wrote to CCI's constituency and described what I felt needed to happen and added, "Russian participants can pay their costs (about $3,000 each) to come to Washington. But to do this project, we need to quickly raise about $15,000 for two part-time salaries for three months to help with logistics and implementation. My time is free. If you believe this is worth doing, your check can be made out to Center for Citizen Initiatives and marked for the '2007 – Washington, D.C. Project.'"

Within 15 days a number of checks had arrived to encourage us. Then an unexpected decision-making contribution arrived. Patricia (Pat) Cloherty, CEO of Delta Private Equity Partners in Moscow, sent a large personal check during the holidays that assured that this "idea-in-germination" would move forward. Without her unexpected generosity, I could not have made plans to organize the Russian delegation to Washington in March 2007. Many, many thanks to Pat!

$\mathcal{Y}ear\ 2007$

As 2007 began, we were moving full speed ahead to bring 100 Russian entrepreneurs to Washington in March. Their responses to our invitations exceeded our wildest expectations, with some hoping to get to see their American host families once more while in the U.S. But most were coming with a determination to have face-to-face discussions with America's decision makers regarding erroneous media coverage about Russia.

This giant project was the most challenging ever launched by CCI due to the agenda—and to complicate matters, at the same time we were organizing 35 more PEP delegations for training in multiple American states.

PEP Nearing Termination Point—February 5, 2007

This was definitely not a good time for bad news, but the inconceivable happened. At the end of January, our three veteran PEP managers—Ashley Owen, Courtenay Carr, and Tiffany Jalalon—informed me they would be leaving CCI at different times during the year. Replacing their combined expertise would be nearly impossible. This situation came as CCI's State Department funds were running out. Moreover, the international economic slow-down meant that most Russian entrepreneurs would be unable to pay increased fees for U.S. training. These combined blows forced me and fellow CCI board members to deal with, and finally accept, our harsh reality.

In early February, I struggled to compose an e-mail to our PEP volunteers across America. It ended with: *"Obsessing over this situation, I finally fell back on biblical wisdom, 'To everything there is a season.' I don't know that this is a truism regarding PEP, but surely it is true in life. Nothing is forever. Perhaps these extraordinary 12 years have been PEP's 'season.' The CCI Board of Directors and I, with great reluctance, studied the situation carefully and have made the difficult decision to phase out our beloved PEP program by the end of November.*

"In 1995, PEP rose out of the legacy of the historic Marshall Plan's training program and took on a life of its own. American 'know how' and the generous spirits of thousands of you volunteers have been implanted in the minds and hearts of Russia's young business owners. These ripple effects will be passed from one generation to the next as Russia's private sector continues to develop. We are overwhelmingly satisfied with what we have accomplished together, and hope you are too.

"Now we begin putting together PEP's last 35 delegations with a deep sense of pride in the program's impact in the lives of all of us involved, and the much needed goodwill that you Americans and Russians have created and spread throughout both countries."

U.S. Administration Pushes Acceptance of Georgia and Ukraine into NATO

While we were reeling from these closure issues at home, our nation's leaders were moving swiftly to further alienate Russia by pushing for the acceptance of Georgia and Ukraine into the North Atlantic Treaty Organization (NATO).

Neither country's citizenry supports NATO membership. Nonetheless, Georgia's President, Mikheil Saakashvili, was received at NATO Headquarters this month in preparation for joining NATO. Ukraine's current President, Viktor Yushchenko, is preparing to take Ukraine into the Alliance in the nearest future. Under NATO regulations, neither Georgia nor Ukraine qualifies for membership.

This effort, which will encircle Russia, is being pushed despite the fact that our long-term allies, Germany and France, oppose it. Russia remains deeply concerned about being ringed by NATO, the largest military force in the history of the world.

U.S. Announces Intention to build Missile Defense Systems in Poland and the Czech Republic

However, recent polls show that 57 percent of Polish citizens don't approve of this plan, and 70 percent of Czech citizens object to defensive systems being placed on their soil. Russia also resists, saying if these systems are built near their borders, they will have to install counterbalance systems nearby.

Russia's Response: "NATO Must Take Russia's Security Interests Seriously"

The Russian Foreign Ministry's message continued: *"We cannot ignore the fact that NATO's military infrastructure is coming closer to Russia's borders or that the U.S. plans to reconfigure its military presence in Europe—plans that will include not just the transfer of military formations to Bulgaria and Romania but also the creation of a third positional area for the global ABM systems in the Czech Republic and Poland*

.... Unfortunately, many of our partners, especially in the West, are still attached to the illusions of the Cold War era and cannot overcome the inertia of 'bloc' approaches and confrontational policies."

Putin's Munich Speech—February 10, 2007
A Trip to Washington to Finalize Meetings for
CCI's Delegation of 100—February 11, 2007

I arrived in Washington during the weekend to begin Monday meetings with Congress members. An incoming e-mail grabbed my attention. It reported that several hours earlier, Russia's President, Vladimir Putin, had forcefully addressed the esteemed 43rd Munich Conference on International Security Policy where, for the first time ever, he lambasted American foreign policy as "unipolar" and dangerous for the future of the world.

My heart sank! How could this happen the weekend before my 25 scheduled meetings in Congressional offices?

Excerpt of President Putin's Munich Speech on February 10, 2007

"I am truly grateful to be invited to such a representative conference that has assembled politicians, military officials, entrepreneurs, and experts from more than 40 nations .... This conference format will allow me to say what I really think about international security problems. And if my comments seem unduly polemical, pointed, or inexact to our colleagues, then I would ask you not to get angry with me. After all, this is only a conference. It does, however, involve the stability of the global economy, overcoming poverty, economic security, and developing a dialogue between civilizations ....

"The universal, indivisible character of security is expressed as the basic principle that 'security for one is security for all.' As Franklin D. Roosevelt said during the first few days that the Second World War was breaking out: 'When peace has been broken anywhere, the peace of all countries everywhere is in danger.' These words remain topical today. Incidentally, the theme of our conference—global crises, global responsibility— exemplifies this."

Putin continued for some 4,000 words in which he called into question American uni-polarism, the intended NATO expansion without Russia's participation, the missile shield in Eastern Europe, enumeration of America's broken nuclear arms treaties, and a call to abide by the Charter of the United Nations. For the full text, check: http://eng.kremlin.ru/speeches/2007/02/10/0138_type82912type82914type82917type84779_118123.shtml.

Meetings on Capitol Hill—Monday, February 12, 2007

Trudging up the steps of the Longworth House Office Building on Monday morning just 48 hours after Putin's speech, I wondered what resistance would greet me. Every Congress member and foreign policy aide would know about Putin's highly targeted Munich remarks.

The mood during the first meeting was surprisingly calm. In the next few offices, responses were quizzical with officials wondering what this speech presaged. And in one key congressional office, the top foreign policy chief remarked, "Putin didn't say anything in Munich that we haven't previously said here in this office."

My fears had been for naught. The Munich speech came at just the right time for CCI's Russians to show up in Washington. Crisscrossing Capitol Hill. I had 25 meetings between February 12th and 16th. All congressional personnel were intrigued with the possibility of discussing issues with a small group of the Russian entrepreneurs soon to come.

Meanwhile American newspapers reported that Russia's president was unacceptably confrontational with the U.S. at the Munich gathering, and questioned what this foretold about dealing with the new "resurgent Russia." This was puzzling: why was there a different reaction between U.S. Congressional offices and U.S. mainstream media headlines?

Did the journalists and their editors assume that a Russian president would continue to ignore the barrage of physical encroachments around their borders and foul media coverage without reacting? And further, what would an American president do if Russians were preparing to put missile systems on Canadian, Mexican, or Cuban soil— or if accused of orchestrating murders by Russian media with no rebuttals from Russia's political elite?

100 Russians to Congress to Speak Their Truth—March 20-30, 2007

The day came; CCI's Russian alumni arrived. One hundred non-English speaking entrepreneurs from 28 of Russia's regions held a total of 72 meetings with American leaders across Washington, D.C., with assistance from PEP's interpreters and facilitators.

In groups of seven, they engaged with Congress members and foreign policy staffs. Some held round table discussions with Senator Sam Nunn, Russia-focused officers in 10 major Washington policy "think tanks," Republican and Democratic Senate Foreign Relations/Affairs Committee officers, National Security Council officials, Thomas Graham (National Security Advisor on Russia until 2006, now with the Kissinger Group), U.S. Department of Commerce officers, U.S.-Russia Business Council, World Bank, International Finance Corporation, the Small Business Association, and numerous other business-related specialists in Washington. They met with German Embassy officers and European Union representatives from seven countries where they dialogued on a range of vital issues.

The incoming American Consul General for the Vladivostok Consulate requested a last-minute meeting with alumni from Russia's Far East regions. The final day started with briefing officials at the Russian Embassy. During their last meeting, they exchanged views at the U.S. Department of State where State's Russia officers created a collegial atmosphere.

Throughout the week, they spoke frankly about the NATO issues, the murder allegations, and the progress that was being felt in their regions across Russia. They emphatically denied that President Putin was involved in despicable acts like assassinations—and reported that Russian citizens are freer today than any have been since the beginning of their history. Moreover they reminded that the West's perceived "freedom" during Russia's 1990s wasn't freedom at all but lawlessness and utter chaos. They continued to share their personal convictions that Russia is moving in a constructive direction.

Fortunately, only one meeting out of 72 was deplorable. At the Senate Foreign Relations Committee, 50 of our seasoned Russian business owners were excoriated by a

Masha Maslova assisting alumni with their complicated schedule of meetings in D.C.

Congresswoman Pelosi's Mike Sheehy questioned CCI alumni when Pelosi was unable to make the appointment. She has been supportive of CCI's work since 1987.

Senator Chuck Hagel discussed U.S.-Russia issues with seven CCI alumni after which he was presented with a piece of Russian children's art. In 2008 Hagel co-led a delegation of American VIPs to Moscow to work on rapprochement between the U.S. and Russia.

Congressman Dennis Kucinich (D) watched a PPT by Sergei Sidorenko making points for closer business relations between the two countries. Kucinich announced later in 2008 that he would lead the effort to establish a Russia Caucus in the House of Representatives, which he did in 2009.

Congressman Thomas Price, flanked by eight Russian businesswomen he took on a tour of the Capitol building after their session on U.S.-Russia relations with him in his office. Price co-led the Russia Caucus effort with Kucinich. His District had also hosted PEP delegations in the past.

The "D.C. 100" delegation of Russian entrepreneurs at the end of 72 meetings on Capitol Hill March 20-30, 2007.

In addition to Congressional meetings, delegates held a wide range of think tank and business meetings.

Well known faces in the field of U.S.-Soviet/Russia relations were present to support the new hoped-for day in relations between the two countries.

Left, Ambassador Jack Matlock, keynote speaker for the D.C. 100 banquet on the final evening.

Right, Marvin Kalb, eminent U.S. CBS and NBC journalist during the Cold War period, discusses modern day Russia with Aygul Mirzayanova and other Russian delegates.

young foreign policy officer who took them to task for Russia's centuries-long problem with corruption, lack of rule of law, high-profile murders, and slowness to democratize. His monologue sounded much like the media's recent opinion pieces. CCI alumni tried to shift the situation to a dialogue with no success. Despite many hands in the air, none were allowed the floor. One alumnus, Alexander Lubyanoi from Volgograd, took the floor anyway and was shouted down by the youthful officer. What transpired was an unforgettable display of arrogance in the U.S. Senate chambers. Afterward, delegates attributed the young man's rudeness to his lack of knowledge and diplomatic skills.

Surveying the spectrum of meetings, they felt their other visits had been successfully handled and hoped that their personal views would influence Congress members' thinking as they made future decisions.

Fifteen CCI volunteers escorted Russian delegates to Congressional meetings. The former traveled to Washington at their own expense from Ohio, Illinois, California, Florida, Georgia, Virginia, North Carolina, and Maryland. They guided the Russian subgroups through the D.C. metros to Capitol Hill and made introductions at official meetings.

CCI volunteers included Allen Kerr, Fran Macy, Enid Schreibman, Larry Miller, Don Chapman, Nancy Glaser, Pat Dowden, Neil Young, Dave Blanch, Lisa Susan, Peggy Simpson, John Muffo, Tommie Whitener, and Jack and Alice Barkan. PEP interpreters flew to Washington and volunteered their professional time to work with the delegations. Masha Maslova, CCI Deputy Director, and I worked in the "communications room" and rarely got out for meetings.

A Democracy Curriculum for Russia's Public Schools—June 11, 2007

Even as CCI is winding down its major programs, Russia continues to command attention in other quarters. One is a democracy education program for Russia's public schools being created by an American military man with a small staff of Russian teachers.

I learned about this unusual project in Evanston, Illinois, where Rotary International was promoting the concept of "Rotary across Russia." At one session a rather large, substantial-looking man stood and introduced himself as Rotarian Charles Heberle, a former NATO man and a retired Colonel in the U.S. military. Charles spoke about a democracy curriculum that he was creating in Petrozavodsk, Russia.

This was a shock to hear. I thought I knew nearly every project of this nature in Russia, but this was off of my radar. Hurriedly I rushed to get in line to talk with this fellow. His quick explanation sounded somewhat far-fetched, so I requested an interview following the evening's celebrations. At 11:00 PM we sat down with my laptop in a quiet corner of the hotel lobby. His strange story poured out.

In 2002 Charles was contacted via email by a man supposedly representing the Putin government. The email inquired if Charles' website curriculum, "You the People," (a democracy program for American schools) might be duplicated in Russia. The contact person reported that Russian authorities were searching for a curriculum consistent with the philosophy of America's Founding Fathers between the years of 1652 and 1775. However, he mentioned that they were not interested in America's current educational system. Next Charles was invited to St. Petersburg for interviews. Eventually, his democracy curriculum won the competition among others who had applied.

Still quite skeptical about this experiment, I asked if I could come to see the program in action. Charles gladly agreed.

Within two weeks I was in Petrozavodsk meeting Charles and his team of middle-aged teachers. They began to fill me in on the history. When it was agreed by his contact persons that he was suitable for the task, he was told that the curriculum would be developed away from Moscow. The area designated was in Petrozavodsk, the capital of Karelia, a city and region noted for their high per capita level of educational degrees. It was arranged that he would work with a group of master teachers who resided and taught there.

Once in Petrozavodsk, Charles and his small group of teachers quietly began the enormous task of creating a K-11 educational program based on the insights of America's founding fathers, the U.S. Declaration of Independence, the Constitution, and the Bill of Rights.

I learned that the new curriculum is not a series of classes "about" democracy; but rather, it trains teachers and children to use democratic interactions and behaviors in everyday classroom situations. Children become fluent in group decision-making and voting on classroom directions. They are encouraged to see multiple points of view, to share information, to be transparent and positive in communications, have respect for diversity, and other non-hierarchical behaviors—these elements are integrated into children's regular history, math, science, and language classes. The program mandates that Russia's tradition-bound teachers give up "authoritarian mentality" in their classrooms and become modern-day facilitators and mentors for their students.

Charles and his teachers showed me stacks of inexpensive handbooks that they had produced, which were already being used in Karelian schools. Witnessing the curriculum in motion, I realized if these extraordinary concepts could be taught in public schools across Russia, this curriculum would quickly produce Russian students academically, psychologically, and sociologically ready for the 21st century.

Alcoholics Anonymous' Twentieth Anniversary in Russia—August 30, 2007

Over 20 years had transpired since the first-ever AA meeting was held in April of 1986 in Kiev, Ukraine U.S.S.R. Following that, it took a year to organize the first real AA group in Moscow.

AA's twentieth anniversary took place in the large indoor Luzhniki Sports Stadium near Moscow's Lenin Hills. Some 3,000 "recovering alcoholics" attended. They came from across Russia's 11 time zones in addition to those who came from America, Australia, Belarus, Canada, Finland, Germany, Latvia, Lithuania, Netherlands, Norway, Poland, Sweden, the U.K., and Ukraine.

The stadium's main stage was decorated with a backdrop of deep blue fabric with large white lettering announcing, "AA 20th Anniversary, Moscow, August - 2007." Further to the right was a huge circle about 12 feet in diameter with the AA's Serenity Prayer in the middle.

God grant us the serenity to accept the things we cannot change,
the courage to change the things we can,
and the wisdom to know the difference.

The "Big Meeting" opened with everyone in the tiered stadium standing and holding hands for a minute of silence. Following that, we repeated in unison the AA Serenity prayer. It was a hallowed reminder of what keeps AA's sober and moving forward with their personal development. Next came the reading of AA's "12 Steps," followed by AA's rather lengthy "12 Traditions." There was absolute silence in the stadium except for the speakers. Following this most serious and meaningful beginning, the event's ambiance suddenly shifted.

Magnificent music filled the air—a dozen live dancers in bright ballroom costumes came onto the floor below and began whirling around. Cheers erupted for the AA "Dance Ensemble." Over the next 30 minutes, classical ballroom dance turned to Spanish flamenco, which turned into flashy modern dance. Earlier those same Russian dancers were in ordinary clothing as they collected tickets and sold AA memorabilia outside the auditorium.

Next came AA's traditional "Flag Parade" with participants from all countries represented carrying flags from their nations. As each country was announced, a representative marched around the basketball floor below amid vigorous applause from the crowd above.

Next came the parade of Russian cities represented at the anniversary. Each representative carried a Russian flag and a large sign indicating the name of their specific hometown; they too paraded below as the crowd responded with joyous approval. The sense of being one world and one AA body without division was absolutely heady.

Another powerful event followed—the traditional AA "Count Down" (or length of sobriety). AA members with 40 or more years of sobriety were asked to stand. In the entire stadium, only one lone American stood. He was honored with hearty applause. Many years earlier, he traveled to the U.S.S.R. Next, 35 years was announced, then 30 years, 25 years ... these who stood were fellow AA's from other countries with years of sobriety before the Soviet movement existed. Each small group stood proudly to enthusiastic cheers.

By the time the countdown got to 20 years of sobriety, the first two Russians stood up. The crowd across the huge expanse went wild! These stalwart souls were the Moscow founders who had put AA on the map for Russia. One was "Big Mary" with whom our early delegations worked in the beginning days. From then forward, as each year was announced, more Russian AA's stood. At the very end, the speakers even recognized those present with only two weeks of sobriety, and then finally a fellow with one week sober stood. The new AA's were called to the floor where they were celebrated amid whistles, shouts, and hugs.

Lastly, a lone member of the very first American AA delegation in April of 1986 was invited to the podium; Loretta walked proudly to the stage clad in a bright yellow pantsuit. She poured out effusive love and joy at seeing so many Russian AA's in the huge stadium. Following heartwarming applause, Loretta addressed the crowd and presented the Moscow chapter with a handmade book of their AA history from 1980s' newspaper articles, journals, photos, and other memorabilia. Barbara O'Reilly, an original CUUI trip traveler and later a CASW delegation leader, had created the history book for the occasion.

To close, Loretta brought a message from Faith S., the visionary who conceived the impossible idea to take AA to the U.S.S.R.—to celebrate the 50th anniversary of Bill W.'s

The 20th Anniversary of AA in Russia. Loretta giving remarks at the Luzhniki stadium to a packed crowd of AA adherents.

Carrying the American flag in the ceremony of countries which were represented at the 20th Anniversary.

AA dancers whirling onto the floor for the Finale.

starting what became Alcoholics Anonymous. The audience was soundless as Faith's words were translated and heard over loud speakers. By the end, the entire stadium burst into applause. Once again I was captivated by *"The Power of One Person's Vision."*

Off stage, another colorful affair was being readied. Russia's famed folk music pealed out over the loudspeakers. Dancers in colorful folk costumes swept onto the floor with the audience clapping rhythmically to their centuries-old melodies.

Good event planning had assured that serious AA traditions were interspersed with explosions of color, music, and dance. It was all so typically Russian.

After two and a half hours of pageantry acknowledging AA's growth throughout Russia, an unexpected finale unfolded before our eyes. Lights lowered across the big stadium. A hush fell over the crowd. Barbra Streisand's captivating voice began to swell majestically throughout the space; dancers in long graceful skirts once again whirled into action.

Finally, when the audience was enamored by the music and rounds of synchronous dancing, flashy fireworks began erupting across the auditorium; brilliant silver, gold, red, and blue streamers rained from the ceiling high above as revolving lights caught their sparkling magic in flight. Streisand's lilting voice reigned over it all.

It was an absolutely breathtaking finale—and a total surprise! Hugs of excitement, exclamations, and squeals of delight resounded throughout the tiers across the big auditorium.

When the music and dancers finished and tinsel covered the floor, somehow, as if on cue, the massive place fell completely silent once more—participants throughout the large stadium quietly reached for the hand next to them. The place was utterly still for a few minutes. The silence was broken as the Serenity Prayer was voiced in unison throughout the crowd. Everyone slowly filed out into adjoining halls where refreshments were waiting.

Following a short break, participants moved back into the auditorium for small group meetings throughout the stadium seats. They seemed self-organizing—with participants glancing around, apparently deciding which group to join. Voices lowered as meetings began. Being a non-AA, I took in what was going on around the big space. Gatherings were taking place in every free spot. Each appeared focused only on itself. Peace prevailed. I had never before witnessed such a spirit among a crowd of this size.

Over the next two days, anniversary events continued at a large health center outside of Moscow. I heard fascinating accounts regarding how Moscow members reach fellow alcoholics far out in the Ural mountains and Siberia. Desperate drinkers contact Moscow's AA website. They organize "car rallies" where half a dozen cars travel to those requesting help. Local meetings are held after which the new hopeful recruits are invited, if possible, to go with them to the next town. The car rallies continue to spread the AA concept for two or three weeks. I learned that AA groups exist in over 100 Russian cities and that the movement is spreading rapidly.

Looking around me at the anniversary events, I observed people who appeared healthy, mentally clear, comfortable with themselves and others around them. I left pondering how it is that this AA program can override all types of addictions, depravities, poor health, mental illness, abusive childhoods, prostitution—and gradually bring human beings into sanity, stability and joy ... many for the first time in their lives. It defies logic ... and is beautiful to witness.

We could have never dreamed what was in store in 1985 when the first group of southern California AA's telephoned requesting help to get them to the U.S.S.R.

A Day in Court—October 17, 2007

The court case against me seemed to drag on indefinitely. I had three lawyers over a span of three years, and none wanted to use mitigation in the court proceedings. I felt it was my only hope for reducing the claims. At stake was $400,000 worth of "damaged property"—far more than I'd paid originally for the wrecked communal flat. If this case were not settled fairly, I would lose everything— the property and the renovation costs that had gone into it. We entered the courthouse once again, showed passports, and marched up to the third floor. I sat at a table for four persons—a court-appointed interpreter, my lawyer Sergei Kuzmin, and the plaintiff's lawyer. Witnesses were elsewhere.

Russia's TV icon, Vladimir Pozner, one of our first contacts in 1983, quietly strolled into the courtroom as though he belonged there. Pozner's face is known and revered by every Russian citizen, so his presence was definitely over the top in this tiny district court. The judge and the plaintiff had no advance notice that he would be present and watching. Having known of CCI's work since the beginning, Pozner had already been greatly helpful during this drawn out case. I was embarrassed that he had taken the time and expense to fly from Moscow to sit in this aging St. Petersburg court. But here he was.

The bell rang; we all stood; and out came an attractive, business-looking young woman of about 30 years in an impeccable black judges' robe. She had a full, dark brown ponytail and a resolute look. If she spotted the court's famous guest, she didn't seem to be rattled. She looked us all over and proceeded in a competent voice to make customary explanations. Throughout the day, she continually questioned both lawyers and me. Periodically, she asked us to meet in a small negotiating room to see if we could settle out of court.

At one point, the plaintiff's lawyer offered to settle for $100,000 plus $40,000 to be paid to their insurance company, plus another $4,000 for court costs—it was a far cry from $400k, but still mitigation of damages hadn't been brought into the court proceedings. I refused the offer and asked my lawyer once more to bring up the mitigation factor. After all, the evening that the pipe burst, the water had drained completely out of her studio below within two hours, leaving only dampness in the air. Most objects claimed as damaged 100 percent had experienced no direct water at all. However, there had been no attempt to move the pianos and valuables, or even aerate the damp space. Being locked up in a cold, dark, damp environment for a month insured that all of the contents would be mildewed.

Hours came and went with both sides arguing—the mitigation issue was still not brought up, and no settlement was in sight. Late in the afternoon, Pozner had to catch the plane back to Moscow. He passed a note, "This won't be over today. I'm ready to return when necessary." His presence was important beyond any words I can express—and his coming most likely had more to do with the case's eventual outcome than we realized at the time. The court adjourned at 7:00 PM. We left exhausted. For some unexplainable reason, I had begun to hope that this young judge with the ponytail might play it straight—and if so, I might have a fair case tried in a Russian court after all. Clearly she wanted us to negotiate, and she didn't want to have to rule on the case. Two more court dates were set. I flew back home to San Francisco.

It would be six more months before a resolution was reached.

Hard Reality Sets in at CCI—November 1, 2007

Our beloved Presidio building had to be vacated within eight weeks. We had brought this space into existence in 1996 when the deserted Presidio buildings were being renovated for Bay Area non-profit organizations.

The historic Presidio had been a prestigious military base since 1776. After the 1950s, it had gradually been vacated. In 1994 the entire area was transferred to the National Park Service. In 1996 CCI signed a 5-year lease as one of the first non-profit organizations to be based in the new national park.

At that time we selected one of the mildewed, asbestos-ridden buildings that had previously been a long hollow ward for post-surgical beds and patients. We designed partitions to separate our program officers, chose paint and carpets, and watched over the renovation like a flock of hens. When it was detoxified and construction was complete, we moved in and made it our CCI home.

Now in 2007, 11 years later, we were leaving it—walking away from all of the diligent work, shared history, and wonderful times experienced within its walls.

We spent the last few days of the year sending our final PEP delegations back to Russia. Over 100 boxes of CCI's history were meticulously organized and moved to Stanford's Hoover Institute's archives for safekeeping and for future Russian analysts. Everyday we held "open house" for non-profit managers who dropped by to scavenge our giveaways—computers, file cabinets, furniture, and office supplies. A new tenant took over our space at the end of December.

Our St. Petersburg office was closed on December 31, 2007. CCI's Leningrad work began in 1983, and since 1986 we had enjoyed an official presence in the city. Closing this operation was painful. CCI's program activity continued in Russia from my St. Petersburg flat.

$\mathcal{Y}$ear 2008

Continuation of CCI Work

Year 2008 was dominated by two overriding goals: to identify well-off Russian companies that could pay full fees (about $7000 per person) for CCI's business training in American firms; and to continue questioning the tone of U.S. mainstream media regarding Russia. The first was critical since so few U.S. programs still existed to keep constructive interactions going between the two countries. The second was crucial to provide reliable news regarding Russia to as many Congress members and American citizens as possible.

CCI moved into a much smaller Presidio building where we set up five workspaces in a large room with other organizations. With American and Russian flags hoisted into place and our favorite photos hung, the new space became cozy and efficient. Remaining with me were Masha Maslova, Olga Tretyakova, Renat Deshuev, and our part-time accountant, Yelena Shklyarevsky. We were receiving a few delegations and hoping to capture more of the large Russian companies in the coming months.

The magic still happens when delegations of Russians come to cities across America. Residents in these cities modify their stereotypes of Russian people through mingling with them in town hall meetings, potluck dinners, and by listening to interviews on TV and radio. Local business trainers, civic club volunteers, home hosts, and mayors turn out to participate in the delegations. Training schedules continue to be intense. Numbers of long-term relations are established between trainees and hosts. Nowhere else was this kind of bi-country goodwill happening at a time when politics between national leaders and medias are so rancorous.

CCI Develops a Blog to Monitor Mainstream Media

At a conference in San Antonio a couple of years earlier, a Rotarian with experience in Russia stood and asked, "Why is it that we don't hold journalists responsible for the inaccuracies and slanted impressions they leave in the minds of American readers? They are never held accountable … I am a businessman. If I gave out bad information and erroneous predictions year after year, I'd be out of business."

What a stunning thought! The notion of holding journalists accountable had never occurred to me. This idea occupied my brain until we could devise a way to address this challenge. We decided to confront the media's inaccuracies by analyzing their articles against accepted journalistic standards.

We contracted Gordon Hahn, a respected, methodical Ph.D. Russian analyst and author, to be our blog expert. Together, by carefully watching the press on Russia, we began to identify the journalistic standards being abused in U.S. media. They follow:

1. Inflammatory and misleading headlines
2. Opinion pieces reported as if accurate news
3. Inaccurate statements/data
4. Omission of key facts
5. Absence of cultural context to explain their accusations
6. Absence of historical content that would explain an allegation
7. Making claims without supporting data/facts
8. Overuse of the same biased Russian sources
9. Overuse of the same biased Western sources
10. Unidentified sources used to make a strategic point
11. Sensational content
12. Jaundiced word choices
13. One-sided perspectives or overstatements
14. Repetitious clichés/rumors
15. Repeating story angles already proven untrue

After settling on the abuses, we developed a system for dissecting articles appearing in *The New York Times, The Washington Post, The Wall Street Journal*, and other major news outlets. Next, we began to design a blog of our own—a task that would take six months with only two neophytes, Masha and me, working on it.

On the blog, questionable assertions in articles are highlighted in yellow, the journalistic standards abused are numbered, then footnotes at the bottom of the page provide the source material with correct information.

In 2010 we also began printing rebuttals to mainstream articles, followed by the original writings. Please check our blog: www.russiaotherpointsofview.com for weekly posts and archived articles.

Farewell to an Angel—February 2008

In late 2007, donor Nika Thayer was told about our 2008 plan for the computer laboratories in the orphanages, which she funded. We had begun to use a steady stream of St. Petersburg University's computer-savvy students to provide after school computer training in the orphanages. The university students quickly grew to love their young pupils, which created a whole new dynamic at the orphanages. The children identified with the trainers as older sibling figures who were closer to them in age and mentality than the "mother figures" who ran their homes. This innovation excited Nika.

Unfortunately by early 2008, we were informed that Nika's health had begun failing. Nadya Klepinina, CCI's Russian director and the children sent her email cards, photos and newsletters prepared on the computers she had provided. These seemed to rally Nika for a short while. On February 8, we were deeply saddened to learn that Nika had peacefully passed away. We made plans to spend down the remaining funds and close the orphanage program.

To our shock a couple of months later, we received a formal letter from an unknown lawyer saying that Nika had included the Angels program in her will. Gratefully, our orphanage work will continue for another several years.

Nika and I never met; she lived in Lyme, Connecticut, far from our offices. The two of us could have passed on a sidewalk and never recognized each other. But we knew each other's minds and intentions. Occasionally she would call to contribute to one of CCI's smaller projects, increase funding to the orphans project, or just to talk about Russia. We had long discussions about the politics and economics of her native country. Since we agreed about what was needed in Russia and in U.S.-Russia relations, these were always pleasant interruptions in my busy days.

After Nika died, her life story surfaced. Nika's father was the Chief of Cavalry for Tsar Nicholas II. Following the 1917 revolution, he was held prisoner to await execution. Her mother was incarcerated elsewhere. By a series of daring maneuvers, both were stolen away and eventually made it out of Russia alive. Nika was born in Vladivostok in 1919. During her early life she traveled from one country to another, finally ending up in America. She was raised speaking the Russian language and carried a deep love for her native country in her soul. She was, however, very American. In our many telephone conversations, she never mentioned her aristocratic roots.

End of Legal Battles in St. Petersburg—April 20, 2008

After a four-year court case, finally a settlement was reached in a small room with our lawyers. It was endless haggling to the very last minute. I paid more than I should have, but much less than the other party expected—and I was able to keep my St. Petersburg apartment. If Russian laws on mitigation had been clearly spelled out in the legal code, I would have had to pay very little in the way of claims, since if the pianos and valuables had been moved from the property within 24 hours, there would have been little, if any, damage.

But, the code's mitigation wording is rather inconclusive, and as a result, it is infrequently used. My lawyers feared the judge would not take it seriously or it would be

Olga Levicheva, Angels Trainer at Orphanage #32. She stands in front of the wall of diplomas awarded to the computer laboratory and pupils for their accomplishments.

Nadezhda (Nadya) Klepinina (standing), Angel's Program Director, explaining a new computer program to a student at orphanage #34 in St. Petersburg.

Above: Pupils at Orphanage #3 begin exposure to computer technology at early age.

Aza Vasilieva with a boy who had just been delivered to Orphanage #32. Many of the children at Russian orphanages have been removed from abusive or neglecting home environments. Aza was courageous enough to risk breaking the law and housing CCI's first computer laboratory without permission. She also has been the perfect mother figure for these wonderful little kids.

Nadya manages, trains, and functions as a substitute when needed. Here she is in Orphanage #8.

too hard to prove. Interestingly enough, the plaintiff wasn't forced to exhibit any of the articles she claimed in the suit. So I never knew the real extent of the damages, or lack thereof.

Throughout this legal process, I grew to understand how difficult it is for a nation to create, or recreate, a totally new set of laws to govern every aspect of public life—particularly a nation the size and complexity of Russia. At the same time, it became obvious why foreigners and local citizens have grave difficulties dealing with Russia's incomplete and uneven legal system of today.

Tips for Americans Dealing with a Legal Situation in Russia
- Study the Russian Civil Code carefully. It is better than I expected but different from ours.
- Judges still have broad discretionary powers, which leaves fertile room for bribery.
- Be assertive. Russian lawyers are less pushy in court than American lawyers.
- Call in your "connections." Human connections and influence still trumps law across Russia.
- Everyone protects cultural icons and authorities. No suggestions here; just be aware of it.
- Judges may use the law fastidiously in some areas but minimally in others.

What I should have done in the beginning:
1. Purchased insurance the day I bought the property.
2. Flown to St. Petersburg on the first plane following the water leak.
3. Gotten a court order for an assessor to enter and document all belongings.
4. Stayed in Petersburg until all portables were moved and claims verified.
5. Screened carefully to get a good Russian lawyer from the beginning.

It may take a decade or more before Russians rely regularly on courts and law. When facing potential legal challenges, they don't think about courts; they think about connections, ways to avoid laws, and bribes. This is understandable—it is faster and cheaper. This inclination may be driven by centuries of conditioning wherein authorities (even local bureaucrats), not the law had ultimate power. If one had connections or could bribe authorities, they could get exceptions to any law on the books.

In the past few years, some ordinary Russians have begun to take their grievances to court. A few of our CCI entrepreneurs depend on the courts today for business-related suits and are satisfied with their results. They say if "equally matched" with a local Russian opponent, one is more likely to get a fair trial. Young Russian friends say that a popular Russian TV show features real-life legal trials, which are making courts seem more normal to average people.

It appears to me that Medvedev and Putin are trying to develop rule-of-law "consciousness" in Russian society. However, it is a near-to-impossible task. Russian friends explain that "law abiding" goes against headwinds of past generational behaviors and expectations. This, they say is true, up to and including within the Kremlin. Also that illegal payoffs travel up and down the vertical chain from Moscow to the lowest level district bureaucrats in small towns.

Corruption is easy to cover up and hard to prove—since transactions happen behind closed doors, and it is to both parties benefit to keep quiet. It is further difficult to prove because Russians won't report on or identify corrupt authorities or other Russians involved with corruption even if they detest them. I'm told this comes from Russians' deep visceral hatred for the ever-present "informers" that existed during the Soviet decades.

So far, these elements, among others, keep the bureaucratic networks lubricated and well off. Unfortunately, these age old practices save time and energy for those wanting favors. Monitoring and cracking down on judges, firing authorities, educating the public, and generational changes will eventually build a new mentality in Russia regarding law abiding. But that time still lies ahead.

Inauguration of Dmitry Anatolyevich Medvedev—May 7, 2008

Amid a fury of Western media protests, the inauguration of Russia's new President, Dmitry Anatolyevich Medvedev, was carried out today in typical Russian grandeur in the magnificent Kremlin palaces. U.S. media angst flared because Putin "groomed Medvedev" to replace himself.

In Russia, grooming and appointment is traditional and is considered completely normal. This is the way Russians have developed or transferred leadership throughout their history. Even if Medvedev had not been Putin's "heir apparent," he would have won by a large margin because he was close to and respected by a departing president who enjoyed high ratings with the Russian electorate. There were no other candidates in the wings in 2008 that would have been at all acceptable to the Russian electorate. This includes Russian chess player Gary Kasparov, who was promoted by U.S. media as an "opposition candidate," while Russian citizens scoffed at Kasparov's street antics and self promotion to attract western cameras.

My View on the Putin/Medvedev Relationship

As President Medvedev took office, Western journalists and pundits obsessed over Russia's future governance—whether Medvedev would kowtow to Putin's whims, whether Putin would wrest power away from him, or whether Medvedev would challenge Putin and "become his own man."

After working and living in Russia for nearly three decades, the following is my view on this topic:

- We in the West need to realize that Russians have a very specific "hierarchical mentality," which is quite different from Americans' and most Europeans' mentalities.
- There has been no real experience with a serious democratic electoral process in Russia in the past, and today Russians still are not ready to make a leap into full democracy.

- Russians were deeply burned by Yeltsin's "democratic" years and the 1990s' oligarch version of democracy. Quite naturally, today they are now extremely leery of democratic experiments, and
- The current Putin/Medvedev coupling for governance has been a practical solution for Russia's citizens and their political elite at this particular time.

As for appointing leaders, even in their educational system, I'm told that Russian teachers appoint class leaders from Grade 1 throughout their schooling. Russian friends tell me that they and their peers instinctively accepted the teachers' decisions. From classrooms to hospitals, the military, scientific institutes, and to politics, this is how leadership in Russia has developed and been passed on to date.

Up to now, Russian citizens are not comfortable with the "rough and tumble" of electoral competition as we know it in America. A personal example of this discomfort occurred with CCI Fellows in 2004. I was facilitating a conference in Moscow hall with 100 successful Russian entrepreneurs, all CCI alumni, from 30 regions across Russia. I suggested that they elect a president and a board of directors among themselves for the new national grassroots association they were planning to create. After considerable discomfort with my suggestion, a natural leader-type among them said that they didn't want to elect a person themselves, but that they would accept whomever I recommended as their leader. I replied that it was their association, not mine, and that a leader elected among them was paramount. Eventually, they managed this unhappy task and reluctantly chose a leader. Then they had the same difficulty electing board members, and they wouldn't have done so had I not pushed them to do it—which looking back, I now regret. This process had nothing to do with their native intelligence or the level of education (all had higher education degrees) or with a hidden desire for autocracy—but it had everything to do with their long historical conditioning. Choosing a leader from among themselves was not familiar to them, and it went against a number of their deeply engrained societal taboos.

Puzzling over this and other similar situations at Russia's grassroots, it became clearer to me that unconscious elements are at work in the Russian psyche that are radically different from Americans' deeply-held instincts and practices. Neither is right, and neither is wrong. They are just simply different.

As far as I can determine, unlike Westerners,

- Russians find it quite difficult to personally promote themselves, and they are suspicious when others promote themselves.
- They are greatly concerned about how power will affect their peers or unknown contenders.
- They don't like elevating one peer above another.
- Russians don't consider it sport to compete with peers for power.
- They are comfortable when someone whom they trust appoints others to positions of power.
- If a leader type has already proven themselves to be responsible in a position of power, Russians generally believe they should continue, not vacate.

While Americans furrow their brows and pen endless articles on Russia's "deteriorating" democracy, it would be well to understand these differences.

Russians tend not to take a chance on a new person. During Putin's eight-year tenure as president, he led Russia out of a bottomless pit of nationwide hopelessness. On the whole, Russians would consider it unconscionable for him to retire to the ski slopes once he had honed his skills and proven that he can handle their country. Most Russians we have spoken with have been comfortable with the combination of Medvedev and Putin leading the country since at least the leader who brought order and stability is still in close proximity to power.

Back to the current tandem relationship, Putin and Medvedev share the same academic and political roots. They problem-solved side-by-side in St. Petersburg during Russia's rocky 1990s. Putin was Medvedev's trusted mentor. This counts big in Russia. They are devoted to the same practical vision and strategy for Russia. Competition isn't an issue. In Russia, such relationships include deference, respect, and trust toward the elder. Trust, promotion, and protection are accorded the protégé. Neither side transgresses these bonds.

In Russia strong bonds form early in life. During their school years pupils frequently stay with the same classmates throughout graduation from secondary school. Many continue on in higher education with each other—and some even end up working together professionally. Such bonds are particularly tight if Russians have been through difficult personal or professional challenges together. Certainly this is true for Putin and Medvedev. Lastly, these types of bonds create life-long loyalties for Russians. In America there is very little of this kind of deeply rooted bonding, particularly among our male population.

In the West we are so accustomed to competition and testosterone politics between alpha males that we do not, or perhaps cannot, comprehend this kind of male-to-male relationship that is common among straight males in Russia.

As for the present and the coming decade, my personal opinion is that Medvedev and Putin will get along collaboratively with give-and-take here and there, and will continue to have a relatively strong connection—and one of them will run for office again in 2012. The other will take the PM role—or another significant position in Russia's leadership. In the interim, Medvedev will have no interest in "besting" his mentor and friend. Putin will continue to support, advise, and trust Medvedev. And they will continue to collaborate on key issues.

Since few, if any, western journalists and pundits understand these dynamics, they most likely will continue to site evidence to insinuate grave tensions between these two leaders, which will say more about the West's mentality than about the Putin/Medvedev relationship.

Launching the CCI Blog: www.Russiaotherpointsofview.com – June 16, 2008

At last, after months of painstaking brainstorming, and figuring out the technology, we launched our blog in mid-June!

Tensions between Georgia and South Ossetia—June 2008

Georgia and South Ossetia have had a long and tragic history with each other. Due to Stalin's capricious carving up of territories to meet political objectives, South Ossetia and Georgia were forced together during the Soviet years. It was an unholy alliance.

When the U.S.S.R. broke up in the '90s, South Ossetia and Abkhazia (a second ethnic group with similar history) determined immediately to free themselves from Georgia's control. The South Ossetians fought battles and won with Georgia at that time. Eventually, U.N. Peacekeepers (Russians, Georgians, and South Ossetians) were installed in South Ossetia to prevent continuous frictions from getting out of control. Recently sniping between Georgian and South Ossetian villagers has been on the rise. Georgia's president, Mikheil Saakhasvili, came into the office claiming he would bring the two "breakaway republics," Abkhazia and South Ossetia, back under Georgia's governance. A Georgian military buildup with support from U.S. advisors had been in process for a couple of years, ostensibly to prepare Georgians to support the U.S.-led military coalition in the Middle East. This did not bode well for Russians who feared Georgia's intentions with South Ossetia for whom they were partly responsible.

The Georgian Invasion of South Ossetia—August 7, 2008

On August 7 Georgian troops and military hardware began the trek toward Tskinvali, the capital of South Ossetia, and proceeded to the border where they crossed over and began an air and ground force invasion of the capital city. In the process, administration buildings, hospitals, the university, and multiple residential houses were left in ruins. Sleeping South Ossetians and Russian Peacekeepers were maimed and killed. South Ossetians tried to protect the population but were woefully outnumbered and out-equipped by the Georgian military. On August 8 Russian forces came through the mountain pass from Russia and pushed them back into Georgia, destroying their ammunition dumps and other facilities necessary for Georgia to launch future attacks. The Russians did not move on Tbilisi, the capital of Georgia. Please go to the Internet for details on the Battle for the South Ossetia, August 2008: http://tinyurl.com/3285u6k.

For two months American mainstream media including CNN, *The New York Times, The Washington Post,* and *The Wall Street Journal* publicized Georgia's invasion of South Ossetia as "Russia's invasion of Georgia," without mentioning that Georgia first invaded South Ossetia where Russia was part of the U.N. Peacekeeping Force.

Hard Facts Regarding the Georgian/South Ossetian/Russian Crisis

- On August 7 Georgia made an unprovoked air and land attack on South Ossetia.
- On August 8 Russia counterattacked after civilians and Russian peacekeepers had been killed.
- Russia has been part of the Peacekeeping force in South Ossetia since the early '90s.
- The U.N., Georgia, and the U.S. approved a Russian "peace force" there 20 years ago.
- South Ossetians fought and won a small war with Georgia in 1991-93.
- South Ossetia had de facto independence as an autonomous area.
- Josef Stalin drew territory lines and separated Ossetia starting in the '20s.
- Ossetians are not Georgian; they are a totally different ethnic population.
- Low-level sniping has occurred between Ossetian and Georgian villagers for decades.

- It would be impossible for Georgia to rule Ossetians; the latter would fight to the last death.
- U.S., Ukrainian, and Israeli military provided Georgia with military hardware, battlefield training, and financial support.

Accurate facts on this war can now be found on the Internet.

To sum up the impact of this debacle, I expect that five years from now this five-day war will be looked upon as the major turning point in the relationship between the U.S., Russia, the regional states bordering Russia, and Europe. A contributing factor to this turning point will be the United States' 2008 financial crisis, which in turn has bled into nearly every country in the world including Russia. Combined, I believe these two events will eventually be seen to have changed geopolitical dynamics in the world from 2008 forward.

E-mail from Senator Barack Obama's Office in Mid-August 2008

"Sharon, what do you know about the Georgia situation?" The query came from Senator Obama's foreign policy person. A lengthy report was emailed to their offices—it contained much that was not being covered by U.S. mainstream media. A response came back within the hour, "Keep us informed." Our track-two reports continued until a couple of months later when *The New York Times* vaguely admitted to what the rest of the world had known from the beginning—that Georgia had invaded South Ossetia, and that Russia, in the role of the peace-keeping agency, had responded in kind.

Early in 2005, we began calling on Senator Obama's foreign policy people and found them to be serious and genuinely curious about the U.S.-Russia relationship although they admitted they weren't well informed about that part of the world.

The Obama team's e-mail searching for information regarding the Georgia/South Ossetia conflict, instilled new hope in me that if Senator Obama was elected to the U.S. presidency, he would slowly begin to feel his way toward a more constructive cooperation with Russia.

Why Divide Russia from her Neighboring States?

Elements in Washington, D.C., have financially supported the independent states of the former Soviet Union to align with the West and encouraged them to reject relations with Russia. Some of the new states (Baltic states, Hungary, Poland, the Czech Republic, and Georgia) were eager for U.S. support since they bristled under Soviet rule with good reason. Other of the smaller less strategic states, which weren't interesting to the West, didn't seem bent on rupturing relations with Russia. All of them, however, were jockeying to see where they could get the most advantage and money—from America or from Russia. Early on there was no contest; America had the big money while Russia was barely able to survive during the 1990s. For those border states in which the U.S. was not interested, Russia was able by the mid-2000s to provide incentives for them to remain friendly trade and security partners. They have remained independent states and have since entered into trade and security alliances with Russia.

Why has the American administration been interested in dividing Russia's neighboring states from Russia? It seems to me these are the main reasons:
- to insure that Russia could not reconstitute the union and become a threat to the United States
- to insure America's energy supply, along with the pipelines that carry it out to the West
- to assure America's hegemony in the world.

As was noted earlier, from the beginning of the 1990s and up to 2007, Russians' top priority was to build the relationship with America and to be accepted by the trans-Atlantic world community. However, America's political elite increasingly ignored numerous opportunities to respond positively to Russia's reasonable overtures. Granted, none knew how to help this largest nation in the world turn itself right side up and quickly learn to build a private sector and democracy. This would be a nearly impossible task in any scenario since communist mentality, the antithesis of democracy, had been methodically instilled into minds of the population for seven decades (or three and half generations).

We at CCI were intimately involved with those years and events. It has been wrenching to watch the genuine political goodwill created by President Reagan and Secretary General Gorbachev go down the drain due to short-sighted political agendas that developed after the two leaders left office.

As of 2008, the geopolitical situation is slowly changing. Meanwhile, Russia is getting stronger by the year—and will no longer acquiesce as they were forced to do in the 1990s. This requires a new political approach for America.

CCI's Twenty-fifth Anniversary

From September 15 through 17, 2008, the Center for Citizen Initiatives celebrated its Silver Anniversary at Asilomar Conference Center, where our work began more than a quarter of a century earlier. For three wonderful days, the clouds of CCI's closure were eclipsed by celebrations as 400 American and Russian leaders met and reminisced the organization's history and their relationships with each other. It was also a welcome respite from the previous month's Georgian invasion and the knowledge that our country was in economic freefall.

Ambassador Jack Matlock was our keynote speaker. He delivered his remarks in English and Russian languages. Matlock was America's Ambassador to the U.S.S.R. during the years when General Secretary Gorbachev and President Reagan were working out their new relationship, the U.S.S.R. finally collapsed, and when the new Russia was born. He has kept an avid interest in U.S.-Russia affairs for over a 50-year period. His latest book, *Reagan and Gorbachev: How the Cold War Ended,* has recently been published.

Large and small group gatherings at Asilomar filled our days and nights. The main celebration on September 16 occurred exactly 25 years after CUUI's first trip to Moscow on September 16, 1983. There were great speeches, toasts, well wishings, singing, dancing, extemporaneous poems, and countless remembrances excitedly told from the

CCI's 25th Anniversary—September 15-17, 2008.

Sharing the magnificent history and warm personal stories around banquet tables.

Jim Aneff (l), Bob Shusta (middle) sharing a toast with Russian colleagues they have now known for years.

Sharing memories at the Anniversary. Larry Miller, second from left, veteran insurance delegation coordinator with Russian friends from earlier trainings.

Allen Kerr, triple PEP delegation coordinator, talking shop about PEP with Jim Aneff, CCI's National Field Coordinator.

Left, Masha unexpectedly diverting the evening from CCI's plan to the alumni's creative plan, which was a colorful, bashy, joyous celebration of song, awards and warm acknowledgements, which Russians do so well. (Below) Alumni from each of CCI's offices created their own programs—sang, played guitars, shared fun stories, and made merry for the remainder of the evening!

An unexpected gift of a Russian pendant from delegates—a lovely memento to keep forever!

Final photo of the wonderful evening. We filed out of the Asilomar great hall into the dark night and crunched together to get one last photo—a tangible memory of a magical time for us all.

How blessed we felt for having been a part of this 25-year experiment in sharing much-needed information and international goodwill.

microphone. It was a gathering, albeit partial, of our huge international family. And it would be the last major event that CCI would ever convene. Few at the time knew that. For me, knowing what was ahead, made the event even more precious.

World Financial Crisis Imminent—September 15, 2008

The very day we opened our CCI anniversary, the U.S. stock market plummeted precipitously starting with the fall of Lehman Brothers. Little did we realize that our financial crisis would take down, not only CCI's hope for future work but also send shock waves throughout the Russian economy. Within a three-month period, from the end of September to the end of December 2008, a seesaw of events developed:

Cancellation of Russian Delegates' 2009 Training—Starting on September 30, 2008

"We are feeling the touch of your financial crisis and cannot risk spending money for U.S. business training right now." One after another, Russian entrepreneurs e mailed to cancel plans to train in the U.S. the coming year. It became clear that CCI would not have a training program in 2009.

The Election of Barack Obama as President of the United States—November 4, 2008

We could only hope for a different kind of foreign policy to emerge after Barack Obama takes over the helm of U.S. policy. Soon it became apparent that quiet changes were in the making.

Ukraine Dropped from Plans to Join NATO—November 28, 2008

Ambassador Bill Taylor, our State Department officer and CCI friend from years past and now Ambassador to Ukraine, called a press conference in Kiev and announced, "For Ukraine the issue of NATO is politically loaded and not particularly expedient at the present time." We sensed the hand of the newly elected Obama.

CCI Downsizing for the Last Time—December 2008

Masha Maslova and I moved into a small room in the historic Presidio hospital building. We could look out the window and see the oversized "Building 1008" that we had occupied for many years … and to the left, the Golden Gate Bridge. Program Officers Olga Tretyakova and Renat Deushev departed CCI on December 31.

Year 2009

This would be CCI's last year to operate an official office. Masha and I continued to run CCI's blog and the Angels Program. We interacted with congressional offices on Russia policy and nurtured myriads of human connections from the past 27 years. Our phones continued to ring; we were busy responding to e-mails from friends and strangers who needed information or assistance with Russia projects. We still envisioned what must be done to achieve constructive relations between the two countries. It seemed fitting that here in our last CCI office, two women, one American and one Russian, worked prodigiously to push this self-imposed mission forward.

Barack Obama Takes Office as President

On January 20, 2009, I was in St. Petersburg and was invited by U.S. Consul General Sheila Gwaltney to attend the festivities inaugurating our new president at the Grand Europe Hotel. A large ballroom and cinema-size screen was provided by the hotel. Amazingly, here we were in Russia, watching the events simultaneously as they were unfolding in Washington D.C. It was 10:00 AM in D.C., and 6:00 PM in St. Petersburg.

The world felt so wonderfully small and beautiful that evening. Brits, Aussies, and Europeans joined us. As events in Washington began, whistles, applause, and exclamations broke out across our space. Hotel attendants whisked in trays of champagne and treats.

President Obama and his family provided a spectacular presidential image on the wide screen; the entire affair was beyond imagining including long shots of the mall's massive crowds and the up-close faces of our chief dignitaries.

The Petersburg crowd was delirious by the time the inauguration ended. Hotel waiters filed in with a huge white cake held high in the air—it displayed embedded firework sparklers and the U.S. and Russian flags. We were so proud to be Americans!

Good Omens

Looking back to 2008 and forward into 2009, positive happenings were in process:

August 2008: Candidate Obama, at the beginning of the Georgia invasion of South Ossetia, remarked that all parties should get to the negotiating table. John McCain accused him as "weak" on Russia. Afterward, Obama took a harder line, perhaps to avoid the issue until after the election.

November 2008: While walking off stage, President-Elect Obama was asked, "What about Russia?" He quietly muttered, "We need to 'reset' the Russia policy," and then faded into the crowd. Later the overused "reset" word was attributed to Vice President Joe Biden, nevertheless, the new president-to-be was the first to use it on national TV.

January 21, 2009: Russia opened an Afghanistan supply route for the U.S. Apparently this offer acknowledged the possibility of a different relationship between the two countries now that a new American president was elected in whom Russians held sincere hope.

February 2009:
- Senior statesman, Henry Kissinger, without fanfare, showed up in Moscow to talk with President Medvedev and Evgeni Primakov, Russia's elder statesman.
- Quiet contacts between Obama and Medvedev were leaked but quickly sealed off.
- A "Commission on U.S. Policy for Russia" with a star-studded board became prominent.
- Hillary Clinton gave Russia's Minister of Foreign Affairs, Sergei Lavrov, a yellow "restart" box. Translation challenges occurred but good humor prevailed.

March 2009:
- America's "wise men," Henry Kissinger, Senator Sam Nunn, George Schultz, and James Baker landed in Moscow for meetings with President Medvedev and Primakov.
- Susan Eisenhower, Russia expert and granddaughter of President Eisenhower, showed up in Moscow for meetings with President Medvedev and Primakov.
- A bi-partisan Congressional delegation led by former Senators Chuck Hagel and Gary Hart went to Moscow for meetings with President Medvedev, Putin, and Primakov.

CCI Russia Specialists to D.C.—April 27- May 1, 2009

CCI initiated a new effort to provide Russia expertise to Congress members in the midst of this new openness. We organized a group of Ph.D. Russia experts from the U.S. and Canada, who held 24 meetings across Capitol Hill in late April. Republican and Democratic Congress members, foreign policy aides, the House Foreign Affairs Committee, the Senate Foreign Relations Committee plus members of the Senate and House Intelligence Committees engaged our Ph.D.'s on issues the U.S. mainstream media had been inaccurately promoting over the past decade. Our fact-based, non-politicized experts proved to be excellent educators. Congressman Dennis Kucinich announced to the group that he would initiate the first-ever U.S. Congressional Russia Caucus before the end of 2009. Congress members now receive weekly updates on Russia affairs from Patrick Armstrong, one of the delegation's Russia experts.

September 17, 2009: U.S. President Barack Obama announced that plans for the U.S. missile shield in Europe had been withdrawn.

September 22, 2009: An official U.S. Congressional Russia Caucus was established. Representatives Dennis Kucinich (D) and Tom Price (R) are the Russia Caucus leaders. CCI has worked closely with both members, both have received delegations of CCI Russian entrepreneurs in their Congressional offices for discussions, and both of their districts have hosted PEP delegations.

As 2009 came to a close, there were small, but continuing signs of progress between the United States and Russia. I am cautiously optimistic that these two countries I care so much about may learn to work together constructively in the future.

Closing CCI's Last Office—December 15, 2009

Closing down our office in the magnificent Presidio National Park was not easy. Moving the last CCI boxes to my car happened on a dark and misty San Francisco evening. The historic Presidio hospital building where we operated for the past year was totally vacated. Only a few hall lights and parking lot bulbs were still on. I walked out onto the veranda leading to the large parking area and put the last box down on the deck. Taking hold of the familiar railing, I looked out toward the Golden Gate Bridge and into the dark night.

It was much like another evening in 1996 when we were moving into the Presidio's Building 1008. I stood on the veranda pondering what our future might be in this grand new setting. The two nights seemed to mesh in my mind.

On this 2009 night, I knew what had been accomplished during those wonderful 13 years in between. Slowly an overwhelming gratitude wafted through me—gratitude for our original vision and mission, the decades working between the two cultures, the dedicated and talented CCI staff who had walked in and out of this parking lot over the years, the 30,000 generous volunteers in over 500 American cities in 45 states who had so willingly taken part in our vision, the multitude of funders who had trusted us with their money, the U.S. State Department officials who had supported and financed several major, multi-year programs, and cheered us on—and for all of our Russian friends across 11 time zones.

Looking out into the darkness, I was totally exhausted ... but something inside felt buoyant recalling all that had transpired throughout these amazing 27 years. Driving away my car seemed to almost float down the highway.

An era had come to an end.

$\mathcal{Y}$ear 2010

It never occurred to me how much work would remain when a large NGO closes its official offices—or that thousands of people would still be intimately tied to CCI's very real but invisible mission and network. In my mind I compare CCI to a big family that grew up and left home—but family members still have bonds to maintain, activities to partake in, work to continue, each other to consult with, and new unexpected opportunities down the time track. So it is with CCI and our large network of participants and volunteers.

The U.S. Congressional Russia Caucus has been established. We are helping organize a Russia lobby to work with Congress. CCI's blog still requires time to analyze western media and edit commentaries—it is now being read far and wide. We still run the Nika Thayer Program in Russian orphanages, and I continue to consult on the region. All remaining work is carried out from my home offices in California and St. Petersburg.

The Book about CCI's Work

This book has been in stages of writing since 1984. For 25 years I've carried a computer to capture interviews, evaluations, and impressions gleaned throughout Russia, with the original plan to try to write a book after the first five years. But there was never time; the workload was enormous and unending. Computerized material kept piling up, but the ability to put it in some coherent form never emerged.

On December 28, 2009, I left for St. Petersburg to bury myself in 31,000 out-going emails and Russia Reports from CCI's last decade. These were the most authentic and exact records available from these intriguing last ten years. Across Russia, small and large miracles had been witnessed and recorded at nearly every train stop.

Putting CCI's three decades and the challenges of the times into a readable book felt like an impossible task for me, a total novice. But there was no one else who had lived through all of these years—and no funds to pay someone else to write the book. So I waded into the process like a blind-folded person, hoping the sequence of events and the stories would adequately describe the many human hopes and hard work that we had all witnessed and in which we had partaken.

A Diversion before Tackling the Book

Before starting the daunting task, Arlie Schardt, CCI's faithful Board Chair for 19 years, and his wife Bonnie, landed in St. Petersburg for three days to celebrate Russian New Year. Heavy snows had begun falling; temperatures were dropping; Nevsky Boulevard was ablaze with tens of thousands of twinkling lights. In my mind's eye, there remains the pre-Gorbachev 1980s, the foreboding gray communist years, compared with present day Russia. St. Petersburg was lighted up like a fairyland that would have been totally inconceivable even 10 years ago.

On New Year's Eve, we sat for hours in the second floor of the historic Singer building on Nevsky Prospect. Singer Sewing Machine Company did a huge business during the pre-revolution period. This elegant building, taken over by the Bolsheviks after 1917, has housed the famed "Dom Knigi" (House of Books) since early Soviet times. Recently, the whole building was exquisitely renovated, and still the first two floors are dedicated to Dom Knigi. Upstairs sits the boutique Singer Café. We got a table looking out of wide floor-to-ceiling windows. The view was spectacular. Just across the Nevsky thoroughfare, sat the fabulous Kazan Cathedral under snow and special lighting. The largest decorated holiday tree I had ever seen in my life graced the church's front lawn.

Below in the snow, shoppers rushed around making last minute purchases before midnight of Russia's most celebrated holiday, New Year's Day. Waiters in the Singer Café were serving up steaming Russian soup, blini with caviar, champagne, and much more. TV monitors scanned similar New Years' celebrations happening across Russia's 11 time zones. Gone were dour faces, drab clothing, and lifeless strolling. Following a couple of hours of tasty holiday foods and drinks, we walked briskly through the snow to the Hermitage's Palace Square, which was lighted up like Times Square. The famous museum buildings glistened in the snow; four huge pavilions had been erected and musicians were preparing night programs for celebrants. This was a New Year's Eve to remember forever.

When my guests departed a couple of days later, I tried to get my mind around the past 10 years of change across Russia. Much forgotten material came alive upon reviewing the e-mails from 2000 forward.

Snow fell each night throughout January. White banks piled up in the streets below. Across the city, thousands of meter-long icicles hung from St. Petersburg's historic buildings. Snowplows and trucks worked 24 hours a day as I agonized over which stories best represented the passing decade. By January's end, stacks of vignettes, reports, and quotes from evaluations had been culled.

Back in America—February-December 2010

The political climate was beginning to shift and this too needed to be covered in the book since it offered the first tangible hope that a working relationship on the horizon was beginning to appear hopeful.

By midyear 2010, evidence continued that rapprochement might slowly but surely be coming about. Still, given the tortuous history between the two nations, one can never be sure what will happen next—especially since so many powerful players are invested in maintaining enmity to sell military hardware—in addition to the geopolitical competition to obtain energy resources, the black gold of the 21st century.

In June a group of prestigious American funders from Silicon Valley came to Moscow. They consulted with President Medvedev regarding his latest dream of Skolkova, a high-tech Silicon Valley-type of operation just outside of Moscow. In late June, President Medvedev came to Silicon Valley to visit the world's renown IT companies. America's giant company, Cisco, pledged $1 billion in business agreements associated with the new Skolkova project.

Next Medvedev went to Washington, D.C., for meetings with President Obama. Both of our nations got to watch their presidents on TV as they munched on hamburgers and fries in a local D.C. restaurant. Their meetings seemed informal and promising.

New Strategic Arms Reduction Treaty (New START) – December 22, 2010

Today, the New START with Russia was ratified by a Senate vote of 71-26. This sets the stage for 2011 with hopes that other evidences of cooperation including Russia's accession to the World Trade Organization (WTO) and the lifting of the barnacled Jackson-Vanik amendment may mean the establishment of normal trade relations—a move that will allow U.S. companies to take advantage of the full benefits of Russia's soon-to-be accession to the WTO.

As this book goes to print in 2012, my hopes are increasing that we may live long enough to see the resolution of the most dangerous country-to-country relationship that the world has ever known; America and Russia being the only two countries in the history of the earth that could have destroyed all life on our planet.

Finally as this bigger than life story ends, please consider ...

The Power of One Idea

Dear Readers,

Please remember that everything you have read herein started with *one* unceremonious and simple *idea*: **"It is time to go and see the enemy."**

Had that idea lain dormant and not been acted upon, every event experienced in the pages in this book would have never happened. Further, this idea occurred to a very ordinary American with no special skills or education with which to carry out such an idea. And it was picked up and nurtured by a small group of ordinary American citizens with no special education or experience with the U.S.S.R. and no clue about how to carry out such an idea. So remember ....

Our seemingly impossible ideas are far more important than we can dream.

Your idea or dream is more possible than you can imagine.

We have far more power to help change the world than we can envision.

I hope this book plants an "exploding thought" in your consciousness about the importance and power of your own idea—even though it may seem far-fetched and may have never been entertained by anyone other than you.

We have seen throughout the CCI story that time after time, totally unexpected "first ever" events took place before our eyes—simply because we took one idea after another and waded forward, educating ourselves as we went along, with the hope that the "waters would part," and seeming miracles would happen ...

. . . and they did.

Further, please remember ...

Our Future Is Too Important
to Leave Up to Politicians and Journalists

Ordinary people can take on extraordinary issues and
succeed beyond their wildest expectations.

You don't need to know what the final outcome will be.
You just need to get started.
Think big—work hard.
Avoid negativity and blame.
Act on your highest visions and deepest concerns,
And you will begin to operate as a *magnet*.

Ideas, people, events, and even money will soon begin to be attracted to your vision.
Stay oriented on your mission rather than giving into your ego pursuits.
The former delivers results larger than you can imagine,
the latter obstructs them.
Much needs to be done in the world to offset human tragedies,
environmental calamities, and future wars.
Governments are not capable of meeting all of these needs.
Too often officials are trapped in entangling alliances that prevent right action.

If something needs to be done,
ponder how you can begin in small ways to address it yourself.
Start the "buzz" with others about what might be possible
and see where it takes you!

Epilogue

I am left at the end of these three decades with a few passions yet to be comprehended or satisfied.

The most challenging one is to understand the reasons behind why there has been so much enmity and fear between Americans and Russians over the last 130 years. Why did our governments come so close to destroying each other in the 20th century? And how can we, at the beginning of the 21st century, uncover the deeply rooted differences in American and Russian mentalities that obscure and prevent efforts to build constructive long-term relations with each other?

In the following "concluding reflections," I venture my humble ponderings on the differences between American and Russian mentalities and the role I believe these differences play in the relationships between the two countries; and secondly, my reflections on the development of democracy across Russia.

Concluding Reflections

Differences Between American and Russian Mentalities

An Obsession to Understand

I have been obsessed to find ways for Americans and Russians, as individuals and as nations, to get to "win-win" relationships with one another. Yes, we should be able to "get along!" Both sides acknowledge that "Russians and Americans are very much alike." We are both hospitable, laugh at the same jokes, enjoy the same sports and cultural activities, and both are down-to-earth people. We are alike in numerous ways … yet in deeper and more profound ways, our instincts and logic are often diametrically opposite. These fault lines become all too obvious when we compete or share serious joint responsibilities for outcomes that are important to both sides.

In the early 1980s, I began to note dramatic contrasts in American and Soviet mindsets and modes of communicating. Being part psychologist, I started to ponder what was behind these differences. The challenges seemed to me to lie deep in the psyches of both populations and their leaders.

By the late 1990s, I was asking others, "Where are the social psychologists and cultural anthropologists who can help us to compare and understand the inner workings of the American and Russian minds?"

Now after three decades, I am still struggling to understand the dynamics that I believe have played a major role in "enemy-making" during the 20th century. To my knowledge, no one has put serious research into these variances that lay buried deep in the psyches of Americans and Russians.

Given the extremely dangerous international challenges between the two nations over many decades … *why have not our best brains been delving into these factors?*

Can Scientists Shed Light?

I believe that social scientists need to meticulously probe the underlying historical conditionings of both populations—which lie in the "unconscious" realms of both nations. *As long as material is in the unconscious—it cannot be accessed or changed.*

Getting to the roots of these conditionings, and making their findings known, could provide insights and solutions that, as yet, have never been explored. They could be enormously helpful in charting a new course between these two nations.

If this unconscious material could be brought to the surface, heads of states and government officials on both sides could openly make allowances for their differences across the polished tables—thereby avoid threatening the other side's needs or security interests. Business representatives contemplating major partnerships could openly discuss how to handle each other's innate proclivities ahead of time—prior to finding themselves in costly, souring business deals.

A whole new science or academic discipline needs to be devoted to this sphere to help us understand the failures of the past—a science which could develop new models of constructive interaction to replace the history of enmity making.

Opposite National Conditionings

As I perceive it: American and Russian histories have produced radically different conditionings of the peoples within their borders. These conditionings have produced unconscious assumptions, reactions, behaviors, and ways of communicating that over many years have derailed the U.S.-Russia relationship.

At this writing, both President Obama and President Medvedev are trying mightily to arrive at a new starting place, a "reset" as they are calling it. But without question, they will face future challenges on the international scene, which will trigger unconscious material in both of them and their support teams—*because they still don't understand each other's deeply-held mindsets and opposite ways of thinking, communicating, and problem solving.*

A Look at American Conditioning

Rugged individualism is part of America's national ethos. Independent settlers came to North America's shores starting in the late 1500s. They had nothing but brains, brawn, and unbroken land stretching before them. They had to survive. There was no one to give them orders or to teach them what to do. Each family had to become creative to keep pace with, or get ahead in, America's rapidly developing capitalist society. It required developing assertive skills. Every generation since has been forced to change and adapt to new circumstances.

As a result, Americans today believe they and others can make anything happen if they try hard enough—that they can make a difference in their own lives and in the world at large. Youth are encouraged to be individualistic, to compete, organize, initiate, plan, lead, and become a part of community life. Life in general has been comparatively easy for most Americans over the past three generations. With only one war on American soil more than a hundred years ago, most Americans were assured of national security until 2001 and had reasonable prosperity up to 2008. The U.S. financial crisis of the past three years has disturbed some of Americans' sense of financial security, but their basic assumptions were developed during earlier decades and still exist deep in their psyches.

Americans value entrepreneuring, innovating, organizing, small business creation, "getting ahead," civic mindedness, volunteerism, good management practices and much more. Most are proud that American tax dollars have helped innumerable people around the world and are convinced that all people deserve the freedoms that they espouse today. On the whole Americans are out-going, confident, and ask a lot of questions. They move residences and cities fairly easily, and enjoy making new relationships and sharing ideas with new acquaintances wherever they are.

A Look at Russian Conditioning

Russians have grown up in a completely different world. They have been conditioned as subjects of higher authorities for some 1,000 years. In the past there were heavy state-induced penalties for going against prevailing norms. Codes of social behaviors have been passed down by parents and teachers, generation after generation. These unwritten traditions have helped their offspring understand how to conduct themselves and how to deal with authorities from local schools up to government officials. Keeping confidences, secrets, and revealing little about oneself or one's family has been critical to surviving across Russia for centuries.

Regarding hierarchical conditioning, it has produced strongly held beliefs that authorities control the fate of nations and of individuals, so individuals need not try to make changes beyond their own personal domains.

In public, Russians instinctively appear aloof and indifferent to their surroundings. A culture of caution and suspicion of others has been prevalent throughout Russia for many decades. There is general lack of trust for fellow Russians with whom they have no strong connection. However, with their immediate families, trusted friends and occasionally foreign guests, Russians are extremely hospitable, humorous, warm, and friendly—even more so than Americans. They spontaneously celebrate, sing, play instruments, and dance with gusto with friends and even on occasion in city parks. In general they abhor noisy and arrogant behaviors—to be called a "modest man" is a great compliment.

Russians are highly intelligent and have produced some of the world's greatest scientific breakthroughs, for instance in space exploration. They have great respect for education for its own sake. They revere Russia's notable authors, poets, composers, musicians, and dancers—and have produced a significant proportion of the world's greatest classical artists. Russians are multi-lingual and for decades have enjoyed one of the highest literacy rates in the world. All of this has deepened and broadened their philosophic outlook on humanity and life.

Finally, Russians have been conditioned by centuries of wars and rumors of wars on their own soil. In the 1940s, they halted the Nazis' attempt to overtake the U.S.S.R. (and arguably the rest of the Western world), which was fought all over western Russia. When WWII ended, Soviet citizens were left with 26,000,000 dead, 25,000,000 homeless, and a country that had to be rebuilt from the bottom up. They had no Marshall Plan to assist them.

The totality of this harsh history has deeply conditioned Russian citizens and their leaders along their own specific lines of thinking and reacting to events and peoples.

Radically Diverse Conditionings Create Challenges

Politics: American leaders, including presidents, have often been bold and confident bordering on strident and inconsiderate. Too often in recent years, they have been short-term thinkers. They grasp the initiative, are comfortable with high risks, and often carry out policy matters on the front pages of newspapers to the dismay of their Russian counterparts. They are comfortable as long as everything projected goes according to their national interests and within their timelines. They are accustomed to success and getting their way.

Russian leaders, on the other hand, are cautious, calculating, and are low-risk takers politically. They are long-term thinkers. They are careful observers of status and protocol. To them, politics is something like a game of chess; they keep their cards close to the chest and make their moves carefully. Russian leaders are known for relying on the inviolability of contracts and treaties to maintain security and are shocked when foreigners break agreements or let them lapse. Russian leaders and citizens have greater tolerance for human ambiguities than do their American counterparts.

Business: American business people are linear thinkers. Personal relationships, in business, matter less to Americans than to Russians; but the "carry-though" and success of the business deal is paramount to them. They require accurate accounting and financial statements, strategic planning, business projections, time management, lawfully signed contracts, and a host of other bottom-line details.

Russians are again different. They first want to build personal relationships and trust, to get to know their future partners, which means dining, vodka, and maybe even a sauna or two together. Toasting and congeniality helps seal the personal relationship and the business deal. After looking at the big picture, Russians decide how to make the business deal go forward one step at a time, depending on changing circumstances. As far as organization, work plans, or deadlines are concerned, Russians' circuitous right brains depend on personal connections, local conditions at the time, lucky breaks, intuition, and "blat" (help from others who can make things happen for a price). In the process of making the deal, timelines may break down; new persons may emerge within the deal; unexpected bribes complicate the situation; finances aren't quite what were projected; and a host of other challenges materialize, seemingly from nowhere. This may be fairly normal for Russians—but not for Americans.

When this kind of business environment becomes obvious, many left-brained, bottom-line Western business partners often forfeit their investments in Russia and flee to more predictable countries. Other Americans, with more balanced left-right brain functioning and determination to make it work, stick out the learning process, insert left-brained methodologies into the mix, and some come out winning big with their Russian partners. And to be candid, some still fail.

The Challenge

Today neither American nor Russia's leaders (or populations) understand the great gap in the underlying mentality of the other; nor do they understand how to interpret predictable consequences of their own actions or of the unconscious assumptions and reactions from the other side.

Lastly, there remains a deep residue of historic distrust and resistance between the two countries that must be dealt with in order to get beyond the tense U.S.-U.S.S.R. and

U.S.-Russia relationships of the past hundred or more years. A cultural amnesty between the two countries needs to be forged. *This would require earnest willingness to honestly look at their own and each other's mentalities and conditionings. Next would be to learn how to deal openly with each other to make room for their counterparts' needs and comfort zones.*

Brain Research Needed?—Untangling the Gordian Knot ...

A cursory study of recent brain research has encouraged me to consider that differences in Russian and American mentalities may be strongly influenced by differences in DNA and brain chemistries—as a result of our centuries of opposite histories and conditionings. If so, this may make it useful to bring in neuroscientists to recommend ways to introduce new response mechanisms into this realm.

Let us briefly consider this possibility: that America is primarily a left-brained society as a result of our history and conditioning; and that Russia may be much more a right-brained society as a result of their history and conditioning. Admittedly, we human beings use both hemispheres of our brains—but one hemisphere is generally more dominant than the other. So let us entertain that this may also true for these two countries.

Left Hemisphere: The left hemisphere is where the circuitries for logic, language, linear thinking, planning, organizing, time management, multi-tasking and other bottom-line practical tendencies exist. The left hemisphere concentrates on getting the details taken care of, rather than being overly concerned with the big picture; left brained people learn primarily from the bottom up. Often left hemisphere people don't need to know much of the big picture in order to act professionally and decisively in their spheres of competencies further down in their companies or organizations.

Right Hemisphere: The right hemisphere houses the circuitries for non-linear, theoretical, imaginative, intuitive, poetic, and the more free-floating creative part of our brains' anatomies. The right brain grasps the overall context of a situation and learns from understanding the big picture, after which it can understand the details if necessary. Generally, right hemisphere people work well with the "big ideas or the big picture and theory, but don't work as well with details or sequential implementation. Russians are known worldwide as unmatched theorists and "big idea" people.

In the mid-1990s, we at CCI were forced to deal with the different learning propensities of Americans and Russians. This occurred as we began training larger numbers of Russian business owners in American companies.

Our American pro bono trainers naturally organized their training modules for Russian entrepreneurs in the manner that Americans learn—from the bottom up. Russians uniformly complained they couldn't learn this way. They urged, "Give us the big picture first, we can't understand where the small parts fit in without first knowing what the big picture is!"

This made no sense to us or to their American counterparts. U.S. business trainers didn't always understand the big picture of their companies or the big picture of the overall industry sector, but they did understand their own management positions.

We began reorganizing CCI training materials to assure that Russians were first given the broad U.S. industry sector, then the company's niche in the sector, followed by the company mission, strategy, and lastly, the constituent parts of lower management of the company. With this background, the Russians could understand the operations and managers responsibilities further down the line.

What Happens When a Society Overuses One Hemisphere?

What happens when a society overuses the left hemisphere in order to survive (as in America) and the right brain gets less attention—or when a society is forced to use the right hemisphere when authorities forbid many left brain activities as with Russians in earlier decades?

A very simplified answer for a complex situation seems to be that one side of the brain gets overdeveloped and the other side remains somewhat underdeveloped. These tendencies, if unaltered, get reinforced in a society's conditioning, and may even, over time, get laid down in their genetic material, which gets passed from generation to generation. This could explain why basic conditioning is so difficult to shift. Some scientists now speculate that such tendencies may be in what has, until recently, been called junk DNA.

Evidence has consistently shown that when a society focuses on what it requires to survive; specific mentalities, assumptions, behaviors, expectations, beliefs, customs, and modes of communication to match survival needs are developed by most of the population.

How then could we begin the work of exploring the deeply buried psychic material in both populations, so that we can get to the roots of what has divided these two nations?

Much work remains to be done in the U.S.-Russia relationship, which will be critical as global competition for resources heightens and countries are forced into new alliances.

If you know of organizations or specialists who are interested in or working with these or similar issues, would you please forward us their contact information. We hope to collect expert opinions and fresh insights from others more knowledgeable than ourselves regarding how these complex dynamics can be analyzed and better understood by citizens and leaders of both countries.

Concluding Reflections on Russia and Democracy

There remains considerable friction between American and Russian political elite over Russia's slowly developing democracy. I wonder if it might be useful to share where I think Russia finds itself with democratic development as the 21st century gets underway. Here are my thoughts:

- From 1250 to 1500, human development in Europe and the Mediterranean went through stages of the immensely important Renaissance—which Russian people missed due to their vast landmass and lack of contact with the developing world.

- Following those centuries, Russians were under a succession of autocratic Tsars until 1917. Most Russians were geographically remote from the clustered centers of developing European societies. A Russian merchant class developed in the 1800s, but it was small compared to the larger Russian population most of whom were cut off from outside influences. Of that merchant class, many of them fled Russia in the early 1900s and took their skills and knowledge to Europe and America. Much of the Soviet Union's intellectual class left in the mid-to-late 20th century and went to Israel or America.

- Following the 1917 Revolution, a fear-driven system of societal controls soon became Russia's fate. In 1945 the Iron Curtain dropped around the entire Soviet world. The communist/socialist system spanned a 73-year period during which the developing world was exploding with new openness, ideas, inventions, laws, trade, and exposure to one another's cultures. Russia was shut off from much of this collective learning period.

- Under the Tsars and behind the Iron Curtain, Russians developed their own societal norms, assumptions, and values based on their hierarchical social life, proverbs, their traditions, and, finally, Soviet standards that were firmly and methodically implanted in their consciousnesses.

- Russia began experiments with democracy a little over 20 years ago, the first 10 years of which were lost to lawless oligarchic capitalism during the 1990s. By contrast, Americans have had 200+ years to develop and refine democracy, and it still hasn't been perfected.

- Are Russians interested in democracy? Yes, very much so. They believe they are working toward a form of democracy, and indeed they are. However, Russian democracy in the future will function differently from American democracy, and will probably look more like the Scandinavian model.

- What do Russians want in the way of governance today? First of all, they want national order and stability, then safe borders, a high degree of social services compared to Americans, reduction of societal corruption and poverty, and to be free to develop along the lines that they choose, not as forces outside themselves dictate.

- Across the nation, young Russians are beginning to push for new reforms.This is heartening and hopefully will result in their particpation in the political life of the country. They have the freedoms that have been important to them so far: the freedom to travel abroad, to live where they wish, to create and build their own businesses, to speak their minds, to raise their children as they wish, and to be free from dogmas and ideologies in society.

- Russia, without a doubt, is becoming more democratic as the new Russia matures. Russians in their 20's and 30's today, often have considerably different mentalities from their parents' generation, yet they are still interested in the same overall values in society.

- Is Russia ready for democracy? Russians on the whole want to live in a democratic society but so far have not been quite ready for participatory democracy. As of 2011, Russian people still have little to no interest in developing or participating together to make constructive changes in local politics. They are busy making a living and openly admit that they leave politics to others, mostly—bureaucrats— for whom they have little respect.

- It seems to me that until Russian people in their districts and cities are ready to participate and begin working together on local issues and public policies, there is little way a participatory democracy can develop—unless it is pushed from the top.

- Further, the skills and openness to develop fresh local leadership from the bottom up have not yet emerged across Russia. This may be due to the general lack of trust existing among fellow Russians. One won't promote an unknown person for a role in leadership if basic distrust is present.

- Russians perceive politics as "dirty business" (as politics in Russia have been). Well qualified entrepreneurs who would be naturals to move into decision making locally refuse to become involved since they fear being suspected of underhanded dealings should they run for, or win, an election. This entire dynamic will need to shift if Russia is to develop participatory democracy.

- If my assumptions are fairly accurate, this means that Russia will have strong top-down leadership until such time as Russian citizens are willing to unite with others to further the public good.

- Americans meanwhile, need to learn to live with Russia's current governance— and to treat Russia as we treat other partners across the world, who have governance practices different from our own.

Your thoughts on these topics will be appreciated if you are interested in sharing them. Readers who wish to receive CCI updates regarding the U.S.-Russia interface are invited to email Sharon@ccisf.org to be put on the CCI e-list.

Board Members

Over the Past Ten Years

Arlie Schardt,
Chair of CCI Board of Directors

Anthony Garrett	Neil Young
Don Chapman	Susanne Campbell
Patricia Dowden	Trevor Gunn
Nancy Glaser	Sharon Tennison

CCI Staff

Thanks to each of the CCI managers and staff members who helped carry out CCI's programs and operations throughout the three decades!

Abbas, Hiam	Cheung, Angela	Freifeld, Douglas
Abrahms Carri	Chin, Phyllis	Galllagher, Rahel
Abril, Christina	Cogley, Jennifer	Galichenko, Irina
Adler, Leah	Collignon, Genevieve	Gandhi, Ruhi
Allen, Cyrus	Cook, Nicole	Garrrett, Milton
Alo, Leilana	Conners, Leonilla	Garrett, Terri
Ang, Faye	Cooper, Dan	Geisley, Gisela
Applebaum, Jody	Cowgill, Jeff	Gelfand, Beth
Atme, Brigitte	Crawford, Billy	Getter, Charles
Bacon, Abigail	Crow, Sabrina	Gilula, Natalia
Bailey, Katherine	Crowley-Delma, Catherine	Glaser, Nancy
Basley, Natasha	Dakin, Adriana	Golden, Kathryn
Bainbridge, Brian	Davis, Eloise	Goloanevskaya, Maria
Behrend, Katie	Demina, Julia	Goodliffe, Gabriel
Birnbaum, Irina	Donovan, Debra	Gordon, Bryron
Blaylock, Rick	Dornhelm, Rachel	Gorman, Eleanor
Borrego, Angie	Donahey, Evan	Graber, Nicole
Bosworth, Natalie	Easton, Will	Graham, Hugh
Broersma, Thomas	Erler, Emily	Haapala, Jennifer
Burch, Amy	Ettkin, Brian	Hart, Moriah
Burnett, John	Evans, Ansley Farinati	Hartman, Heidi
Carlton, Kim	Feiman, Eli	Hedges, Kim
Carr, Courtenay	Feltman, Tatiana	Henry, Christina
Chan, Bernadette	Foley, Tom	Heventhal, David
Chavez, Natalie	Friedman, Andrea	Hillis, Heidi

Hinds, Sally
Houd, Elizabeth
Hoverter, Terry
Hughes, Matthew
Immanuel, Bradley
Immanuel, Catherine
Insalaco, Michael
Jaunakais, Marisa
Jones, Bob
Jones, Brandon
Jones, Courtney
Kachovsky, Artyom
Kane, Meeghan
Karol, Meredith
Khan, Wendy
Knupp, David
Kohlmyer, Carter
Kroutovskaya, Alissa
Kuchins, Noah
Kyser, Rachel
Lacey, Ingrid
Lane, Maura
Lange, Liz
Lange, Jeremy
Lee, Wynetta
Leung, Maria
Lipkina, Natasha
Lozowy, Lesia
Macgowin-Pitman, Olga
Mair, Lucy
Malone, Gillian
Mantynen, Michele
Maslova, Masha
Mayton, Craig

McClellan, Charles
McDonald, Gordon
McCoy, Lara
Melnikova, Sonia
Messmer, Michael
Moore, Tonya
Moskina, Anastasia
Motta, Donna
Mowrer, Andi
Mullane, Rachel
Navaro, Juan Carlos
Needles, Dale
Nelson, Arthur
Ng, Dawn
Ng, Sterling Duck
Noel, Anna
Norberg, Derek
Odenwald, Timothy
Owen, Ashley
Pawlick, Catherine
Pitcher, Latoya
Potter, Chris
Pointer, Dawn
Potter, Sarah
Price, Julia
Redd, Meghan
Reese, Sabrina
Reddy, Grace
Roen, Elizabeth
Roney, Leslie
Rothrock, Kevin
Saindon, Nikki
Saum, Steve
Saunders, Allison

Schwartz, Ellen Augustine
Mizenin, Heather
Shornik, Paula
Simakulthorn, Araya
Skvir, Nika
So, Minna Ling
Sokhor, Olga
Soustin, Dmitry
Sprague, Tiffany Jalalon
Stewart, Erica
Starrett, Susan
Sullivan, Catherine
Swalley, David
Talis, Anna
Taylor, Kristina
Taylor, Stacy
Tailor, Wendy
Teets, Robert
Thayer, Teli
Tilley, Matthew
Trapp, Ellen
Tretyakova, Olga
Unger, Serena
Vakhroucheva, Elizaveta
Vossbrinck, Amy
Weber, Christina
Webster, Walter
Weidner, Erika
Werner, Gedeon
Wilson, Richard
Wink, James
Wright, Tracy
Wu, Susan
Young, Nancy

*There may have been other staff not listed here since records
from some of the years may not have been perfect.*

Interpreters and Facilitators

CCI was extremely fortunate to have attracted excellent professional Interpreters and Facilitators who traveled with the PEP delegations, usually coming with them from Russia, and assisting them by being the voices though which the non-English speaking delegates were able to absorb management principles and a host of other cultural activities during their stay in American companies, communities and host families.

The following were our permanent Facilitators and Interpreters:

Bennett, Ella	Kopinec, Marina	Shekhter, Valery
Bernblit, Mikhail	Kotchetkov, Max	Startseva, Galina
Dyatlovskaya, Irina	Kutuzov, Andrei	Stepashkin, Slava
Finkel, Matvei	Nelyubova, Irina	Vasilieva, Svetlana
Generalova, Zina	Goldberg, Elena	Yakimenko, Natasha
Ivanova, Natasha	Polyakova, Elena	Zavolokina, Irina
Karaldina, Irina	Puzyreva, Katya	Zlotnikov, Ilya

The following worked as needed with the delegations:

Afonin, Peter	Gussseva, Tamara	Ponomarov, Sergei
Alexeenko, Alexandre	Horkan, Nadya	Pritchard, Vita
Bathori-Tarczy, Zita	Irko, Ludmila	Pushkareva, Larisa
Bekzadian, Igor	Kachkovsky, Artyom	Renner, Elena
Belyaeva, Irina	Kalugin, Sergei	Samsonov, Pavel
Berkovich, Anna	Klochkov, Yuri	Sherstyukova, Irina
Bikbulatova, Madina	Kolchugina, Tatiana	Shimonenko, Sergei
Bolotikov, Vladimir	Krainii, Sasha	Shornik, Edward
Bonnischen, Mila	Kulikov, Yelena	Skorik, Adrey
Bunich, Gregory	Lemov, Vladimir	Smith, Alan
Buzetskiy	Leontieva, Natasha	Solovieva, Yulia
Chtchoukina, Nelli	Loukiantchik, Victor	Stepanova, Irina
Chuprina, Larissa	Mazel, Irina	Strelkova, Natalie
Cole, Dasha	Mikhalskaya, Milena	Sukhomeylo, Tatiana
Dolgapolova, Zhanna	Mosher, Ludmilla	Tchernovsko, Yuri
Drapkina, Ludmila	Motalygo, Valo	Temkin, Gregory
Entchevitch, Masha	Novomeiskaya, Lena	Terra, Kristina
Fesseko, Rom	Ozhekh, Maria	Tetradze, Avtandil
Forbes, Marina	Palek, Inna	Uvarov, Andrey
Frolov, Alexander	Peppard, Victoria	Valushkin, Anatoly
Gavrilov, Alexander	Pershina, Elena	Vaubel, Marina
Grindle, Julia	Petrosyan, Violet	Vayan, Marina
Gurevich, Mikhail	Pokatilova, Ludmila	Yurova, Alexandra

American Civic Organizations

We are deeply indebted to the American civic clubs, official offices, educational institutions and churches and their 30,000 volunteers who sponsored and implemented CCI's business management trainings throughout 45 states and over 500 American cities. They were the local organizers and the executors on ground, without which these trainings could have never taken place. Further there is no way to mention the tens of thousands of U.S. businesses which these clubs and institutions depended on to carryout the trainings in local environments. To all, we are so grateful!

Abilene North Rotary Club—Abilene, TX
Abilene Rotary Club—Abilene, TX
Alameda Rotary Club—Alameda Rotary Club
Alamo Rotary Club—Alamo, CA
Alamo Rotary Club—San Ramon, CA
Albany Kiwanis Club—Albany, GA
Albuquerque Kiwanis Club—Albuquerque, NM
Albuquerque Kiwanis Club—Albuquerque, NM
Albuquerque Metropolitan Board—Albuquerque, NM
Alcoa Rotary Club—Alcoa, TN
Alexandria Rotary Club—Alexandria, MN
Allentown Rotary Club—Allentown, PA
Aloha Rotary Club—Lake Oswego/Aloha, OR
Alpine Kiwanis Club—DeKalb, Rochelle
Alpine Kiwanis Club—Rockford, IL
Amarillo West Rotary Club—Amarillo, TX
American Society of Interiors—Grand Rapids, MI
Amherst Rotary Club—Amherst, OH
Ames Rotary Club—Ottumwa, IA
Anderson Rotary Club— —South Carolina
Ankeny Rotary Club—Des Moines, IA
Annapolis Rotary Club—Annapolis, MD
Appleton Downtown Rotary Club—Appleton, WI
Arlington Kiwanis Club—Arlington, TX
Arlington North Rotary Club—Arlington, TX
Arlington Rotary Club—Poughkeepsie, NY
Arlington Rotary Club—Riverside, CA
Armonk Rotary Club—Armonk, NY
Asheville Kiwanis Club—Asheville, NC
Asheville Kiwanis Club—Asheville, NC
Asheville Kiwanis Club—Asheville, NC
Ashland Rotary Club—Ashland, OR
Ashland-Lithia Springs Rotary Club—Ashland, OR
Athens Rotary Club—Athens, OH
Austin Northwest Rotary Club—Austin, TX
Baltimore League of Women
   Voters—Petersburg/Richmond VA
Baltimore Life Underwriters—Baltimore, MD
Bangor Rotary Club—Bangor, ME
Bartlesville Daybreak Rotary Club—Bartlesville, OK
Bath Rotary Club——Portland, ME
Barbara Van't Hoff—Grand Rapids, MI
Bay Area Rotary Club—Roseburg, OR
Belfast Rotary Club—Belfast, ME
Belfast Rotary Club—Belfast, ME
Bellefontaine Rotary Club—Bellefontaine, OH

Bellingham Kiwanis Club—Bellingham, WA
Bellingham Kiwanis Club—Bellingham, WA
Bellingham Kiwanis Club—Bellingham, WA
Beloit Noon Rotary Club—Janesville, WI
Belton Rotary Club—Temple, TX
Benton/Bauxite Rotary Club—Benton, AR
Berkeley Rotary Club—Berkeley, CA
Berkeley Rotary Club—Berkeley, CA
Bettendorf Rotary Club—Eldridge/Davenport, IA
Bismarck Noon Kiwanis Club—Bismarck, ND
Bismarck Noon Kiwanis Club—Bismarck, ND
Bismarck Noon Kiwanis Club—Bismarck, ND
Bismarck-Mandan Realtors—Bismarck, ND
Blue Springs Rotary Club—St.Joseph, MO
Boardman Rotary Club—New Philadelphia, OH
Boise Sunrise Rotary Club—Boise, ID
Boulder Kiwanis Club—Boulder, CO
Boulder Foothills Kiwanis Club—Boulder, CO
Boulder Rotary Club—Boulder, CO
Boulder Rotary Club—Thermopolis, WY
Boulder Valley Rotary Club—Boulder, CO
Bowling Green Rotary Club—Richmond, KY
Brandon Rotary Club—Brandon, FL
Brush Rotary Club—Brush, CO
Burnsville Breakfast Rotary Club—Burnsville, MN
Canton Rotary Club—Canton, GA
Canton Rotary Club—Ripon, Wisconsin
Canton Rotary Club—Canton, OH
Canton Rotary Club—Canton, OH
Carbondale Breakfast Rotary Club—Carbondale, IL
Carbondale Breakfast Rotary Club—Mt. Vernon, IL
Carbondale Noon Rotary Club—Carbondale, IL
Carbondale Noon Rotary Club—Carbondale, IL
Carmel Rotary Club—Carmel, CA
Casper Kiwanis Club—Casper, WY
Casper Gillette Rotary Club—Casper, WY
Cedar Park Rotary Club—Austin, TX
Center for Citizen Initiatives—San Francisco, CA
Centerville Rotary Club—Centerville, OH
Cereal City Sunrise Rotary Club—Charlevoix/
   Battlecreek, MI
Champaign Rotary Club—Champaign, IL
Charleston Rotary Club—Mattoon/Charleston, IL
Charlotte Sister City Committee—Charlotte, NC
Charlotte South Rotary Club—Charlotte, NC
Chattanooga Rotary Club—Chattanooga, TN

When Club names are duplicated, it means they have participated several times.

Chaska Rotary Club—Chaska, M

Chico Rotary Club—Chico, CA

Chico Rotary Club—Colusa, CA

City of Lakes Rotary Club—Minneapolis/
St.Paul, MN

Clarkston Rotary Club—Clarkston/Waterford,

Clayton Valley Rotary Club—Clayton Valley, CA

Clayton Valley/Concord/Lafeyette Rotary—Concord/
Walnut Creek, CA

Clemson Rotary Club—Clemson, SC

Cleveland Rotary Club—Cleveland, TN

Clinton Rotary Club—Clinton, IA

Coles County Sunrise Rotary Club—Coles
County, IL

Colorado Farm Bureau—Greeley, CO

Columbus Noon Rotary Club—Columbus/
Norfolk NE

Columbus Noon Rotary Club—Lincoln, NE

Columbus Rotary Club—Columbus, GA

Columbus Rotary Club—Columbus, GA

Columbus Rotary Club—Columbus, GA

Colusa Rotary Club—Colusa, CA

Colusa Rotary Club—Colusa, CA

Concord Rotary Club—South Bend, IN

Concord Rotary Club—Elkhart, IN

Concord Sunrise Rotary Club—Concord, CA

Constantine Rotary Club—Constantine/Marcellus MI

Cookeville Breakfast Rotary Club—Cookeville, TN

Cookeville Noon Rotary Club—Cookeville, TN

Coos Bay – North Bend Rotary Clubs—Coos
Bay, OR

Copperas Cove Rotary Club—Temple, Texas

Coralville-North Corridor Rotary—Iowa City, IA

Cordelia Rotary Club—Cordelia, CA

Corry Kiwanis Club—Corry, PA

Corvallis Sister City—Corvallis, OR

Coshocton Rotary Club—Coshocton, OH

Crescent Rotary Club—Greensboro, NC

Crescenta Valley Technology—Glendale, CA

Cupertino Rotary Club—Cupertino, CA

Dallas League of Women Voters—Dallas, TX

Dallas Women Lawyers Assoc.—Dallas, TX

Danville Rotary Club—Danville, CA

Davenport Rotary Club—Davenport, IA

Davis Rotary Club/Davis Sunrise Club—Davis, CA

Dayton Rotary Club—Dayton, OH

Decatur Rotary Club—Decatur/Macomb, IL

Denton South Rotary Club—Denton, TX

Denison Rotary Club—Denison, IA

DePere Rotary Club—Rhinelander/Waupaca WI

Des Peres Rotary Club—St. Louis, MO

Division 10 of Kiwanis—Lexington, KY

Dougherty County Kiwanis Club—Albany, GA

Dougherty County Kiwanis Club—Cordele, GA

Dover Rotary Club—Youngstown, OH

Downtown Optimist Club—Columbia, MO

Downtown Rockford Kiwanis Club—Rockford, IL

Downtown Towson Rotary Club—Baltimore/
Towson, MD

Dublin Breakfast Rotary Club—Dublin, OH

Duncanville Rotary Club—Dallas/Fort Worth, TX

Dunsmuir Rotary Club—Dunsmuir, CA

Dunn Loring Rotary Club—McLean, VA

Durango Kiwanis Club—Durango, CO

Durango Kiwanis Club—Durango, CO

Durango Rotary Club—Durango, CO

East Madison Rotary Club—East Madison/WI

Eaton High Plains Rotary Club—Eaton, CO

El Cerrito Rotary Club—El Cerrito, CA

El Paso Rotary Club—El Paso, TX

El Paso Rotary Club—El Paso, TX

El Sobrante Rotary Club—El Sobrante, CA

Elkhart Rotary Club—Elkhart, IN

Episcopal Church of the Ascension—Hickory, NC

Escanaba Kiwanis Club—Escanaba, MI

Eugene Emerald Rotary Club—Eugene, OR

Eugene Metropolitan Rotary Club—Eugene, OR

Fairbanks Rotary Club—Fairbanks, AK

Fairbanks Sunrisers Rotary Club—Fairbanks, AK

Fairbanks Sunrisers Rotary Club—Fairbanks, AK

Fairfield Suisan Rotary Club—Fairfield, CA

Florence Pee-Dee Kiwanis Club—Florence, OH

Florissant Rotary Club—St. Louis, MO

Florissant Rotary Club—St. Louis, MO

Foothills Rotary Club—Fort Collins, CO

Forest Grove Daybreak Rotary Club —Oswego, OR

Forest Grove Rotary Club—Forest Grove, OR

Forrest City Rotary Club—Forrest City, AR

Fort Atkinson Rotary Club—Fort Atkinson, WI

Fort Collins Breakfast Rotary Club—Fort
Collins, CO

Fort Dodge Rotary Club—Fort Dodge, IA

Fort Worth Rotary Club—Fort Worth, TX

Franklinton Rotary Club—Franklinton, LA

Franklinton Rotary Club—Franklinton, LA

Franklinton Rotary Club—Franklinton, LA

Fredericksburg Morning Rotary
Club—Fredericksburg, TX

Fremont Rotary Club—Fremont, NE

Fremont Niles Rotary Club—Fremont, CA

Fresno Airport Rotary Club—Fresno, CA

Fresno Metropolitan Rotary Club—Fresno, CA

Friendswood Rotary Club—Friendswood TX

Ft. Atkinson Rotary Club—Ft. Atkinson, WI

Gainesville Rotary Club—Gainesville, TX

Galesburg Rotary Club—Galesburg, IL

Galesburg Rotary Club—Galesburg, IL

Garden City Rotary Club—Garden City, KS

Genesee Division Kiwanis Club—Rochester, MY

Gettysburg Rotary Club—Gettysburg, PA

Novato Rotary Club—Novato, CA

Gillette Rotary Club—Casper, WY

Glendale Kiwanis Club—Glendale, CA

Glenwood Springs Kiwanis
Club—Glenwood Springs, CO

Glenwood Springs Rotary Club—Glenwood
Springs, CO

Globe Rotary Club—Globe, AZ

Grace Fellowship Church—Baltimore, MD

Grand Forks Kiwanis Club—Grand Forks, ND

Grand Junction
Rotary Club—Grand Junction, CO

Grand Rapids Golden K
Kiwanis Club—Grand Rapids, MI

Granger Sunrise Rotary Club—Goshen, IN

Greeley Rotary Clubq—Greeley, CO

Green Bay West Rotary Club—Green Bay, WI

Green Bay West Rotary Club—Green Bay, WI

Green Bay West Rotary Club—Green Bay/
    Madison, WI
Greensboro Kiwanis Club—Greensboro, NC
Greensboro Rotary Club—Greensboro, NC
Greensboro Rotary Club—Greensboro, NC
Greensboro Rotary Club—Greensboro, NC
Greenville Rotary Club—Greenville, SC
Gulfport-Orange Grove Rotary Club—Gulfport, MS
Hanover Rotary Club—Hanover/New London, NH
Hartford Rotary Club—Hartford, CT
Harlingen Rotary Club—Harlingen, TX
Harlingen North Rotary Club—Harlingen, TX
Hastings Rotary Club—Hastings, NE
Hastings Rotary Club—Hastings, NE
Hattiesburg Sunrise Rotary Club—Hattiesburg, MS
Hayward South Rotary Club—Hayward/San
    Leandro, CA
Hermiston Rotary Club—Lake Oswego, OR
Hickory Rotary Club—Hickory, NC
Holland Rotary Club—Holland, MI
Home Builders Association—Ann Arbor, MI
Hood River Rotary Club—Columbia OR
Huntsville Rotary Club—Huntsville, TX
Hurst-Euless/Bedford Rotary Clubs—Ft. Worth, TX
Hyde Park Rotary Club—Poughkeepsie, NY
Independence Rotary Club—Kansas City, MO
International Exchange Council—Grand Rapids, MI
Institute for Management
    Accountants—Charlotte, NC
Iola Rotary Club—Iola, MO
Iowa City Morning Rotary Club—Iowa City, IA
Ithaca Sunrise Rotary Club—Ithaca, NY
Ithaca Noon Rotary Club—Ithaca, NY
Jackson Township Rotary Club—Jackson, OH
Janesville Noon Rotary Club—Janesville, WI
Jefferson City Downtown
    Rotary Club—St. Louis area, MO
Johnson City Rotary Club—Johnson City, TN
Kalamazoo Rotary Club—Kalamazoo, MI
Kalamazoo Rotary Club—Dowagiac/Kalamazoo, MI
Kalispell Rotary Club—Kalispell, MT
Kankakee Valley Rotary Club—Kankakee, IN
Kansas City Kiwanis Club—Kansas City, KS
Kennebunk Rotary Club—Kennebunk, MD
Kennebunk Portside Rotary Club—Kennebunk, MD
Kent Rotary Club—Kent, OH
Killeen Heights Rotary Club—Killeen, TX
Kingsport Rotary Club—Kingsport/Abington, TN
Kirkwood Rotary Club—Kirkwood, MO
Kirkwood Rotary Club—St. Louis, MO
Kirkwood Rotary Club—St. Louis, MO
Kishwaukee Kiwanis
    Club—Sterling,/Rockford, IL
Kiwanis Capital District Division—Baltimore, MD
Kiwanis Clubs Division II—Lima, Ohio
Kiwanis Clubs of Division 19—Mt. Pleasant/
    Saginaw, MI
Kiwanis Division 1—Washington, D.C.
Kiwanis Division 14—Pasadena, MD
Kiwanis International Club —Kansas City, MO
Kiwanis International MO-ARK—Kansas City, MO
Klamath Falls Rotary Club—Klamath Falls, OR
Klamath Falls Sunrise Rotary Club—Klamath
    Falls, OR

Kruse Way-Lake Oswega Rotary—Medford/
    Portland, OR
Kruse Way-Lake Oswego Rotary Club—Oswego, OR
Lafayette Rotary Club—Lafayette, CA
Lafayette Rotary Club—Lafayette, Orinda, CA
Lafayette Rotary Club—Lafayette, CA
Lafayette/Concord/Clayton Valley
    Rotarys—Lay/Con/Clayton, CA
Lake Ozark Rotary Club—Lake Ozark, MO
Lake Charles Rotary Club—Lake Charles, LA
Lakeland South/Sebring Rotary Clubs—Lakeland, FL
Lakeshore Rotary Club—St. Joseph, MI
Lakeview Rotary Club—The Dalles, OR
Lakeview Rotary Club—Klamath Falls, OR
Lakewood/Rocky River Rotary Club—Lakewood/
    Rocky River, OH
Lamar Rotary Club—Lamar, MO
Lamorinda Sunrise Rotary Club—Moraga, Lafayette,
    Orinda, CA
Lamorinda Sunrise Rotary Club—Pleasant Hill, CA
Lander Rotary Club—Lander, WY
Lancaster West Rotary Club—Lancaster, CA
Lake Charles Rotary Club—Lake Charles, LA
LaPlace Rotary Club—LaPlace, LA
LaPlace Rotary Club—New Orleans, LA
LaPorte Rotary Club—Northwest, Indiana
Lebanon Rotary Club—Lebanon, NH
Lee's Summit Sunrise Rotary Club—Lee's
    Summit, MO
Lee's Summit Sunrise Rotary Club—Lee's
    Summit, MO
Leominster Rotary Club—Leominster, MA
Lewis Center Rotary Club —Athens, OH
Lexington Rotary Club—Lexington, KY
Lincoln Rotary Club—Lincoln, CA
Livonia Rotary Club
Locust Valley Rotary Club—Sacramento, CA
Logan Rotary Club—Logan, UT
Longmont Rotary Club—Longmont, CO
Los Gatos Rotary Club—Los Gatos, CA
Lynnwood Rotary Club—Lynnwood, WA
Macon Rotary Club—Macon, GA
Madison Area Builders Assoc.—Madison, WI
Madison Horizons Rotary Club—Madison, WI
Madison West Rotary Club—Madison, WI
Madison West Rotary Club—Madison, WI
Madison West Rotary Club—Madison, WI
Mankato Downtown Kiwanis Club—Mankato, MN
Mansfield Rotary Club—Mansfield, OH
Marietta Golden K. Kiwanis Club—Marietta, GA
Marietta Kiwanis Club—Marietta, GA
Marin Evening Rotary Club—Mill Valley, CA
Marin Sunrise Rotary Club—Mill Valley, CA
Marion Rotary Club—Marion, OH
Marquette Rotary Club—Marquette, MI
Marshall Rotary Club—Marshall, MO
Marshalltown Rotary Club—Marshalltown, IA
Marshfield Rotary Club—Wausau, WI
Maryland Assoc of CPAs—Baltimore, MD
Maryville Rotary Club—Maryville, TN
McComb Rotary Club—McComb, LA
McKinney Rotary Club—McKinney, TX
Medford Rotary Club—Medford, OR
Media Rotary Club—Media, PA

Memphis Rotary Club—Memphis, TN
Memphis Advertising Federation—Memphis, TN
Menomonie Rotary Club—Menomonie, WI
Metairie Rotary Club—Metairie, LA
Metairie Rotary Club—Metairie, LA
Metairie Rotary Club—Metairie, LA
Metairie Rotary Club—Metairie, LA
Miami Rotary Club—Globe, AZ
Midland Morning Rotary Club—Bay City, MI
Midland Rotary Club—Midland/Saginaw, MI
Midland West Rotary Club—Midland, TX
Midlothian Rotary Club—Midlothian, TX
Middlebury Rotary Club—Middlebury, VT
Milbrae Rotary Club—Milbrae, CA
Milwaukee Downtown Rotary Club—Milwaukee, WI
Mill Valley Rotary Club—Mill Valley, CA
Milton-Freewater Rotary Club—Pendleton, OR
Modesta Sister City International—Davis,
    Modesto, CA
Modesta Sister Cities International—Davis/
    Santa Rosa, CA
Modesto Sister Cities International—Modesto, CA
Modesto Sunrise Rotary Club—Modesto, CA
Monterey Rotary Club—Monterey, CA
Moorhead Noon Kiwanis Club—Moorhead, MN
Monmouth-Independence Rotary
    Club—Monmouth, CO
Monroe Rotary Club—Monroe, WI
Monticello Rotary Club—Monticello, IA
Morrisville Rotary Club—Morrisville, VT
Montgomery Rotary Club—Blacksburg, VA
Moultrie Kiwanis Club—Moultrie, GA
Mountain Road Kiwanis Club—Jessup/
    Pasadena, MD
Mt. Shasta Rotary Club—Mt. Shasta, CA
Muncie Sunrise Rotary Club—Muncie, IN
Murray Rotary Club—Salt Lake City, UT
Murfreesboro Noon Rotary Club—Murfreesboro, TN
Murfreesboro Noon Rotary
    Club—Murfreesboro, TN
Muskegon Rotary Club—Muskegon, MI
New London Rotary Club—New London, CT
Nashville Kiwanis Club—Nashville, TN
New London Rotary Club—New London, NH
New Mexico Society of CPAs—Albuquerque, NM
New Philadelphia Rotary Club—New
    Philadelphia, OH
New Orleans Mid-City Kiwanis Club—New
    Orleans, LA
New Haven Rotary Club—New Haven, CT
Newnan Kiwanis Club—Newnan, GA
Newnan Kiwanis Club—Newnan, GA
Marietta Kiwanis Club—Newnan, GA
Newton Rotary Club—Newton, NJ
Newton Rotary Club—Newton, NJ
Niles Fremont Rotary Club—San Leandro, CA
North Colorado Springs Rotary
    Club—Colorado Springs, CO
North Kansas City Rotary Club—Kansas City, MO
North Platte Rotary Club—Lincoln, NE
North-East Green Bay Kiwanis Club—Green
    Bay, WI
Northshore and Slidell Rotary Clubs—Slidell, LA
North River Rotary Club—Chattanooga, TN

North Roseburg Rotary Club—Roseburg, OR
Norwich Rotary Club—Norwich, CT
Novato Rotary Club—Novato, CA
Novato Rotary Club—Novato, CA
Novato Rotary Club—Novato, CA
Oakland Rotary Club—Oakland, CA
Oconomowoc Rotary Club
Odessa Rotary Club—Odessa, TX
Olive Branch Rotary Club—Olive Branch, MS
Orange Rotary Club—Orangeburg, SC
Orangeburg Morning Rotary Club—Orangeburg, SC
Oshkosh Rotary Club—Oshkosh, WI
Ottumwa Rotary Club—Ottumwa, IA
Ottumwa Rotary Club—Ottumwa, IA
Overland Park Rotary Club—Overland Park, KS
Palo Alto-University Rotary Club—Palo Alto, CA
Parker Rotary Club—Denver, CO
Pensacola/Gorlovka Sister Cities —Pensacola, FL
Petal Rotary Club——Hattiesburg, MS
Philadelphia Rotary Club—Philadelphia, PA
Piedmont-Montclair Rotary Club—Piedmont, CA
Plant City Rotary club—Plant City, FL
Pleasanton Rotary Club—Pleasanton, CA
Portland Rotary Club—Portland, ME
Prescott Valley Rotary Club—Prescott Valley, AZ
Preston Center Rotary Club—Dallas, Texas
Princeton Rotary Club—Princeton, KY
Provo Rotary Club—Provo, UT
Purdue Co-Op Extension Service—Kass &
    Carroll Counties, IN
Rancho Cucamonga Rotary Club—Rancho
    Cucamonga, CA
Rensselaer Rotary Club—Valparaiso/Renseller, IN
Redding East Rotary Club—Redding, CA
Redding Sunrise Rotary Club—Redding, CA
Rexburg Rotary Club—Rexburg, ID
Rice Lake Rotary Club—Rice Lake, WI
Richmond Kiwanis Club—Richmond, CA
Richmond Rotary Club—Richmond , KY
Rigby Rotary Club—Rigby, ID
Ripon Kiwanis Club—Ripon, WI
Rockford Downtown Rotary Club—Rockford, IL
Rock Island Kiwanis Club—Rock Island, IL
Ross Valley Rotary Club—San Ansalmo, CA
Rosslyn-Fort Myer Rotary Club—Rosslyn, VA
Rotary Club of Greece—Greece/Rochester, NY
Rotary Club of New Orleans—New Orleans, LA
Rotary Club of New Orleans—New Orleans, LA
Rotary Club of Provo—Provo, UT
Rotary District 563—Grand Island/Lexington, NE
Rotary District 5170—Santa Clara, CA
Rotary District 5890—Houston, TX
Rotary District 6460—Peoria/Springfield, IL
Rotary District 6650—Youngstown/Warren/
    Canton, OH
Rotary District 7250—Locust Valley/Long
    Island, NY
Rotary District 7610—Washington, D.C.
Rotary District 7950—Cape Cod Area, MA
Rotary District 7950—Providence, RI
Rotary International Dist 636—St. Joseph/South
    Lansing, PA
Rotary International Dist 636—Sturgess/Fort Custer/
    LakeGrass, MI

Salinas Rotary Club—Salinas, CA
Salem Rotary Club—Salem, OR
Salt Lake City Rotary Club—Salt Lake City, UT
Salt Lake City Rotary Club—Salt Lake City, UT
Salt Lake City Rotary Club—Salt Lake City, UT
San Bernadino Crossroads Rotary
   Club—Highland, CA
San Francisco Golden Gate Rotary
   Club—San Francisco, CA
San Francisco Fisherman's Wharf
   Rotary—San Francisco, CA
San Mateo Rotary Club—San Mateo, CA
San Ramon Rotary Club—San Ramon, CA
Sandy Rotary Club—Salt Lake City, UT
Santa Clara County Committee—Santa Clara, CA
Santa Cruz Sister City Committee—Santa Cruz, CA
Saratoga Rotary Club—Saratoga, CA
Sausalito Rotary Club—Sausalito, CA
Scottsboro Rotary Club—Scottsboro, AL
Sebastopol World Friends—Sebastopol, CA
Sebring Rotary Club—Sebring, FL
Sepulveda University Church—Pasadena, CA
Shelby Township Optimist Club—Shelby
   Township, MI
Silverton Rotary Club—Silverton, OR
Silverton Rotary Club—Silverton, CO
Slidell Rotary Club—Slidell, LA
Slidell Rotary Club—Slidell, LA
Slington-Allenton Rotary Club—Slington, WI
South Bend Rotary Club—South Bend, IN
South Salem Rotary Club—Salem, OR
South Pittsburg Rotary Club—South Pittsburg, TN
Southhaven Rotary Club—Southhaven, MS
Spokane Rotary Club—Spokane, WA
Spokane Rotary Club #21—Spokane, WA
Springdale Rotary Club—Sterling, IL
Springfield North Rotary Club—Springfield/
   Branson, MO
St. Cloud Rotary Club—St. Cloud, MN
St. Cloud Rotary Club—St. Cloud, MN
St. Lukes United Methodist Church—Hickory, NC
Sterling Rotary Club
Stillwater Rotary Club—Stillwater, MN
Storm Lake Rotary Club—Storm Lake, IA
Sugar House Rotary Club—Salt Lake City, UT
Summit Rotary Club—Greensboro, NC

Sun Lakes Rotary Club—Sun Lakes, AZ
Swarthmore Rotary Club—Swarthmore, PA
Tellico Village Kiwanis Club—Loudon, TN
Tallahassee Sunrise Rotary Club—Tallahassee, FL
Thrope Memorial Church—Orange County, CA
Tomball Rotary Club—Tomball, TX
Toms River Rotary Club—Toms River, NJ
Towsontowne Rotary Club—Towson, MD
Troy Rotary Club——Troy, Michigan
Tullahoma Rotary Club—Tullahoma, TN
Tucson Rotary Club—Tucson, AZ
Tulsa Rotary Club—Tulsa, OK
Tulsa Rotary Club—Tulsa, OK
Tulsa North Rotary Club—Tulsa, OK
Tulsa Midtown Rotary Club—Tulsa, OK
Tuscaloosa Rotary Club—Tuscaloosa, AL
Tyson Foods International—Springdale, AR
Tyson Foods International—Springdale, AR
Uman/Davis Sister City Int.—Davis/Uman, CA
Uman/Davis Sister City Int—Davis/Uman, CA
Uman/Modesto SCI—Davis, Modesto, CA
Unitarian-Universalist Church—Annapolis MD/
   Arlington VA
Urbana Rotary Club—Urbana, IL
Vacaville Rotary Club—Vacaville, CA
Valparaiso Rotary Club—Northwest, IN
Victoria Rotary Club—Victoria, TX
Victoria Sunrise Rotary Club—Victoria, TX
Visalia Rotary Club—Visalia, CA
Washington Rotary Club—Washington, IN
Waupaca Breakfast Rotary Club—Waupaca, WI
Wellington Rotary Club—Wellington, FL
Wenatchee Downtown Rotary Club—Wenatchee, WA
West Des Moines Rotary Club—Des Moines, IA
West Memphis Rotary Club—West Memphis, AR
West Knoxville Rotary Club—Knoxville, TN
Westport Sunrise Rotary Club—Westport, CT
Wichita Falls North Rotary Club—Wichita Falls, TX
Wichita Falls Rotary Club—Wichita Falls, TX
Wichita Falls Southwest Rotary—Wichita Falls, TX
Wilbur Smith Rotary Club—Texarcana, TX
Woodland Sunrise Rotary Club—Berkeley, CA
Wooster Rotary Club—Wooster, OH
Yakima Rotary Club—Yakima, WA
Zanesville Kiwanis Club—Zanesville, OH

Index